# DATE DUE

13 DEC ☒☒ D   A R

JUN 18 2000     JUN 28 2001

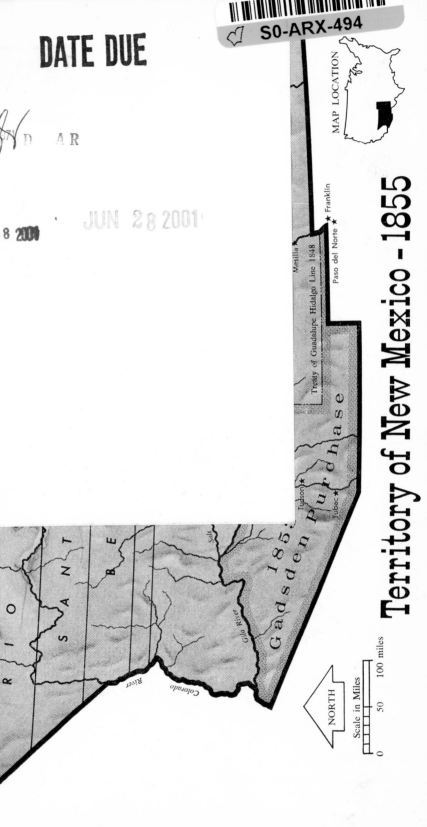

S0-ARX-494

MAP LOCATION

★ Franklin

Mesilla

Treaty of Guadalupe Hidalgo Line 1848

★ Paso del Norte

G a d s d e n   P u r c h a s e

1853

Tucson ★

Tubac ★

R I O   S A N T E   B E

Salt

Gila River

Colorado River

NORTH

Scale in Miles

0    50    100 miles

## Territory of New Mexico - 1855

SYRACUSE UNIVERSITY   11420380
The march of Arizona history.
F 811.P36

3 2911 00172740 3

# THE MARCH OF
# ARIZONA HISTORY

OTHER BOOKS BY
ANNE MERRIMAN PECK

*Young Mexico*
Dodd Mead & Co., 1934

*The Pageant of South American History*
Longmans Green, 1941

*The Pageant of Canadian History*
Longmans Green, 1943

*The Pageant of Middle American History*
Longmans Green, 1947

*Southwest Roundup*
Dodd Mead & Co., 1950

# THE MARCH OF
# ARIZONA HISTORY

*by*

ANNE MERRIMAN PECK

☆

DRAWINGS BY THE AUTHOR

☆

ARIZONA SILHOUETTES
TUCSON, ARIZONA
1962

END MAPS
*by*
DONALD H. BUFKIN

INDEX
*by*
DON POWELL

Library of Congress Catalog Card Number: 61-17810

☆

*Text and Illustrations Copyrighted*
1 9 6 2
*by* ANNE MERRIMAN PECK
*All Rights Reserved*

PRINTED IN THE UNITED STATES OF AMERICA

Book 4 Pages 63 direct (Geog)

51

J. Brmmy. Hall 11/11/71

hi: 2GApG3

# FOREWORD

History is the story of people. In this vital section of the Southwest it was people of three basic cultures who explored, settled and developed the land: the native Indians, the Spaniards and Mexicans, and finally, American pioneers from various parts of the country.

I have not been a resident of Arizona long enough to claim the title of "Oldtimer," but during the years since the state became my home I have known all kinds of people in many parts of the state. I have learned of the courageous struggles of their forebears, and themselves, to win a difficult land for civilization, and have delighted in the dramatic natural beauty of that land. My deep interest has been enriched through reading history, archeology, anthropology, and folklore. Arizona has a remarkable prehistoric past that may be studied not only in rocks, canyons and mountains, but in the artifacts and dwellings left by long-vanished inhabitants. For that reason I have begun the story with prehistoric geology, animals, and man, and have carried it through into mid-twentieth century.

While I traveled in Latin America for the purpose of writing books I learned to steer for museums and libraries to acquire knowledge and understanding. Arizona has provided similar sources, and I am grateful to the staff of each institution where I have worked.

Members of the faculty at The University of Arizona

were kind enough to consider and approve my plan for the book and to read certain chapters to check for authenticity. I am indebted to Dr. Emil W. Haury, director of the State Museum and head of the Anthropology Department; to Dr. John F. Lance, geologist and paleontologist; and to Dr. John Alexander Carroll, historian. Patricia Paylore, Assistant Librarian of The University of Arizona Library, and Donald M. Powell, head of the Reference Department, gave of their time to read the manuscript and make valuable suggestions. William R. Hardwick of the United States Bureau of Mines helped me with information on modern mining. Ralph Patey, manager of the Kitt Peak National Observatory offices, supplied material.

I am grateful to Mrs. Alice B. Good of the Arizona State Archives for her interest, her counsel and excellent reference material. My thanks go, also, to Dr. Paul Hubbard, Associate Professor of History at Arizona State University, for his historian's counsel on the book.

The staffs of the museums where I have worked have been invariably interested and helpful: the State Museum and Arizona Pioneers' Historical Society in Tucson; the Museum of Northern Arizona in Flagstaff. In particular, I appreciate the suggestions for research given by Dr. Edward Danson, director of that museum, and Dr. Katherine Bartlett, librarian of their Research Center.

Many individuals have given me encouragement, among them teachers in the Tucson Public Schools and personal friends. Douglas D. Martin, former head of the Journalism Department at The University of Arizona, started the book on its way with his counsel; and Enid Johnson, fellow writer, has helped with suggestions and belief in the project.

This book is offered to the people of Arizona, of any age, with the hope that they will find it a rewarding and authentic narrative of their state's dramatic history.

Tucson, 1961.

ANNE MERRIMAN PECK.

# CONTENTS

## PART I.
### Prehistoric Arizona

## PART II.
### Spanish and Mexican Arizona

## PART III.
### Anglo-Americans Take Over Arizona

## PART IV
### Territorial Arizona

## PART V.
### Arizona the Forty-eighth State

# PART I.
# PREHISTORIC ARIZONA

## Chapter I

### Earth-making in Prehistoric Ages

Arizona's rugged surface, wrinkled with mountain ranges, cut into deep canyons, spread out in plateaus and desert plains, reveals more of its geologic past than many parts of the nation. Nature's sculptor, Erosion, has been at work through the ages, using the tools of wind, sand, and water to wear down mountains and carve the colorful sandstone plateaus of the north into buttes, mesas, and cliffs. Rivers have done their share of this sculpturing as the powerful force of water gouged out deep canyons.

The masterpiece created by the Colorado River, the Grand Canyon, is an open book of earth's geologic history for those who know how to read it. Exposed in the walls of the huge gorge geologists find layers of limestone that were once sea bottoms, and in the rocks are fossils of corals,

1

shellfish, sponges, and sea plants. They find layers of sandstone and shale formed from sand dunes or wet plains or the shores of prehistoric seas. Other rocks were made after mountains had been thrust up and worn down by erosion, or from lava spread by volcanic upheavals.

A ride down the trails from the rim of Grand Canyon is a journey in time, for geologists find evidences of earth-making in the rocks of the walls, reaching back through many million years. Down at the bottom of the Canyon, where the Colorado River rushes in rapids through the dark walls of the Inner Gorge, it has cut its way through the oldest rocks on earth. They were formed in the Archeozoic Era when our earth, a spinning globe, was acquiring a crust of rock over its molten interior.

This story of geologic ages, shown in the rocks, proves that Arizona land went through turbulent millenia of changes, and that it is, geologically speaking, a very ancient land.

During the long third era of geologic time, lasting millions of years, called the Paleozoic, shallow seas washed over the low flat land and then retreated, leaving thick layers of mud filled with primitive forms of sea life, or great areas of sand dunes and plains. The sea bottoms became limestone, containing fossils of crab-like trilobites, primitive fish, shellfish, and coral. In the Grand Canyon area this deposit from ancient seas, called the Kaibab lime-stone, is a mile or two thick. Since fossils of sea life are also found in the limestone cliffs of southern mountains, it is likely that parts of this region were under water at times from invading seas.

Before the end of the Paleozoic Era, land areas were acquiring vegetation, thickets of reed-like plants, ferns, and some trees. Over wide muddy plains meandered rivers, and ponds glistened among the swamps. In the waters lived prehistoric turtles, snakes and other primitive creatures. Ugly amphibian lizards, something like crocodiles, aired themselves on stream banks, watching for food, such as insects. Overhead flapped reptiles with bat-like wings attached to their legs.

In this strange, watery landscape of damp, warm climate, the great reptiles, dinosaurs and others were the rulers. In many parts of the earth where this warm climate prevailed, the great reptiles flourished during the fourth era of geologic time, the Mesozoic.

Over the plains and swamps lumbered the huge, grotesque dinosaurs. Largest of them were the diplodocus that stood twenty feet high, and their enemies were the meat-eating tyranosaurus and allosaurus. The diplodocus were mild, stupid monsters who walked on thick legs dragging along spiny tails. Tiny heads on long necks reached out to browse on plants and leaves. They were attacked by the meat-eating creatures who were not so large but more active and intelligent. They tramped over the earth on great hind legs, using their short front legs to seize their prey. They sprang on the stupid monsters, crushing them with great jaws and sharp teeth, tearing their flesh with their claws.

Year after year and century after century the giant reptiles searched for food, fought each other, wallowed in the swamps, and died. Their skeletons were buried deeply under sediment. In some areas of damp earth they left their huge footprints, and these in time hardened into rock and were buried under layers of soil.

In the Mesozoic Era wet, sandy plains extended over southern Utah and Colorado and northern Arizona, and, in the course of time, this earth became sandstone, and the relics of prehistoric monsters were preserved. Colorado seems to have had a large population of dinosaurs, for many skeletons have been unearthed by excavation. The bones were studied and assembled by scientists and the skeletons placed in museums. In Arizona people may see their actual huge, three-toed foot prints. Near Cameron, in Dinosaur Canyon, and in the Painted Desert, near Tuba City, there are dinosaur tracks and their bones have been found not only in northern Arizona but in the Santa Rita Mountains and the San Pedro Valley as well, indicating that the southern region must have been a suitable habitation for the reptiles. The Smithsonian Institute has a skeleton of a dinosaur, taken from the San Pedro Valley, near Benson, Arizona.

Late in the Mesozoic Era great geological changes occurred as the Rocky Mountains were being built, different types of plants were evolved, and the North American continent was being blocked out basically in its present form. At this time the giant reptiles disappeared by degrees, perhaps because they were too stupid to adjust to changes.

During the warm, wet era of the Mesozoic there was higher land to the northeast, above the plains where rivers spread their sediment. Forests of great coniferous trees, a sort of primitive pine, grew on this higher land. After heavy rains the rivers tore down the hillsides, uprooting trees on their banks. The trunks were carried along with masses of debris, stones and sand to be strewn over the plains and piled up in log jams. Through the ages the logs were buried deeply under many feet of sediment. Minerals in the water, such as silica, finally turned the wood cells to jeweled stone. After centuries of erosion the sediment and rocks, covering the great logs of prehistoric forests, were worn away and they were revealed. The ends of the logs glowed with colors of semi-precious stones: agate, carnelian, onyx, and jasper. They were scattered over acres of land, a wonder to generations of people until geologists figured out their history. So we have today the Petrified Forest.

The multi-colored cliffs and valleys of the Painted Desert were also carved by erosion from the rocks that were once muddy plains. North of this area wind, sand and water sculptured the red, orange and creamy cliffs, mesas, rock windows and arches on the Navajo Indian Reservation and in southern Utah.

When mountain-building began in ancient Arizona crustal movements from deep within the earth thrust up mountains, such as the Bradshaws around Prescott, the ranges to the east near Globe, the Santa Catalina Range. In the west and south other mountains rose gradually, from the Gulf of California to New Mexico, with wide valleys between them. Geologists think that the great areas of dried, cracked mud called playas, in the Sulphur Spring Valley, are the remains of prehistoric lakes. They are near Willcox. After a big rain, when they are seas of mud, they look like lakes. Sometimes a mirage is seen above them.

In the north, the Kaibab limestone in the Grand Canyon region, formed from the mud of ancient seas, had been buried through the ages under deep layers of soil and rock, then slowly worn down again until the limestone was laid bare. It made the surface of a great flat plain, and across the plain flowed the young Colorado and other streams.

Then began one of the mighty upliftings of the earth's surface in crustal movements. The deep layers of rock

were bent and tilted as the land slowly rose, century after
century.   This probably occurred during the fifth and
last era of geologic time, the Cenozoic, that began about
60,000,000 years ago.   The land rose into a high, dome-
shaped plateau over northern Arizona, from 4,000 to
8,000 feet in altitude.

While the land grew higher, the Colorado River
gouged its course ever deeper through the rocks, grinding
with the forces of water, sand and boulders to create its
awesome canyons; the most marvelous of all is the Grand
Canyon itself.   The San Juan and Little Colorado rivers
also began the cutting of their canyons at this time.

It was during the long period of crustal movements
that the bending and breaking of rocks created the
steep escarpments of the Mogollon Rim.   Along this edge
of the plateau streams and water carved the canyons and
cliffs which make such a barrier between the plateau and
land below it.   At the same time erosion began to carve
the gloriously colored cliffs of Oak Creek and Sycamore
Canyon country.

Volcanic eruptions, during the Cenozoic Era, made
more changes in the northern plateau.   Crustal movements
cracked the rocks, providing vents for lava and cinders
from within the earth.   The plateau must have been a
terrifying place when dark clouds of dust obscured the
sky, and fiery spouts shot from many vents to build up
what are called cinder cones.   They are there to this day,
among the pines near Flagstaff, rounded hills of dark red
or black cinder, sometimes thinly covered by grass.   The
San Francisco Volcanic Field, as it is called, extends over
some 3,000 square miles.

The tall mountains of the plateau were created during the second period of volcanic activity.   The highest

of the volcanoes are the San Francisco Peaks, 12,611 feet above sea level. Other volcanic mountains are Bill Williams, Sitgreaves, O'Leary, and Kendrick. Much later in time another eruption created Sunset Crater and the lava fields around it.

There was also great volcanic activity in the central and southern parts of Arizona, when a series of eruptions created volcanoes, and time and weather wore them down. The interesting Chiricahua Mountains in the southeast were raised up from low land by volcanic disturbances, and the low peaks of jagged shapes west of Tucson are eroded ancient volcanoes.

After the long ages of mountain-building and volcanic action Arizona began to acquire its final physical form. The climate was changing, as huge ice caps covered the northern part of the continent at periods from one million to ten thousand years ago. Glaciers spread downward over North America, but there is little evidence of glacial activity in the Southwest. However, icy air cooled the climate and mountains shut off moisture so that the land became drier. The vegetation of the past was replaced by grasses, plants, and trees more suited to a dry climate. The great reptiles had disappeared, but mammals and birds were developing.

The Colorado River and its tributaries was not the only river system to create areas of Arizona geography. The Gila River, and streams that fed it, was a great maker of canyons, as it forced its way downward through mountain masses and carved out gorges in its passage. It flowed westward to the low land and finally joined the Colorado. The Salt River, too, was a strong and cutting stream. It forced a passage through the eastern mountains, creating gorges almost as startling as the Grand

Canyon. The modern highway twists up and down and across the river in these canyons, giving spectacular views. The river brought its waters to the broad valley that is now the region around Phoenix.

The tumultuous ages of mountain-building and volcanic action created rocks rich in minerals that were to be a source of wealth to the modern state. In the mountains the marvelous variety of rocks, minerals and crystals make Arizona a paradise for "rock hounds." Fossils that were preserved in rocks help in the understanding of plant and sea life that existed millions of years ago, and footprints in sandstone prove that prehistoric creatures walked over dunes and muddy plains. Few places in the country show such an extent of geologic history, plain to be seen in Arizona's canyons and mountains. Museum displays and geological collections aid in understanding the past. The Museum of Northern Arizona in Flagstaff has a most interesting exhibit, visualizing the story of Arizona's geologic changes throughout the ages by means of dioramas, charts, and rock samples.

As centuries rolled on in the Cenozoic Era toward the coming of man, the warm-blooded animals, the mammals, took over the continents, and many of them flourished in the Southwest.

## Chapter II

### Prehistoric Animals and Early Man

The Southwest was not a bad home for the many varieties of primitive beasts that replaced the giant reptiles as inhabitants. The shallow bodies of water had drained back to the sea; mountains had been uplifted; and there were rivers, grassy valleys and uplands.

Animals of that far-off time were great migrants. At some periods there was a land bridge from Siberia to Alaska, where the Bering Straits lie today. Over this bridge animals of Asia crossed to North America. Later, when water covered this strip, animals could still cross on the ice in winter. At the other end of North America the Isthmus of Panama rose to make a bridge between North and South America. Up to that time the continents had been two big islands. Over this land bridge animals

9

passed back and forth from one continent to the other.

There are no camels in North America now, but South America has animals of the camel family: the llama, alpaca and vicuña. Perhaps they are descendants of the small camels without humps that frequented the pleasant valleys of the Southwest in prehistoric times. The opossum, the deer and prong-horned antelope settled on each continent. The giant sloth originated in the southern continent but migrated north.

In the Southwest the prehistoric sloth was a large, bulky, hairy animal. Recently, a cave was discovered in the cliffs that frame Lake Mead where these animals had taken shelter. The floor was deep in prehistoric dung, and skeletons of the beasts were found. The remains of sloths have been found in other places, and there is a skeleton of the clumsy creature in the Museum of Northern Arizona.

Herds of animals, some of them very large, roamed the hills and valleys of the Southwest and California. There were huge animals of the elephant type, mastodons and mammoths. The mastodons had short tusks and hairy bodies, but the mammoths were really prehistoric elephants with long trunks and great curling tusks. There were prehistoric bison, much like the bison of the present that are generally called buffalo.

Small horses, prong-horned antelope, and deer raced across the country. There were tapirs, wild pigs and many smaller animals. Predatory beasts, such as the dire-wolf and sabre-toothed tiger, pursued the feeding herds.

In southern California, between the coast and the mountains, there was a good feeding ground for animals. Near modern Los Angeles, a district now called La Brea, there were many pools to attract thirsty beasts. The water of the pools looked innocent enough on the surface, but underneath bubbled liquid tar.

Large and small animals came to drink, waded into the pools and were caught in the tar. Their struggles and cries attracted predatory beasts who leaped into the water, only to be caught in the tar themselves as they attacked the mired-down animals. Vultures swooped down to feed on the dying creatures, and they, too, met their death. This may have gone on for hundreds of years.

In modern times men, who were digging into the pools for tar, discovered that there was, deep down, a regular museum of prehistoric animals: horses, elephants, camels, lions and others. They had been preserved in oil for centuries. Bones were taken out, cleaned, and assembled by scientists, and the skeletons are in the Los Angeles County Museum in Exposition Park. From these skeletons scientists have gained much of their knowledge of the size and character of animals that inhabited the Southwest in the great Age of Mammals.

Southern Arizona, in the valleys of the San Pedro and Santa Cruz rivers, was a delightful place those thousands of years ago. The climate was cooler than at present and not so dry. There were plains of tall grass, pools and rivers, bushes and trees. Above this landscape rose craggy mountains not unlike those of modern times. But in all this wild, fertile country of sun, grass and mountains were there no human beings to compete with the animals?

For many years scientists have been studying the problem of when early man arrived in North America. It is now believed that the first men were primitive hunters from Asia, who crossed over the land bridge at Bering Straits, or later on the ice, to enter North America.

During the last Ice Age, when upheavals and breaks in the ice cover created corridors for travel, many migratory groups of men, women and children wandered into North America and eventually spread out eastward and southward. Probably some groups came in pursuit of animals they were hunting for food. In the course of centuries, some groups crossed the Isthmus bridge into South America. These primitive people hunted animals with stone-tipped wooden darts, or they gathered nuts, berries and seeds for food. Skins of animals they killed were the only materials they had for clothing.

Scientists were convinced that some of these migratory people must have reached the Southwest about 11,000 years ago, but they could find no proof of human presence. Many bones of prehistoric animals were dug up from time to time. Sometimes collections of bones came to light after flash floods had washed away banks of soil in creeks or river beds. Bones were found in caves, and these places were searched with special care, because if men had been present they would have used caves for shelter.

At last, at a place near Folsom, New Mexico, an important collection of prehistoric bison bones was found in a cave, and with the bones were chipped stone spear points, certainly man-made. In Sandia Cave, New Mexico, charcoal ashes of ancient fires were found in a stone-lined fireplace, together with stone tools. This was positive evidence that man had been there. In Gypsum Cave, Nevada, painted dart shafts and spear points were found in the same layer of debris with dung, claws, and hair of the prehistoric sloth. It seems likely that these men followed the river valleys southward from Nevada.

Now the searchers knew that primitive hunters had

been in the Southwest at the same time as the prehistoric animals, although they had found no human bones. But, questioned the scientists, did the hunters leave the spear points beside animals they actually killed, or did the men occupy the caves at a later period? They kept on searching for further knowledge.

Another cave that provided a great deal of information was the huge Ventana Cave on a mountainside of the Papago Indian Reservation, west of Tucson. Here archeologists from the State Museum, directed by Dr. Emil W. Haury, worked for some years, digging down through fifteen feet of trash, debris, sand and stones. In the lowest level they found bones of prehistoric animals, ashes of fires, stone knives and scrapers. Men must have occupied the cave farther back than 10,000 years ago, because soon after that period these animals became extinct. Other levels in the excavations at Ventana revealed remains of human occupation in later centuries.

In the Arizona State Museum, in Tucson, displays of the discoveries and artifacts from Ventana Cave have been set up to explain the story of ancient human occupation.

Then, in 1951, a discovery of mammoth bones was made at Naco, a small settlement at the Mexican border near Bisbee. North of the settlement was a creek with steep clay banks through which flood waters rushed after summer storms, although it was dry most of the year.

After one of these storms the Navarettes, father and son, who lived at Naco, discovered large bones protruding from the clay soil in the creek bed. They had found ancient bones before and realized their importance. Carefully, they dug around the exposed bones until they found the shape of a skull and a spear point. This was something to be reported, they decided, and promptly notified the State Museum in Tucson.

Archeologists, led by Dr. Haury, and paleontologists from the University gathered at the site to dig and study. They were well rewarded by their discoveries. With infinite care they cleaned the clay from the group of bones which proved to be the fore part of a mammoth: ribs and shoulder blade and huge jaw. Then — triumphant discovery — they found eight spear points embedded among the bones, just where they had penetrated the hide of the ancient elephant!

Here was proof that prehistoric hunters had killed this very mammoth. Geologists and paleontologists, who knew the period when these beasts flourished, could give an approximate date for this elephant hunt. It was between 11,000 and 10,000 years ago. Now, it was certain that men had arrived and were functioning in southern Arizona at that period.

After the meticulous work of cleaning, preserving, and transporting the bones to the State Museum was completed, the scientists speculated about that ancient elephant hunt. Most likely the arroyo had been a stream where the mammoth came to drink. When the hunters attacked the huge beast it could not get away easily because it was hemmed in by the high banks of the creek. The hunters hurled their spears at the creature from all sides, wounding the great beast until he fell and could be finished off at close range. Since no hind quarter bones were found, the hunters must have carried off these sections to eat at a later time. During thousands of years, the bones were buried deeply in the creek bed under water and clay. Thus they were preserved until erosion, caused by flood waters over a long period, exposed them.

In 1955 another important discovery was made at the Lehner Ranch on the west bank of the San Pedro River. The owner of the ranch, investigating a deep arroyo, found bones and a mammoth tooth in a layer of black soil.

Once more the scientists gathered to excavate and study, with exciting results. Evidently this had been a water hole where animals were accustomed to drink, for there were bones of several extinct types, covering a large area of the arroyo bed — bones of mammoth, bison, tapir and small horse. The excavators found thirteen spear points and eight cutting and scraping tools as well as ashes of fires. It seemed to prove that this had been a place to kill and cut up big game. Here too came the small brown men, agile and skillful, with their spears to attack the great beasts. What a wild scene it must have been as the small men darted in to throw their spears, and the great elephants trumpeted and thrashed, their tusks clashing. As the animals fell the hunters rushed in to kill, to cut up the meat, and to start it roasting. Fires blazed while the hunters squatted on their haunches to devour the good meat.

The story of the discoveries at Naco and at the Lehner Ranch has been written by Dr. Haury, leader of the study for the archeological magazine, *The Kiva*.

People who are not scientists may also follow the story of the men and beasts of prehistoric times at the Arizona State Museum. There are the mammoth bones from Naco, displayed in a case with replicas of the spear points placed just where they were found among the bones. The actual prehistoric points are displayed below the case where they may be easily studied.

There are bones and points from the Lehner site and

a lively model of the brown men cutting up a carcass. A fine diorama gives an exciting picture of a mammoth hunt. In another diorama prehistoric animals are seen feeding on the plains, and here the great mammoth lifts his huge head and curling tusks, an Arizona elephant of 10,000 years ago.

## Chapter III

### The First Southwesterners

Wherever men and women settle, find food and shelter, and raise families, they leave signs of their presence. In Arizona, stone tools and spear points are the only relics of the first primitive inhabitants. Those who came later, who had learned to make useful things and to farm, left their woven baskets and sandals, also pottery made from clay and painted with designs. Ruins of the villages they built on hilltops, or clusters of houses in caves, show the skill in building that was achieved by some of the prehistoric groups.

When archeologists undertook the study of bygone peoples in the Southwest they found that the dry climate had preserved many articles that would otherwise have been destroyed by rain and damp. In the dry shelter of

17

caves where people had lived, baskets, sandals, and pots were found, even prehistoric corn cobs and bits of fabric kept intact through the centuries. Many articles were preserved in the ruins of villages that had been buried under many feet of soil.

Groups of people lived near each other in villages or cave homes and accumulated tremendous ash heaps. All the refuse of the houses — ashes from fires, bones, broken pottery — was thrown into these dumps. Each generation of housekeepers threw out more rubbish, until there were huge mounds outside villages or below cave homes. The contents of these mounds were undisturbed through centuries.

Archeologists are skilled detectives in their study of how and when ancient peoples lived. They take particular delight in the trash heaps, digging through them with the greatest care. Each bone or tool or bit of pottery is lifted out and cleaned for study. They learn a great deal about how people lived from these relics of things they used, and from the kind of pottery each group made.

The question of when the various tribes lived in prehistoric ages is judged partly by these things, partly by the sort of dwelling they had, but most particularly by the science of tree-ring dating.

This method of dating was developed by Dr. Andrew E. Douglass, a scientist at the University of Arizona, when he was making a study of cycles of climates. In the Southwest, a land of little rain, Dr. Douglass made a study of tree-ring growth from pines. A tree produces a ring of cells each year, a thick one in years of good moisture, a thin one in dry years. After long study and experimentation the science of tree-ring dating, called dendrochronology, was developed.

It was discovered that this method of dating could be applied to ancient roof beams taken from prehistoric Indian dwellings. By boring into these logs the tree-ring specialists could determine when those logs were cut to become roof beams. This was done by comparing the rings in the pieces of wood with their charts. In this way the archeologists could obtain approximate dates for the various prehistoric dwellings.

Year by year, the archeologists have pieced together a story of prehistoric Indian life from some centuries before the time of Christ to the thirteenth and fourteenth centuries A.D., when the Indian civilizations reached their height.

Arizona of so long ago, when prehistoric Indians lived here, looked more or less as it does today. Centuries of geologic changes had created the mountains, river valleys and desert plains. In the north was the spectacular region of glowing colored cliffs, mesas and canyons. In the central and eastern part, rivers surged down to the valleys from the mountains.

The huge prehistoric beasts had disappeared, but there were plenty of animals for the hunters to pursue: deer and antelope, mountain sheep, mountain lions, wild pigs, and among the small animals were gophers and rabbits.

Through the centuries, many different groups of copper-skinned, sturdy people with coarse black hair wandered into Arizona to hunt the game, to gather wild plants, and eventually to farm. In the southern valleys the clans may have been descendants of the first brown men who hunted the prehistoric beasts, or they may have been groups who entered the region later.

Southern Arizona valleys and those in neighboring

Sonora, Mexico, are all the same kind of semi-arid land with good grass cover and a variety of desert vegetation. This whole region is called the Sonoran Desert.

The inhabitants, who depended on wild plants for much of their food, harvested the red-meated fruit of the saguaro cactus, fruits of other cacti, and beans of the mesquite tree, just as the Indians of the country do at the present time. In the wooded foothills of the Chiricahua Mountains they found acorns and juniper berries to add to their diet. Archeologists call these early people the Cochise tribes.

In time, the people of the San Pedro Valley and those in Mexico met each other. The Arizonans acquired from their neighbors the idea of cultivating wild plants for food.

Some thousands of years ago, inventive tribes of the highlands of Mexico or Guatemala learned to cultivate a wild grass plant with nourishing seeds that grew into small ears. This was maize or corn, the basic food of all Indian inhabitants of the Americas. Learning to cultivate corn was the beginning of agriculture for the native Americans. The maize plant passed from one group to another over much of North America. It reached the people of southern Arizona before the beginning of the Christian era.

By this contact with more advanced groups, the people of the southern Arizona valleys began a new way of life. They were the first farmers. When they could raise crops of corn and beans and squash, which also came from Mexico, they had an improved diet. Families or groups could settle in one place instead of wandering hither and yon in search of food.

Human beings have always bettered themselves by trying new things. So, when these Arizonans began to settle in groups in order to grow their corn and beans, they developed the idea of a house to live in, something better than a brush shelter. The first crude dwellings are called pit houses. A circular or rectangular space was dug out in the ground and posts were set up to support a roof of poles and brush, then plastered with mud. Walls were also of stakes, held together by mud plaster. Entrance was by an inclined runway facing the east, or sometimes by a ladder of sticks lowered through a hole in the roof.

Men and boys went off with their spears to hunt game for meat, but the hunt was not so desperate when they had additional food from the crops. Women had time to think of ways to make housekeeping easier. Some wove baskets or trays to hold food or, when lined with pitch, to store water brought from streams. When the cotton plant was introduced by tribes of Mexico, women learned to weave the fiber into cloth for garments.

As they went on experimenting, the women molded pots with clay from the river banks. These pots were rough brown things, useful for storing seeds, nuts or other food. Perhaps by accident, some pottery-maker discovered that her pots could be hardened in fire, so they could be used for cooking vessels. Or this knowledge may have come to them from more advanced tribes to the south. A decorated pot is more attractive than a plain one, and before long the pottery-makers ground up red or black earth or used vegetable juices to make paint. They painted the first designs on their jugs or bowls, using a brush made from yucca fiber.

These busy housekeepers invented a grinding stone for mashing up seeds, corn kernels, or mesquite beans. They used a large rock with a flat surface. With a small rounded stone that fitted the hand, they rubbed the grains back and forth until they had them ground into meal. Moistening the meal with water, they patted it into flat cakes to be cooked on stone slabs over the fire. Constant grinding with the small stone wore down the flat surface of the rock until it had a trough-like shape. Those early Arizonans ate so much pulverized rock with their corn meal that their teeth were worn down.

Through later centuries, the grinding stone developed into a well-shaped trough called a metate, and the rounded grinding stone is called a mano. Native women of the Americas, through hundreds of years, have ground their corn and other grains on the metate. Many Indian women in modern Arizona still use the metate and mano.

While these tribes were learning better ways of living, another clan had come in to make homes in the semi-arid Gila River Valley. The Pima Indians of today, who believe these prehistoric people were their ancestors, called them Hohokam, "those who have departed." No one knows definitely where these wanderers came from or when they arrived. Some students believe they came from Mexico, bringing with them the knowledge of farming and pottery-making. Others think they were primitive people when they arrived, like the other inhabitants of the southern valleys.

In their desert land there was little rainfall. Often, after winter snows or rains in the mountains, the Gila overflowed its banks. When the water receded the flooded plains made good soil for farming, but this could not be depended upon. Some ingenious farmers of the tribe thought of digging ditches from the river to water their fields. They were able in this way to increase their crops.

Near their farms they built villages of mud-walled

huts with roofs of brush and mud. These Hohokam were settled people, busy with their crops and crafts. As the years passed, the men became excellent engineers. Although they had only digging sticks or stone hoes, and woven baskets for moving dirt, they built a network of canals from the river to their settlements, and ditches from the canals to their fields. They made dams of brush and rock in the river to control the flow.

For miles over the once-desert valley there were flourishing fields of corn, beans, squash, and cotton. Eventually the settlements spread to the Salt River Valley as well.

While groups of farmers were learning how to live in the south, the northern part of the Southwest was also becoming populated. Bands of wanderers drifted into the wild, rugged country of mesas, canyons and plains in northern Arizona and New Mexico and southern parts of Utah and Colorado.

In the canyons, wind and storms had worked on the walls until shallow caves were hollowed out under overhanging ledges. These places made excellent shelter from weather and a place to sleep. In the Arizona caves of Canyon de Chelly, Tsegi Canyon and others, traces have been found of the first people who used them for shelters.

These early wanderers were hunters with few skills, but they did weave excellent baskets and sandals from plant fibers. The name Basketmaker has been given to them because baskets were the relics found buried with their dead. Many skeletons and some mummies, dried by the climate, were discovered in trash heaps or in the back of caves.

These people, the Basketmakers, acquired corn and beans to plant and learned to make pottery. The women were skilled in making cord from plant fibers or strings from their own hair, which they had to chop off with stone knives. There were string bags for carrying things, and there were ties for sandals. Strips of rabbit fur were tied together, wound around fiber cord, and sewed together to make fur robes for warmth.

The hunters used the spear which was attached to a throwing stick held in the hunter's hand. This gave extra force to the swing of the spear as it flew toward the hunted animal. Later, they learned to hunt with bow and arrow.

In small fields near the streams, corn, beans, and cotton were grown by the groups who lived in pit houses on mesa tops or in valleys, as well as by those who lived in cliff dwellings.

Archeologists have a general name for all the inhabitants of these northern regions who lived there century after century. They call them Anasazi, a Navajo name meaning the Ancient Ones. Some of these people wandered southward and met groups from southern valleys, who had traveled into the upper Gila Valley and eastern mountains. Called Mogollon people by the archeologists, these groups built their pit houses on ridges above the valleys where they grew their crops. They wandered northward as the Anasazi came southward, and the two tribes influenced each other.

There were villages of pit houses in the high plateau country near the San Francisco Peaks. These people lived in valleys below extinct volcanoes. Then, suddenly, about 1064 A.D., a tremendous eruption burst forth! Fire, red-hot rocks, clouds of volcanic ash soared into the sky and showered over the pit houses and fields. They were buried deep in cinders and ashes. Streams of boiling lava spread over large areas, adding to the destruction.

In this eruption lava and cinders created Sunset Crater.

The survivors of the eruption were joined years later by farmers from other regions. The black volcanic ash and cinder, covering 1,000 square miles, made good farm land after it settled, because the cinders held water and made a good mulch for crops. When word of this got around from clan to clan, there was a prehistoric land rush to the vicinity of Sunset Crater. The new inhabitants brought a variety of ideas and skills to the pit house people who were already inhabiting the country.

Centuries passed while all these groups of hardworking brown people in prehistoric Arizona acquired new skills. Time had no meaning in their world; all the work of their hands, with primitive tools, was slow and painstaking.

When we study in museums their stone tools, baskets, pottery, and ornaments, it is evident that everything they made required slow, patient labor. Stone ax heads and hammers, stone knives, finely chipped spear points — all required infinite labor in chipping, shaping and smoothing. The women had bone awls to help them in making baskets or sewing together the deerskins they had patiently cleaned with stone scrapers. It was endless work for the men to chop down trees and trim branches with stone axes.

The women were always busy with grinding corn kernels or seeds, sewing deerskins, weaving baskets or cotton cloth. Slowly, they molded their pottery jars and bowls, fired them and painted delightful patterns on them with earth and vegetable paints.

From earliest times all peoples, no matter how primitive, have loved adornment. So the prehistoric craftsmen worked with carved bone, shells, stones, and turquoise to make necklaces and bracelets. Turquoise, the sky stone, was valued above all others by the native Southwesterners.

The people of all these groups obtained materials they needed through the traders who were hardy, strong-legged men, able to travel far and wide over the vast country to exchange products. It seems likely that tribes of Arizona, Mexico, and those across the Colorado in California communicated with each other through these sturdy travelers. In this manner the inland dwellers of Arizona received shells from the Gulf of California, perhaps even from the Pacific Coast. They also received bright tropical bird feathers, copper bells, and parrots from Mexico. Perhaps the mountain people traded deerskins and turquoise for shells and feathers. Different types of pottery were also spread from group to group through these traders.

The prehistoric Arizonans had no written language, but they liked to express their ideas in drawing, as children do. Sometimes on the walls of their caves they painted, with crude earth colors, the figures of animals, hunters, or designs that had some meaning for them.

They had no chalk or paper, but when they found a smooth face of rock or boulder they "drew" on it by pecking out lines on the rock with a sharp-pointed stone. Animals and hunters, the round face of the sun, footprints, or strange signs were outlined on the rock. In many parts of Arizona these picture rocks, called petroglyphs, may be seen. They are the attempts of primitive artists, centuries ago, to tell stories in pictures.

By about 1100 A.D., most of the prehistoric inhabitants had made great progress in building homes. They used whatever stone was available for walls of houses, built above ground instead of over a pit. Stone rooms were also built in caves. The walls were laid up in rows of stone slab or rocks, firmly cemented with mud plaster.

Having learned the skill of masonry, the people could construct snug houses for shelter.

Instead of scattered groups of one-family pit houses, the idea of living in communities was adopted by most of the tribes. In the next few centuries the prehistoric people of the Southwest reached the height of their civilization.

## Chapter IV

### Farmers, Builders, Craftsmen

Indian towns in Arizona, seven or eight hundred years ago, were busy, crowded communities. Generally they were built on ridges or hilltops above the valleys where the people farmed. These towns did not have separate houses, but were built in long rows of small apartments, one level set back above another with fewer rooms on the upper levels. The inhabitants climbed to each group of apartments by crude ladders, and the roof of each row made a terrace for the people in the apartments above. It was a set-back type of architecture something like that of skyscrapers on a small scale.

In the bright, strong sunlight of the Southwest, the people spent most of their lives outdoors. The cramped, dark rooms were useful mostly for sleeping or refuge from storms. On the roof terraces, or in the plaza before the houses, women cooked for their families or sat in groups busy with their craft work. They made beautiful pottery, wove cotton for garments, made baskets, and prepared deerskins for various uses.

Women went to the spring or stream to fetch water in large clay jars which they carried home on their heads, or slung over their backs secured by a band, called a tump line, across their foreheads. Up the ladders to the higher levels they carried the water jars, or anything else needed for their rooms.

Children scampered up and down the ladders, or played in the plaza where turkeys scratched in the dust. The turkeys were kept for their feathers more than for food. Women made soft robes from feathers by wrapping them around cords that were sewed together. Sometimes bright-hued parrots added their squawks to the gobbling of turkeys. Turkey feathers and those of the parrots were precious to the people, as they were used for ornaments and in making religious objects and decorations for their ceremonies.

The large plaza of the village was the center of activities. Here there was an underground room, reached by ladder from above, called the kiva. This was the gathering place for the men to discuss affairs of the village, to prepare costumes, ornaments, and sacred corn meal for the dances that were prayers to the nature gods they believed in. People who were close to the earth, who were so dependent for their welfare on natural forces, thought of sun, rain, thunder and lightning as spirits to whom to pray. These spirits would provide sufficient rain for the crops, give the people good health, protect them from evil and disaster.

The families worked for the good of the whole village without personal ambition. They shared the use of the stream that provided water; they shared the fields where they raised food. The elderly men of the tribe were leaders of the communities. They directed the activities, the social behavior, and the religious ceremonies.

During the centuries from 1100 to 1300 A.D., the tribes of the northern regions became the most expert builders and townmakers. For this reason the archeologists call the Anasazi of this period Pueblos, or builders. Pueblo is a Spanish word meaning village. When Spaniards first saw the terraced Indian towns of the Rio Grande Valley they called them pueblos, and the name has been applied to Indian towns and their people ever since.

A real building boom was going on in these last few centuries of prehistoric civilization. The population was increasing, and although some groups continued to live in clusters of houses in the open, large numbers of people crowded into the towns. Pueblo Bonito and Chaco Canyon in New Mexico were very large towns. Tuzigoot and Wupatki in Arizona were also well-built communities.

It was at this time that the marvelous cliff dwellings of Mesa Verde in Colorado and those of northern Arizona and New Mexico were built. The caves were high on the walls of canyons, reached only by steep trails, ladders, or toe-and-hand holds cut into the face of the cliff. Up and down these trails the people went to reach their fields and water supply below. The cliff dwellers also built houses and raised crops on the tops of mesas above their cave homes.

Various elements in the style of building suggest that the Pueblo people feared enemies. The towns built on ridges often had strong walls around the whole settlement.

Inhabitants could climb the ladders to the upper levels of their buildings and draw them up to keep marauders from reaching them. From the upper terraces they had a wide view over the country. Enemies could not approach unseen.

Archeologists think it is likely that during these centuries Athapascan tribes from the north, ancestors of the Navajo and Apache, were drifting down through mountain valleys, filtering into the prosperous farming settlements of the Southwest. The fields of corn, beans and squash must have looked good to these primitive hunters and warriors.

There were other things to worry the Pueblo people besides raiders. They moved around frequently, seeking to improve their living conditions. Often in drought years the springs and creeks dried up. Sometimes the earth of their fields became exhausted. The families then wandered over the land in search of better soil, good water, and a sheltered place in which to live.

Some Pueblo bands moved down into the valleys of the Mogollon country, settling among the people already there. Apparently there was no trouble. They lived side by side, and the new settlers taught their neighbors the art of building. A number of strong towns, occupied by large groups of families, were built over the years. There was sufficient food from their fields and from hunting; they were secure in their walled towns to carry on their crafts and social life. Kinishba, a large town that has been excavated and studied under the direction of Dr. Byron Cummings, was such a community.

The University of Arizona Summer School, directed by Dr. Emil Haury, has excavated and studied prehistoric ruins for fourteen years at Point of Pines, on the Apache

Reservation. Their work has brought to light much information on prehistoric settlements. Evidently a large population lived in the region over a long period.

Other groups wandered through the canyons of the Salt River to join Hohokam tribes in the irrigated valleys. Here, too, it seems to have been a friendly migration. The newcomers joined the settlements of the desert farmers and brought them new ideas in building. These people from the north are called Salado, the Spanish name for the Salt River.

Those interesting but rather mysterious groups, the Hohokam, had gone on quietly with their own methods and customs for centuries. Their canal system of irrigation and their villages extended over the lower Salt and Gila valleys. Altogether they built over 200 miles of canals to serve the farmers of a prosperous civilization.

Their villages were collections of mud and brush huts, too perishable to exist through centuries as the stone houses have done. Archeologists, in excavating mounds of earth, discovered the foundations of rooms, also large mounds that they believe had houses or store-rooms for food products on top of them.

Recently, at Gila Bend, an unusual mound was unearthed. It had sloping sides, faced with the hard desert earth, caliche, and a flat top. The construction was like that of the pyramid temples built by ancient people in Mexico, with steep steps leading to the temple on top.

The Hohokam seem to have had a close relationship with Mexican people in various ways. One of these was the ancient ball game, played in rectangular walled courts. The Maya people of Mexico had ball courts with walls of stone and a large stone ring set in one wall. The object of the players was to put a hard rubber ball through that ring, a sort of prehistoric basketball. Apparently this game was popular in the Hohokam settlements, for several walled courts were uncovered by investigators. To confirm their belief that these were ball courts, a ball was found made from the rubber of the guayule plant that grows in Mexico.

A place half-buried under the earth, called Snaketown, revealed many interesting things when archeologists dug into it. Besides learning about the construction of houses, the investigators found some of the finest handiwork of these talented people. They carved stone bowls and decorated bone and shell with carved designs and turquoise mosaic. The women, who made their interesting pottery, took pleasure in the small animals and birds of their desert land. Painted on the buff surface of bowls with red paint were delightful little figures of lizards, horned toads, birds, and turtles. Around some shallow bowls were painted amusing rows of figures, sometimes a line of people dancing, again figures carrying baskets on their backs.

These small figures of people give the only idea of what the Hohokam were like, since they cremated their dead instead of burying them. It is difficult to imagine their way of life when their homes are gone, and there are no relics of clothing, only the works of their hands to study.

By the time the Salado groups moved into their territory, the desert farmers were ready to learn from them new ways of building. In their arid valleys there was a scarcity of wood, but they learned to build with adobe and caliche, as other inhabitants of arid regions have done.

The most impressive remains of a settlement built by these mixed groups is the collection of ruins called

Casa Grande. There it stands to this day in the desert near Coolidge, a massive tower with remains of houses and compound walls around it. The tower, called "The Great House," is four stories high with walls of amazing thickness. The builders constructed those walls with great blocks of stiff caliche mud that hardens into a rocklike substance. The walls were strong enough to survive the centuries, although the floors are gone.

In its day, Casa Grande was probably a community center for the villages around it, a fort, and a storehouse for surplus food. The ruins are now a National Monument.

Another group of buildings, called Pueblo Grande, stands on a high knoll above a main irrigation canal between Phoenix and Tempe. The foundation of the ancient canal was used in building the modern waterway. Pueblo Grande is now the Municipal Prehistoric Monument. This town, like Casa Grande, seems to have been a center for villages and farms around it. In excavating the ruins, it was discovered that many of the rooms had been granaries or storage rooms. In the lowest level, bins lined with stone slabs were found.

After some prosperous centuries, disaster began to threaten the desert farmers. All over their irrigated valleys the soil was becoming waterlogged by seepage back into the earth from irrigation. For hundreds of years they had planted and harvested crops on the same land. This theory seems logical because modern farmers in the Salt River Valley have had the same trouble with irrigation. The Indians had no pumps or other means of getting rid of surplus water.

Families began to move away, but where they went is a mystery. Some may have wandered into the desert region now occupied by the Papago Indians. Those who remained were, perhaps, the ancestors of the Pima Indians the Spaniards found in the Gila Valley. The Pimas occupied mud and stake huts and raised crops in irrigated fields. However, the Salt River Valley and part of the Gila Valley were deserted by 1400 A.D. The excellent system of canals fell into ruin.

Tree-ring studies show that the thirteenth century in the Southwest was a very dry period. There was an extreme drought that lasted for twenty-three years, from 1276 to 1299 A.D. In this arid country rain is always of supreme importance, and when such a long cycle of drought occurs the streams dry up, the fields turn to dust, the crops will not grow.

Northern Arizona had been well populated with farming people. They could not live without water for crops, and perhaps there were other troubles, such as epidemics of disease or fear of enemies. At any rate, the inhabitants of the great pueblo towns and cliff dwellings began moving away, year after year. Leaving most of their possessions behind them, groups of families wandered across the country seeking new homes.

Some traveled eastward to the valley of the Rio Grande River in New Mexico. In earlier years, exploring families had found this valley a good place to live and had started settlements. The refugees from northern Arizona applied their skill in building to construct new villages. That prehistoric type of architecture may be seen now in some of the Indian villages, particularly in Taos and Santo Domingo. Many of the Pueblo clans in this valley are believed to be descendants of the prehistoric Pueblo people.

Other wanderers joined the scattered groups who were occupying the mesas now belonging to the Hopi tribe in northern Arizona. Migrations, from all directions, swelled the population of stone villages built on mesa tops. These people were to become the ancestors of the modern Hopi.

There were farming settlements in the New Mexico valley now occupied by the Zuñi tribe. Some of the migrating people joined them, causing such an increased population that six villages were built, the chief one named Háwikuh.

In Arizona the remarkable cliff villages of Betatakin and Keet Seel in Tsegi Canyon, those in Canyon de Chelly, and Montezuma's Castle in Verde Valley were deserted. The hilltop towns of Tuzigoot and Wupatki near Flagstaff and Kinishba in the White Mountains stood empty. Roofs fell in, walls crumbled into heaps of rubble; the rooms were inhabited only by chipmunks, lizards and other small creatures.

The time was coming, in the sixteenth century, when this country would be invaded by Spaniards. They would find some inhabited towns, many groups of simple Indians living near water courses where they could grow their small crops of corn and beans. They would find nomadic groups of Navajo and Apache, but the desert valleys and mountainous regions would be sparsely inhabited, and the dwellings of the Ancient Ones would be deserted.

Arizona has a prehistoric past of great interest. Thanks to the devoted work of scientists, people of today may visit the settlements of bygone inhabitants. They may learn from books the ways of life of the ancient people. Many hilltop towns or cliff dwellings have been excavated, studied and partly restored, and the most valuable are preserved as National Monuments. There are excellent museums at these sites where visitors may study the articles of daily use and fine craft work, discovered by excavators. Treasures from the life of the past are displayed in the museums of the state: the Arizona State Museum on the campus of the University of Arizona in Tucson; the Museum of Northern Arizona in Flagstaff; the Heard Museum in Phoenix; and the Amerind Foundation near Dragoon.

# PART II.
# SPANISH AND MEXICAN ARIZONA

Chapter V

Spanish Adventurers Reach the Southwest

For many centuries the copper-skinned natives of
North and South America lived undisturbed by invasions
from other races. In Mexico and Central America there
were tribes who advanced far in civilization: the Toltec,
Aztec, and Maya people. Many artistic tribes lived in
South America during prehistoric centuries, and the powerful Incas had developed a wonderful kingdom before
the Spaniards entered the continent.

Spaniards of the sixteenth century were bold, arrogant, adventurous men. Spain was powerful in Europe,
and Columbus had presented the rulers with a New World
across the ocean. Knights, captains and soldiers were
ready to sail the seas, to explore the wilderness. They
dreamed of more land, more wealth for Spain and them-

selves. The Catholic Church and the Spanish rulers were equally resolved to win heathen souls of the new lands for the True Faith.

On the islands of Cuba and Hispaniola the Spaniards soon had flourishing towns and great plantations where the primitive Indians slaved for them. Various captured Indians told of rich kingdoms, whose chiefs had quantities of the yellow metal, gold, that the Spaniards prized so greatly. One of these stories described the mighty kingdom of the Aztecs, in a land called Mexico, ruled by powerful Montezuma, whose warriors had conquered many other tribes.

It was this tale that led the Spaniards into an era of conquest and glittering visions. And it was Hernando Cortés, a clever, ambitious knight, who became the hero of one of the greatest adventure stories in history.

Cortés obtained permission from the governor of Cuba to lead an expedition with several ships for the discovery of the kingdom of the Aztecs. In the spring of 1519, Spanish soldiers, horses, and arms were disembarked on the sandy shore of Mexico, near the site of modern Vera Cruz.

Faced with a jungle wilderness, above which rose terrific mountains, Cortés and his men set out to win a kingdom. There were less than five hundred men, both horsemen and foot soldiers, with their lances, swords, and arquebuses. For their outpost the Spaniards built a small fort on the shore which they named Villa Rica de Vera Cruz, the Rich City of the True Cross.

Helped by friendly Indians who hated the Aztecs, the bold adventurers then began their invasion. Following Indian foot-trails, they struggled upward through forbidding mountains, hampered by their armor and horses. It was an incredible journey. At times, they had to fight hostile tribes to prove the superiority of guns, horses, and armor over arrows and war clubs. One tribe, the Tlascalans, joined with them to fight the Aztecs.

At last they came through a pass into the great Valley of Mexico. The invaders were overawed by the beauty of the country, its cultivated fields, its shimmering lakes with white towns on the shores. Mountains circled the valley, highest of all soared the snowy crowns of Popocatepetl and Ixtaccihuatl. In the largest lake lay the magical island city, Tenochtitlán, Montezuma's capital. It was connected with the shore by several causeways.

Over one of these causeways a gorgeous procession streamed out to meet them. Montezuma himself, in a litter trimmed with gold and feathers, came accompanied by proud chieftains. The Aztec ruler knew of the advancing invaders from his scouts, but chose not to attack them.

The Spaniards were invited into the city, housed in a palace and shown the whole beautiful town of canals, palaces and temples. In the great marketplace, crowded with people, the Spaniards saw all the rich products of the land. Astounded by these evidences of civilization, the Spaniards were yet anxious and afraid. Well they knew that these haughty warriors had them in a trap. That was the plan of the chieftains when they urged Montezuma to invite the invaders into the city. The warriors were fiercely hostile, but they could not attack the strangers without an order from their revered lord, and Montezuma would not give permission.

The Aztec ruler was a strange character; he was superstitious and greatly influenced by the priests of the gods and the magicians. He believed their prophecy that in a certain year their hero-god, Quetzalcoatl, would return from the East, where he had vanished, to take over the rule of the Aztecs. It was in that year that the Spaniards arrived. To Montezuma's superstitious mind, these white-skinned, bearded strangers, who came from the East in ships with wings, might be representatives of Quetzalcoatl. He was afraid to make a move against them, even though his warriors could easily have destroyed them.

Months passed while Cortés played his clever game to win the kingdom by impressing Montezuma with the might and splendor of the King of Spain, the greatest ruler in the world, to whom the Aztecs must give obedience. Although Montezuma knew by then that the Spaniards were not supernatural beings, yet he was haunted by the fear that their coming meant the doom of the Aztecs. It was their fate; it was useless to resist. Cortés was on the verge of victory when he was called to the fort on the coast to deal with a ship's captain, sent by the governor of Cuba to arrest him for proceeding to the interior without orders. He left his captain, Pedro de Alvarado, in command.

This captain was an impetuous man with none of his leader's diplomacy. While the people were celebrating a festival in honor of the war god, a festival that included human sacrifices, Alvarado decided it was time to give these heathen a lesson in the power of Spain. He led his horsemen into the dancing, singing crowd before the temple. Ruthlessly, the men slashed with their swords and trampled people under the horses' hoofs. Many were killed and wounded.

By this brutal act, all the skillful work of Cortés was ruined. The whole city rose against the invaders. When Cortés returned, he found his men imprisoned in their palace, cut off from food, bombarded day and night with arrows and stones. Cortés had persuaded Montezuma to take up residence in the palace with the Spaniards for their safety, but even the presence of their ruler did not keep the warriors from their attacks.  As a last resort, Cortés ordered Montezuma to appear on the roof to tell his people they must let the Spaniards leave the city.  It was too late for the weakling, Montezuma, to control his people.  Yells and curses greeted him; stones and arrows flew toward him.  Montezuma was hit by a large rock and died of the wound.

Now the only hope for the Spaniards was to try escape by night.  They slipped out with their horses and bags of loot but were soon discovered.  In a terrible night of fear, they were slaughtered by swarms of warriors who attacked from canoes in the canals.  The bridges were lifted, and men and horses drowned in the canals.  Cortés, with a few men and horses, managed to reach the lake shore by one of the causeways.

They took refuge with the Tlascalans, who were bitter enemies of the Aztecs.  From Indian messengers, Cortés learned that a few ships had arrived at the fort with men and supplies, and these were led up the mountains by Indian guides.

Cortés would not recognize defeat.  He was determined to reconquer Tenochtitlán.  During the winter, a Spanish shipbuilder of the company taught the Tlascalans to shape timbers for small ships from the trees of their forests.  In the spring, the timbers were carried down the mountains on Indian backs to the lakeside city of Texcoco, which had been abandoned.  Cortés planned to besiege the Aztec city from the lake.

The tiny fleet sailed out into the lake loaded with soldiers and Indians.  Swarms of warriors in canoes darted out to stop them, but the ships plowed over the canoes, spilling the warriors into the lake. Day after day the small vessels cruised around the island city, cutting off canoes that were bringing food from the shores. The ships sailed on both sides of the causeways as Spanish soldiers crossed to camp on the outskirts of the city.

The Aztecs were commanded by the proud young chief, Cuauhtémoc, Montezuma's nephew, who was a splendid type of brave, intelligent Aztec. Under his leadership the warriors fought valiantly, but the people were dying of starvation and wounds. Street by street and canal by canal, the Spaniards made their way into the city, until they won the great marketplace near the temples. In 1521, Cuauhtémoc was captured, and the siege was over.

The fabulous Aztec city, Tenochtitlán, was destroyed, but it would be remembered in legend for its beauty. On the ruins rose a solid Spanish town called by the conquerors Mexico City. The stones of the pyramid temples were used to build Spanish churches. Spanish buildings and plazas were constructed over the ruined canals. Indian Mexico was divided into provinces with Spanish governors, while Spanish towns and plantations replaced Indian settlements. Mexico became a Spanish colony called New Spain.

The conquest of the Aztecs roused a storm of excitement in Spain. Crowds of knightly adventurers and soldiers hurried to this new land of wonders, eager to make conquests of their own. Captains went out in all directions, subduing tribes.

Meanwhile, more wondrous lands and stores of treasure were discovered. Pedro de Alvarado conquered the civilized Maya people. In 1531, a tough adventurer from Spain, Francisco Pizarro, won control of the marvelous empire of the Incas in Peru. He followed Cortés' pattern of daring, combined with underhanded dealings and treachery, but won his ends in a more brutal manner than Cortés.

When Spanish minds were fed on all these true tales of kingdoms and treasures, it is not surprising that they were ready to believe any story, no matter how fantastic. Another golden legend was being prepared in a most unusual way.

Far across the Gulf of Mexico, Spanish explorers discovered the peninsula of Florida. In 1527 a shipload of men, with Panfilo Narvaez for governor, was sent to establish a colony. On the Gulf Coast of Florida the ship was wrecked, Narvaez was drowned, and the local Indians rejected the shipwrecked men. With the ingenuity of sixteenth century Spaniards, these men constructed rafts from the ship timbers, bound together with strips of horsehide. In these strange craft they pushed out into the Gulf of Mexico, hoping to float all the way across the Gulf to New Spain.

Off the coast of Texas their rafts were sunk in a storm and only four men survived. They were three gentlemen, Nuñez Cabeza de Vaca, Castillo de Maldonado, Andres Dorantes and his black Moorish slave, Estéban.

They managed to reach shore, only to be captured by Indians, who carried them along as slaves in their travels. The direction was westward, however, and these forlorn waifs swore they would walk until they reached New Spain. Cabeza de Vaca apparently had some small medical knowledge and, after making a few cures, the Indians thought he had magical powers and treated him like a medicine man. Estéban, the slave, had a knack for picking up Indian languages, so he was useful to his companions.   By ingenuity and courage they survived.

For eight long years the sun-blackened, ragged men drifted on across coastal Texas, passing from tribe to tribe, and were received as medicine men.   They crossed the Pecos River, then the Rio Grande, and at last they reached the northern territory of New Spain, or Mexico.   Here, too, the Indians they met took care of them and honored them.   From each group Cabeza de Vaca asked for news of men like themselves, the Spanish.

Finally, they met Indians who said they had seen men who had beards, who rode great animals and had weapons that spit fire.   They feared these men because they came into the Indian country hunting for slaves, but they agreed to lead the wanderers to a place where they might find the hunters.

The day came when the desperate waifs saw men of their own kind, men on horseback.   The Indians vanished into the forest while Cabeza de Vaca and his companions spoke to the horsemen.   It was hard to believe that these weatherbeaten men, half-naked, with long, shaggy hair, were Spaniards, but the language was convincing.   Their tale was accepted and they were taken to the frontier town of Culiacán, where the mayor believed their story in spite of their appearance.   After the wayfarers had been washed and dressed in Spanish clothes they were escorted to Mexico City to give their report to the Viceroy, Antonio de Mendoza.

The Viceroy listened to the story of these men with amazement.   But when they described rich cities in the north, a tale told to them by Indians, he was really impressed.   The Indians who had been companions of the wanderers had said that they traded parrot plumes for turquoise and buffalo skins with the inhabitants of these towns, which they declared were very rich. Although buffalo skins and turquoise were not signs of wealth, the mention of rich cities could excite a credulous Spaniard. The Viceroy decided to investigate the story told by the wanderers.

Chapter VI

The Seven Cities of Cibola

Among the romantic legends, popular in sixteenth century Spain, was the tale of seven Spanish bishops who fled from attacks by the Moors. On an island, somewhere in the mysterious ocean, they had built seven golden cities that had never been found. When this tale was circulated in Mexico City, treasure-hunting Spaniards decided those seven cities might just as well be hidden in the New World as on an island.

This idea was confirmed when an Indian from the north, who traded with many tribes, told Spaniards that in his travels he had seen tall cities. They were cities belonging to people called Cibola. This fitted in well with the story Cabeza de Vaca had heard from Indians about rich cities. In no time at all, the story had grown to a belief in the Seven Cities of Cibola, somewhere in the unknown country north of Mexico.

Cabeza de Vaca and his companions were not interested in more exploration; they were eager to return to Spain. Viceroy Mendoza, however, kept the slave Estéban to act as guide in the exploration he was planning. This was to be a scouting party, and for leader the Viceroy chose a certain Franciscan friar.

Fray Marcos de Niza was a missionary brother who had traveled over much of Mexico and Peru. He was a veteran frontiersman who could be trusted to explore the wilderness. Fray Marcos, the black slave Estéban and a troop of Indians set out in 1539. He was given the usual instructions for explorers: the Viceroy expected him to report on the resources of the country, souls to be saved for the Christian faith, and above all, to discover if the seven rich cities existed.

The company followed the route by which Cabeza de Vaca and his companions had traveled to reach the Spanish towns when they entered Mexico. Estéban and his admiring troop of Indians led the way, marching fast. The black slave was feeling important. He was a guide, an interpreter, he might even become a chief in the golden cities. Decked with feather headdress and with little bells around his ankles, he shook his rattle, trimmed with feathers and bells, and gained new Indian followers in each village. Fray Marcos let the troops go ahead while he proceeded more slowly, studying the country as he had been instructed to do. Estéban was told to send back messages by Indians. If prospects were not good he should send a small cross, but if he found rich cities he was to send a cross as large as a man.

The good friar plodded along with a few Indians,

always days behind the picturesque black and his attendants. At various settlements, Estéban left instructions
about the trail for the father and went tramping on. The
two groups crossed mountains, plains and rivers, north-
eastward, until they came to the headwaters of the San
Pedro River, which rises in Mexico and flows north into
Arizona. First the advance troop, then Fray Marcos,
crossed into what is now Arizona. A white man from
Europe and a black slave from Africa were the first "for-
eigners" to set foot on Indian Arizona soil.

Finally, there came a messenger carrying a cross as
tall as a man, saying that there were rich cities. Delighted,
the friar pushed on as fast as he could, through the river
valley and mountains, trying to catch up with his fantastic guide. Then came the shock of his life. A wounded
Indian came running over the trail with the terrible news
that when they reached the first city, named Háwikuh,
the inhabitants had killed Estéban and many of his followers. Soon more Indians came hurrying in a state of
terror, because they thought the Cibolans were pursuing
them. Fray Marcos was stunned by the news. His guides
wanted to join the fleeing Indians, to get away from that
place as soon as possible.

Fray Marcos was in a bad spot. He ought to go
forward to see for himself what had happened, to report
on the famous cities, but he did not want to be killed.

Most historians believe, judging by Spanish documents, that Fray Marcos never saw the Seven Cities of
Cibola, that he turned back with the frightened Indians.
On the long journey to Mexico City he concocted a good
story to tell the Viceroy.

He was given to dramatizing experiences, and he felt
sure the cities were really beautiful and rich. Accord-

ing to his story, he had proceeded until from a hilltop he had seen Háwikuh, with walls shining like gold. He even added details such as walls and doors studded with turquoise. If he did view the city he was fooled by the sun shining on adobe walls, but if he turned back without seeing it he proved himself to be one of the most accomplished liars in history.

The return of Fray Marcos created a sensation in Mexico City. To be sure, Estéban had been killed, but undoubtedly the kingdom of the Seven Cities was as marvelous as they expected. Each time Fray Marcos told the tale it became more alluring. Probably he believed it himself in the end. All the adventurous young men in the city were eager to set forth to the conquest of this new kingdom.

Viceroy Mendoza was so anxious to win glory for himself by a new conquest that he was ready to believe the story and to spend money for an expedition. All this land north of the Spanish settlements in Mexico was unknown. How far it extended, what riches it contained, was still a mystery. For leader of the expedition the Viceroy chose a gallant young cavalier, Francisco Vasquez de Coronado, the younger son of a noble Spanish family. He had settled in Mexico and married a wealthy wife, Doña Beatriz. The Viceroy had appointed him to be governor of the province of New Galicia.

There was a furor of excitement as the young knights and captains hurried to enlist for the adventure. Each one provided his own riding horse, supplies, arms, and pack animals. Doña Beatriz contributed from her wealth to equip Coronado with splendor. There was also a large company of foot soldiers, hundreds of mules and burros for pack animals.

The head of the Franciscan Order sent Fray Marcos and several other brothers as missionaries. Fray Marcos was to be the guide, since he had been over the route before.

Viceroy Mendoza, although enthusiastic, was cautious enough to check on the friar's description of the country and trail. While the expedition was assembling, he sent a veteran frontiersman, Melchior Díaz, to take some horsemen and scout ahead over the trail, to bring back a report. The Viceroy also arranged for a ship captain, Hernando de Alarcón, to sail up the Sea of Cortés, as they called the Gulf of California, with a small group of ships loaded with supplies for the expedition.

Spaniards had explored the Gulf of California and landed on the opposite shore, which they thought was a great island. They named it California from a romantic tale about a California Island inhabited by Amazon women. They had not yet discovered the mouth of the Colorado River.

It was thought that Alarcón could sail up the Gulf to some point on the west bank of the mainland, where he could land supplies for Coronado. Fray Marcos had given the Viceroy the mistaken idea that the expedition would be traveling only two days' journey from the coast. Having never explored this northern land, they knew nothing about its geography and had no maps to guide them. They could not know that Coronado's company would never be anywhere near the coast. A great deal would be learned about this land to be claimed for Spain by the time Coronado and his courageous men were through exploring it.

## Chapter VII

### The Adventures of Coronado

On a spring day in 1540, the people of Compostela were filled with pride and were enjoying a festival in honor of their governor, Francisco Vasquez de Coronado. Compostela was the capital of his province. Here Viceroy Mendoza held an impressive review of the expedition about to start for the Seven Cities of Cibola. The people crowded the streets to watch the magnificent company march by.

At the head rode Coronado, a handsome, brave young man. Mounted on a prancing horse, he wore a suit of gilded armor with a gilded helmet topped by plumes. After him came two hundred and fifty horsemen, the knights and captains. There were long lines of foot soldiers, of pack mules, burros and horses, accompanied

55

by Indians.    Fray Marcos and the other Franciscans marched on foot following this cavalcade.

At the end of the procession herds of cattle and sheep, food on the hoof, filled the air with their bellows and bleats.    Clouds of dust rose from the feet of men and the hoofs of animals.

The company took the trail to Culiacán, the frontier town where Melchior Díaz was mayor.    On the way they met this gentleman, returning from his scouting trip to report to Coronado.    The leader tried to keep this report from reaching his men, for Melchior Díaz told him that the way was long and difficult, nothing like the fine description Fray Marcos had given the Viceroy.    After this report, Coronado thought best to leave part of his company and supplies in Culiacán, to follow him when he sent the word.    He would take a company of horsemen and foot soldiers to go ahead, exploring the route.

The expedition crossed into Arizona, went down the San Pedro Valley and across to a pass in the mountains. There an Indian ruin, called the Red House, was pointed out by Fray Marcos as a landmark on the trail.    They traveled by Indian paths, up mountains and over plains, guided by the cheerful friar, who told the grumbling men they would find plenty of everything and easier going very soon.

The men were increasingly disheartened and discouraged.    Burdened by heavy armor and clothing, they sweated in hot summer days as they struggled through canyons and over rocky passes, short on water and food.    Often the horsemen had to walk and lead the exhausted horses over difficult trails.

Worse was to come after they passed through the upper Gila River Valley and crossed the plateau through

a region that is now the Apache Indian Reservation. At
that period it was a desperate place for men on the trail.
Spaniards later came to call it the Desplobado, the uninhabited place. There were no Indians to give them food
or to help them. Men and animals were worn out and
half starved, as supplies were giving out.

Coronado had been six months on the trail. It was
July, and he had given up hope of ever finding Alarcón
and the ships. They came into the mountainous country
before reaching the Zuñi River, where the Cibola cities
were located. Indians met on the trail told them the
Cibola people had heard of their coming and were preparing to attack them. This was not encouraging. The
company advanced cautiously, seeing smoke signals here
and there.

At last they came in sight of Háwikuh, the longed-
for city in the river valley. At first shouts of joy went up,
to be changed in a few moments to curses and shouts of
anger. Was this the city of golden walls described by
Fray Marcos — this hilltop Indian town of brown adobe
walls and bare terraced houses? Where were the golden
walls, the signs of treasure?

The chronicler of the expedition wrote in his account: "Such were the curses hurled at Fray Marcos that
I pray God to protect him from them."

It was a bitter disappointment to the adventurers,
who had endured the hardships of the trail in the hope
of abundance to come. For Coronado it was a great
shock, but he was a courageous man and set to work to
make the best of the situation. Fray Marcos seems to
have retired into the background, as well he might.

The Indian town they saw ahead of them in the river
valley was Háwikuh, one of the pueblos of the Zuñis, de-

scendants of the people who took in refugees from the
Great Drought of the thirteenth century. The people called
Cibola, with whom Coronado dealt, were Zuñis.

Coronado exhorted his angry followers to march on
to investigate this wretched town. They proceeded into
the valley and camped before Háwikuh. On the roof tops
and terraces above the walls they could see warriors
massed, and an advance guard of sturdy brown men,
armed with bows and clubs, was drawn up before the wall.

A few captains were sent by Coronado, with an interpreter, to speak peace to the warriors. They approached,
laid down their arms and asked by signs that the Indians
do likewise. The Indians refused and shouted to the Spaniards to be gone. The chief sprinkled sacred corn meal
in a line before their group, showing by signs that the
Spaniards should not cross it. When the captains moved
forward the warriors rushed at them with showers of
arrows until they retreated to the Spanish camp.

Now, Coronado prepared to impress these Indians.
Mounting his handsome horse, in his gilded armor and
plumed helmet, he was a splendid sight, but the Indians
refused to be impressed. He lectured them, telling them
it was their duty to submit to his great lord, the King of
Spain, and to receive the religion of the Christian god.
He assured them no harm would come to them if they
made peace with the Spaniards.

Probably the chiefs understood little of this speech
through an interpreter. In any event, they did not intend
to let these strangers enter their town. They remembered
the great black man who claimed to be sent by a powerful king. Coronado's offer was rejected with yells and
flights of arrows.

Coronado would have preferred to conquer peacefully. He had orders from the Viceroy to win the towns by gifts if possible instead of battle. However, the situation was desperate; his men were starving. If they must fight for the town they would.

Shouting the Spanish battle cry, "Santiago and at them!" he led the horsemen and foot soldiers in a charge on the town. The warriors outside the gate retreated within the walls, while others on the housetops showered missiles on the horsemen. The Spaniards found it difficult to get into this town of narrow alleys and terraced houses. From every housetop stones beat down upon them; arrows hit them. Coronado was knocked from his horse by a boulder that hit his helmet. Indians leaped on him with clubs, but some of his men rescued him and carried him out to the Spanish camp. The horsemen attacking outside the walls were driven back by a rain of arrows and stones.

The men were desperate, however. They returned to the attack, and before long firearms and metal armor overcame the primitive weapons of the Indians. They surrendered the town and fled to their sacred mountain, leaving the Spaniards in possession. The hungry men found stores of corn, beans, and a flock of wild turkeys. They filled their empty stomachs and rested from the fatigues of the trail and battle.

Coronado wrote a report to the Viceroy, telling of their disillusionment, saying that not a word of Fray Marcos' tale was true. The letter was sent back to Mexico City by the friar himself, who thus passes out of the story.

In a few days, head men of Cibola towns came to interview Coronado, who was resting from his wounds in Háwikuh. Gifts of buffalo hides, turquoise, and mats of woven yucca fiber were presented. These must have seemed poor presents indeed to the invaders who had expected gold and jewels such as the Aztecs possessed. This was the end of another golden legend, the Seven Cities of Cibola.

Spaniards occupied some of the Zuñi towns, while the inhabitants preferred their refuge on the sacred mountain.

Through some of his Indians, Coronado learned the fate of black Estéban. He had marched to the gate of Háwikuh in all his glory of tinkling bells and feather ornaments, demanding gold, jewels, and women, in the name of the greatest lord on earth. The chiefs locked him up while they took council. When they decided he was an enemy, he was killed and many of his Indian followers as well. Thus ended the career of the slave who dreamed of becoming a savage chieftain. The Zuñi Indians of the present time have a legend that long ago their ancestors were visited by a big black Mexican who tried to conquer them, and they had killed him.

Coronado was determined to explore the new land in every direction. He must find something worth reporting to the Viceroy. From the Indians he learned that to the north were tribes like themselves, who lived in stone towns on mesa tops. They called the region Tusayan. These were the Hopi towns.

Captain Pedro de Továr was sent with a company of soldiers to investigate. At first the Hopis came out to defend their towns but were soon driven back by Spanish firearms. The next day Hopi chiefs came down from the mesa to make peace and give presents, for these people have always tried to live without fighting if it could be avoided.

The Spaniards discovered that they lived like the

Zuñis in houses of stone, and raised crops in the desert plain below the mesa. They explored the towns of Walpi, Oraibi, Awatobi and others. Walpi and Oraibi are still in existence. Oraibi is supposed to be the oldest continuously inhabited village in the United States.

Pedro de Továr had some news for Coronado. Besides telling of the Hopi towns where they received gifts of food and blankets, but no gold, he learned that, far to the west, there was a very great river, and along its banks lived tall, strong Indians. This tale must be investigated, for by that river the explorers might find Alarcón and the ships.

Captain Lopez de Cardenas and a small band of men were sent to look into this story. The Hopis helped them with food, and told them the country they must pass through was uninhabited. For twenty days the small band of men traveled through desert country, through rocks and cactus and scattered pines. Then, to their amazement, they came to the brink of a tremendous chasm that looked to be miles across. At the bottom of the canyon they could see the river, narrow between towering cliffs. Cardenas and his companions were the first white men to see the Grand Canyon.

For several days the men scrambled, slipped and toiled, trying to get down to the river, but the cliffs were too steep and rugged, even for their agile strength. There was no food in the region, no water so far as they could find. Reluctantly, they returned to Coronado's camp. It was the opinion of all the captains that the huge chasm they had seen and the wilderness around it was a totally useless piece of country.

Coronado had sent a messenger to Culiacán, ordering the remainder of his company and the flock of animals to join him at Háwikuh. When they arrived, plans were made for further exploration. Coronado could not return to the Viceroy with nothing to report but vast wilderness inhabited by farming Indians, who lived in bare stone towns. He must find treasure to justify the expedition.

The Zuñis assured the gold-hungry Spaniards that if they traveled to the east they would find prosperous towns. Their object in telling this story was to rid themselves of their unwelcome visitors. The Spanish cavalcade traveled eastward across New Mexico until they reached the Rio Grande River and found more Indian stone towns. There the Spaniards spent a miserable winter, cold and hungry, huddled in Indian villages. The Pueblo Indians, who had been friendly at first, soon became resentful as the Spaniards constantly demanded food from their sparse stores.

A certain Indian, called by the Spaniards the Turk because of his long mustache, roused their hopes with another fantastic tale of a rich kingdom named Quivira. Led by this prize liar, the eager adventurers traveled for months across the vast, grassy plains of the Texas Panhandle, Oklahoma, and Kansas. They passed huge buffalo herds and learned to hunt the animals for food, but discovered few Indians and no kingdom. When, finally, they found that Quivira was a group of mud huts, they killed the lying Turk for his deception.

In 1542 the bedraggled, exhausted army was on the way back to Mexico. To the Viceroy and to the treasure-hunting Spaniards, the expedition was a failure. Coronado was ill and discouraged. He had done his best; he had led his company through journeys of terrific hardship, but nowhere had he found gold or kingdoms, nothing but vast wilderness and simple Indians.

Nevertheless, in the history of the Southwest Coronado had won his place. He brought to Mexico precise accounts of mountains, valleys, rivers, resources of the country, and information about the great extent of territory to the north, west and east. He had prepared the way for Spanish exploration and settlement in the Southwest.

## Chapter VIII

### Other Spanish Explorers

What happened to Hernando de Alarcón and his ships, carrying supplies for Coronado's expedition? While Coronado's company was tramping over plains and mountains, going ever farther from the coast, the ships were sailing up the Gulf of California. Captain Alarcón entered several harbors to look for signs of the expedition, but found none. While Alarcón sailed northwest in the Gulf, Coronado was traveling northeast, away from the coast.

Far up the Gulf the ships ran into fierce conflicting currents, where turbulent waves tossed them like leaves and then grounded them on hidden sandbars. They had met the tidal bore of the Colorado River. When the tide from the sea met the forceful current of the river it caused a wild battle of waters. Waves dashed over the ships; the men could not lower boats to escape, so fierce were the conflicting currents. The captain calmed their fears, and after some time a huge surge of sea lifted the ships off the sandbars, sending them on into deeper waters.

Only once before had Spaniards met these raging waters. That was when Captain Ulloa, sent by Cortés to explore the Gulf, had nearly lost his ship in the tidal bore. As soon as the tide turned he sailed away, hoping never to see that place again.

Hernando de Alarcón realized from the strong current that the ships must be in the mouth of a great river. He was an adventurous explorer, not to be stopped by obstacles. Perhaps along its banks he would find news of Coronado.

He ordered the steersmen to turn the ships into a small bay where they could anchor. Then he ordered the sailors to lower two small boats and fill them with supplies. He would explore with these, although his sailors clamored to return to safer waters. Hernando de Alarcón and his sailors were the first white men to enter the great Colorado River.

Since they could make little headway against the current by rowing, Alarcón soon sent the boats to shore. There, ropes were tied to them and the sailors had to tramp along the shore, towing the boats.

In a few days they met a crowd of Indians who were greatly excited over the strangers. These natives were tall, strong men with painted faces, who wore nothing but feathers around their middles and on their heads. Their bodies were scarred by burns that came from the practice of carrying burning brands to warm themselves. The captain had an Indian interpreter along, but he could not understand the language of this tribe.

As the crowd increased, Alarcón thought it best to keep the boats in the river. From there he harangued the crowd, making signs of peace, dangling trinkets to interest them. A few Indians swam out to investigate. By signs, they invited the strangers to come ashore. Here the Spaniards were nearly smothered by swarms of friendly natives, touching everything they wore, but in a childlike way. It was easy to understand that they regarded these white men as miraculous beings. They were persuaded to take over the job of towing the boats upstream.

They crept up the river from village to village. At each place they were greeted by excited natives. At last, they met an Indian who understood Alarcón's interpreter. He told them that he had heard on his travels that in a distant Indian town a big black man, wearing bells and feathers, had been killed. That must be Estéban, Alarcón decided. He was further encouraged when a trader Indian told them that in a town far to the east there were men with beards and white skins, who carried guns. Evidently, Coronado was there, but how far away it was impossible to judge.

Alarcón wanted to set off across country at once, but the Indians refused to guide them because they would have to pass through hostile country, and the sailors were set against starting such a trek. There was nothing for the anxious captain to do but proceed up the river, hoping for more news.

Finally, they came to a place where another large river entered the Colorado. This was the junction of the Gila and Colorado rivers. Now the Spaniards were among the Yuma Indians, who controlled the crossing of the Colorado at this point. The Indians swam across, resting on small rafts of reeds. They were not at all pleased to have these strangers cross their river, but Captain Alarcón had his boats, and he rowed across to see what was on the other side.

The intelligent captain must have understood from his journey up the river that the land the Spaniards called California was not an island but a long peninsula with the Gulf and the river on one side of it. He must have set down the idea in his report to the Viceroy. However, Spanish officials paid no attention to this piece of news for many years to come.

Hernando de Alarcón had found the place where Indian tribes for ages past had crossed the great river on their trading trips. In times to come, it would be a crossing for Indians and white men alike, between Arizona and California. However, Alarcón had not found Coronado, and it seemed necessary to return to his ships, anchored far down the river. He left a message for Coronado by constructing a large cross from tree limbs. This he planted firmly in the earth. On the bark he carved a record of his visit for Coronado's information if he should reach this place.

Meanwhile, Coronado had sent word from the Cibola villages to the good Captain Melchior Díaz, asking him to search for the coast and the ships. Melchior Díaz and some soldiers, with a flock of sheep for food, made a wearisome trip across deserts and barren hills until they found the east bank of the Colorado. He followed it up to the Yuma villages and to the junction of the Gila and Colorado. Here he found Alarcón's big cross and its message.

The Yumas were angry to have more white men invading their territory and crossing their river. They assembled warriors to attack the Spaniards, but they were beaten back by Spanish guns. The invaders crossed the river on Indian rafts, swimming their animals. Melchior Díaz started to explore the countryside, and might have added much to Spanish knowledge had he not been killed by his own lance; he fell on it as he was driving off his dog from attacking the sheep.

All this happened in the year 1540. The map of Arizona was growing. Spaniards had found the Colorado River. To the east, Coronado had beaten out a long trail, and his men had discovered the Grand Canyon. Many years later, explorers from the east would find a way across Arizona to the Colorado.

In 1542, after Coronado and his company had returned to Mexico, the Arizona Indians were left in peace for about forty years. They continued their life of farming, trading, and religious ceremonies. White soldiers with guns and horses, and missionaries with crosses became a dim memory.

The Pueblo Indians of the Rio Grande Valley, who had been visited by Coronado, were also left alone except for two Franciscan friars who persisted in their attempts to convert the people.

Spaniards had found valuable silver mines in what is now the Mexican state of Chihuahua, and mining camps were booming. Antonio de Espejo was one of the prospectors who gained wealth from his mines. He wanted to explore the mineral resources of the north country, using as an excuse his intention of finding out what had happened to the Franciscan friars.

In 1582, he won permission to make a trip up the Rio Grande. From Indians he soon learned that the two friars had been murdered. With that off his mind, he turned westward by Coronado's route, visiting the Zuñi and Hopi towns. He went on, exploring mountainous regions, hunting for valuable ore. Somewhere he discovered rich silver ore. After staking some claims, he returned to Chihuahua.

The Spanish authorities now renewed their interest in the northern regions. Explorers discovered the pass they called Paso del Norte and crossed the Rio Grande River at the place where El Paso is now situated. Don Juan de Oñate was commissioned to take settlers up the river. He founded a small town, then went exploring. Although he could not find Espejo's claims, he helped Spanish exploration by working out a route across Arizona to the Colorado River.

Don Juan de Oñate did not remain to be governor of the new province, called New Mexico. About 1609, the new governor, Juan Martinez Montoyar, founded Santa Fé as capital of the province. So this Spanish colony had a capital town some years before the Pilgrims landed on the coast of Massachusetts. Spanish towns, villages and farms grew in the Rio Grande Valley. Missionaries preached to the Indians and built churches in their villages.

Over the years, resentment increased among the Pueblo Indians because of Spanish attempts to change their way of life and interfere with their religion. The harsh domination of Spanish officers and soldiers added to Indian anger. The missionaries were included in their hatred, as well.

In 1680 a great rebellion broke out, organized by a clever Indian called Popé. Secretly he worked among the tribes and, on a given day, they rose as one against the white men. People were murdered in towns and countryside. The furnishings and statues of the churches were pulled down and destroyed. Those Spaniards who escaped death retreated down the river to Paso del Norte. The Zuñi and Hopi people joined the rebellion by killing the missionaries who were preaching to them. New Mexico was all Indian for thirteen years.

In 1692, the Viceroy commissioned the dashing, aggressive Captain Don Diego de Vargas to reconquer the province. With his troops de Vargas proceeded up the river and took possession of Santa Fé with little resistance from the Indians. They gave up, and New Mexico became a permanent Spanish colony. Don Diego de Vargas was too busy rebuilding the Spanish settlements to pay much attention to lands farther west, so the Indians of Arizona continued to pursue their ancestral occupations.

## Chapter IX

### Padre Kino: Missionary, Explorer, Cattleman

The first visitor to the Pima tribes of southwestern Arizona came not with soldiers and guns, he came astride a sturdy horse, accompanied by a few Indians and some pack animals. No shining armor clothed this visitor. He wore a severe black robe and a wide black hat.

This man of big heart and keen mind was Eusebio Francisco Kino, a Jesuit missionary, a member of the Company of Jesus. He had been assigned to the mission field of Pimería Alta, after working with the primitive Indians of the barren land of lower California in an unsuccessful colony.

Pimería Alta was the name given to the land of the Pima Indians and various other tribes in northwestern Sonora and southwestern Arizona. It was a land north

73

of Spanish settlements, unknown and unexplored, with countless Indians to be converted.

Sonora was a frontier province, growing rapidly in importance because of the discovery of rich silver ore. Settlements were built at the mines; there were towns and seaports, cattle ranches, and established Jesuit missions in the lower province.

Here among the gentle Pimas of northern Sonora, Padre Kino found great satisfaction. The Indians lived in villages of round-domed huts made of stakes and mud. They knew how to irrigate their small fields of maize, beans and squash from any available stream.

Padre Kino rode with an Indian guide over the country, preaching to the friendly natives, laying the foundation for future missions. On a hill surrounded by fertile valley fields he founded his home mission, called Nuestra Señora de Los Dolores. This place became his pride and joy.

Eusebio Kino was a man of enthusiastic energy and many talents. From missions in lower Sonora he obtained stock to fill the corrals and pastures of Mission Dolores with horses and mules, cattle, sheep and goats. Hitching up his robe, he taught Indian converts to ride and rope, brand cattle and butcher animals. Fruit trees and grape vines were planted by the practical father, and wheat was added to their crops.

Father Kino taught the Indians to make adobe bricks with which to build a small church and a house for him to live in. In a surprisingly short time, Mission Dolores became a prosperous farming and stock-raising center, with a large population of contented Pimas.

The tribes to the north heard by word of mouth, passed from group to group, about this Black Robe. He

was a man who had the magic symbol of the cross, who
had a good heart toward the Pima Indians. Before long
a delegation of Sobaípuris reached Father Kino. They
were a Pima tribe who lived at the large ranchería or village of Tumacácori, on the Santa Cruz River. At this
time, Father Juan Salvatierra was visiting the missions.
He had been sent by headquarters to inspect Kino's work.
The Indians, holding little crosses made of sticks, knelt
before the fathers, begging them to visit their village.

It was an appeal the fathers could not refuse. Soon,
in the year 1692, they were on the road to Tumacácori.
They rode down the valley of the Santa Cruz, impressed
with the scene of peace and fertility. Huge cottonwoods
shaded the river; the Indian fields were well tended, and
the whole valley was rich with grass. There were about
forty stick-and-mud huts in the ranchería, and the Indians
had built brush shelters for the visiting fathers.

Padre Kino baptized the children, conducted Mass
under the brush shelter before a wondering crowd, and
talked to them tenderly of the love of God. While the
missionaries were at Tumacácori, chieftains of the larger
ranchería of Bac arrived to ask for a visit.

The two fathers continued down the valley to Bac,
the Place Near the Well. They found a village of about
eight hundred farming Indians, who had fertile fields and
many huts. Gladly the people listened to Padre Kino's
"good words" about the Christian God. He organized the
village and taught the men to make adobe bricks with
which to build a small house, where Mass could be said
when he visited them. He promised to send them animals
from his herds at Dolores.

From that time on, the lean father with the kindly,
weather-beaten face was almost constantly on the trail,

riding from village to village, teaching and inspecting the work in fields and pastures. Generally the "padre on horseback" traveled with a few Indian attendants and pack animals carrying supplies for the settlements.

Word of his coming went ahead from village to village. At each one the people came joyfully to meet him, carrying arches of green branches and crosses, or gifts of food. They swept the dusty trail over which the father's company must pass.

In his explorations, Padre Kino founded several small visitas, as the missionaries called the villages where they came occasionally to teach. One of these Padre Kino called San Cosme de Tucson, a village near Bac. He established a visita and small church at Tumacácori and at Guevavi.

Headmen of a Sobaípuri group, living in the San Pedro River Valley, came to Kino, asking for a visit to their village of Quíburi. Once again the father rode into new country and found an energetic group of Indians living in a village on the bank above the river. There was an earthen wall around the village for protection, for these Sobaípuris lived on the edge of Apache territory. The Apache warriors had arrived in the Southwest and were occupying eastern mountains in Sonora, the Chiricahua Mountains and upper Gila Valley in Arizona. They were a constant menace to Spanish settlements and peaceful Indian villages.

The people of Quíburi welcomed the Black Robe and his teaching, and their chief, Coro, became his fast friend. The father made several journeys in the San Pedro Valley, escorted by Chief Coro and throngs of his people.

Each mission settlement became a little island of civilization in the vast region of Pimería Alta. The country was well populated with Pimas, Sobaípuris, and Papagos.

The Papago Indians lived in the desert land which is still the home of their descendants. These tribes were all primitive farmers who generally lived at peace among themselves. The good missionary taught them animal husbandry, carpentering, building and other skills.

Eusebio Kino was the first rancher and cattleman of Arizona. From his large herds he supplied all the mission villages with cattle, sheep, horses and mules. Life was changed for all the Indians who learned to use animals for food and in their daily activities.

This devoted friend of the Indians stood up for their rights with all the authorities in Sonora. He was a thorn in the flesh to Spanish mine owners and ranchers who wanted to exploit the Indians and use them as slaves. Often the Indians were brutally treated by soldiers, or wrongfully accused of stealing cattle, for which they were punished by beatings. Padre Kino always went to the defense of Indians who were abused.

What lies beyond? That was the question in Padre Kino's mind as he rode over the trails day after day, through weeks and months. In his vigorous character the explorer's keen interest in new lands was almost as strong a force as the missionary's loving care for his Indian children. He had been educated in Jesuit colleges of Europe, well-trained in astronomy, geography, mathematics, and map-making. Everywhere he went he made maps of the territory and questioned the Indians about the land beyond their villages. Pimería Alta extended to unknown distances. To his keen mind there were great possibilities for Spanish settlement and civilization.

One time, some Indians told him that to the north there was a river running westward, and near it a Great House that had been built by people in the far distant past. The exploring father determined to see this. He started from the village of Bac with some pack animals and the visiting Indians for guides. They journeyed over desert plains to the Gila River, beginning a trail that would become well-traveled in later years.

Padre Kino was impressed by the wide river, the flourishing fields irrigated from the river, the friendly Pimas of the villages. They welcomed him as all others had done and listened to his teaching. With some of them he visited the Great House, a massive tower with ruins of houses around it, standing in the desert. The father was astonished to find ruins of such well-built structures among these simple Indians. Padre Kino, the first white man to see it, named the place Casa Grande, a name it has held ever since. It was, of course, the ruin of a pre-historic Hohokam town center. To the Indians it was legendary.

Kino's visit to the Gila River spurred his mind to questions about the geography of this part of Pimería Alta. The Pimas told him that their river, the Gila, joined another great stream far to the west. This must be the Colorado, Padre Kino realized. His exploring spirit was set on investigating and mapping this territory.

Another question preoccupied him — was California an island or a peninsula? Much argument was going on among Spaniards over this question. As a missionary, Kino hoped it was a peninsula, because then it might be possible to send supplies by land to the barren country of lower California where his friend, Father Salvatierra, had started a mission.

About this time the military commander of Sonora became concerned about the missionary's persistence in traveling all over the wild desert country with only a few

Indians. He needed military protection. He also realized that Padre Kino was working for Spain as well as for the Church, for his explorations pushed the Spanish frontier farther north.

Padre Kino accepted as companion a young officer and a few soldiers of the Flying Company who were organized to fight the Apaches. This man was Lieutenant Juan Mateo Manje, young, enthusiastic and intelligent. He loved the country and saw eye to eye with Padre Kino on the importance of converting the Indians. When they visited the villages, he was to represent the Spanish government, count the number of people, appoint native officers, and instruct the people in loyalty to the King.

From 1694 to 1701 he accompanied Padre Kino on nine journeys of exploration. On these trips he kept a journal that has become a treasure-trove to historians. Lieutenant Manje was a man of the frontier, a worthy companion to the dauntless missionary. They became good friends, and the father regarded his companion almost as a son.

The two explorers criss-crossed the desert country of the Papagos many times. One of the trails they worked out was later called Camino del Diablo, the Devil's Highway. It passed through bone-dry desert and rocky hills where the only water to be obtained was in rock tanks in several canyons, which were filled by rain water or springs and frequently went dry. These two hardy men traveled over the dangerous trails without complaint.

The missionary and the soldier made their way to the Gulf Coast several times, because the California problem obsessed Father Kino. On one trip they climbed an ex-

tinct volcano, now called Pinacate, to get a good look
at the country. They scrambled up to the top, slipping
and crawling through lava rock and cinders. Before them
stretched an area of sand dunes and beyond lay the blue
waters of the Gulf. But beyond the water they saw land
extending north, south and west as far as they could see,
with mountain ranges running north and south.

Padre Kino wrote in his report, "I descried plainly and
without a telescope the junction of these lands of New
Spain with those of California, and the land passage."

Now he must continue his explorations, to find a route
and a place to cross the Colorado. Before he could do
this, Padre Kino had the happy task of organizing the
village of Bac as the mission of San Xavier del Bac, named
for his patron saint, Francisco Xavier. Lieutenant Manje
distributed trinkets and gave the chief men of the village canes of office. Padre Kino conducted Mass and gave
the natives loving talks on the True Faith.

The whole population joined, under Kino's direction,
in the work of building a proper church. This was in the
year 1700. Men carried stones from a nearby hill and
mixed mud plaster with water from their irrigation ditches.
Day by day the walls rose and before long the church was
finished. There were statues of the saints, altar cloths, and
vessels for the Mass, all tended with devotion by the
Indians.

Then the determined explorer followed his desire to
trace the course of the Gila to its junction with the Colorado. Escorted from village to village by friendly Indians, he reached the large Yuma village at the junction.
The tall, spirited Yumas made much of their Black Robe
visitor. He was surrounded with crowds and spent nights
around the camp fires, while the Yumas danced and

chanted with burning brands flickering in their hands.

Padre Kino had come to the place where Captain Alarcón had left the message on a tree-limb cross for Coronado, the place where Melchior Díaz had crossed the river, far back in 1540.

Among the gifts offered by the Yumas were large, beautiful blue shells. Where had he seen such shells before, the Padre wondered. Then he remembered that, when he was ministering to the Indians in the desert land of California and had traveled to the Pacific Ocean shore of that land, he had seen shells like these.

He questioned the Yumas about the shells. They said that Indians who lived across the river had traded them for Yuma products. The shells came from the shore of the great sea, many days' journey to the west from the river. That must be the Pacific Ocean, thought Kino, and the shells had been brought overland to the Colorado.

As soon as he returned to San Xavier del Bac, Padre Kino sent out his messengers to summon the chiefs of tribes from far and near to meet him at Bac. They came, bearing gifts of blue shells, because the beloved father wanted them, baskets and necklaces of blue abalone shells from the Pacific Coast. There were night talks at Bac under the brilliant stars of the Arizona sky. The Padre talked to his children of the joy of being Christians and living in peace; but he also talked about the blue shells, asking where they came from, what tribes brought them, and how far it was to the great sea.

Now, Padre Kino was determined to make another journey to the Colorado, to study the head of the Gulf and the land on the opposite side of the river. When he arrived at the Yuma village the rejoicing among the Indians was so great it was difficult to continue the journey. Crowds of Yumas accompanied him to the villages of the Quíquima Indians near the head of the Gulf. Here the Padre could study the conformation of the land and the Gulf; he could take measurements and record the latitude.

The river was very wide at this point, but the waters were quiet. Padre Kino was determined to get across. Quíquima Indians from their village across the river swam over, towing great round baskets filled with gifts of food for the visitor. The father and his Indians were at work making a raft from logs, tied together with ropes he had brought for the purpose.

The crude raft was launched, but it was very leaky and insecure. The Quíquima Indians had the solution. With much chatter and vivid signs they offered one of their great baskets. This was lashed to the raft and the father was invited to go aboard. Without a qualm Father Kino seated himself in the basket and was towed across the river by swimming Indians.

He spent the night with them and explored some of their marshy country and little villages. Then he was towed back to the other side and started on his homeward journey to Bac. He had set foot on the earth of California. He had seen the sun rise in the east across the waters of the Gulf. He had proved his point — California was a peninsula and the land passage was possible.

After assembling the notes and records of all his journeys over the land, Padre Kino, the cartographer, used his skill to draw a map of Pimería Alta. It showed the land on both sides of the river Colorado, its junction with the Gila and the head of the Gulf. This map he sent to the authorities with an explanation of his theory that California was a peninsula, and that a land route could be worked out to join Sonora and California. Although the missionaries and military authorities were deeply interested in his work and its results, nothing was done about this land route.

In the next few years, the missionary of inexhaustible energy was constantly on the trails, riding from mission to mission. He had spells of illness because the years of exhausting toil had sapped his strength, but he would not reduce his work.

In 1711 he was called to Magdalena, Sonora, where a new chapel was to be dedicated to his patron saint, San Francisco Xavier. The horseback journey tired him greatly. While he was conducting Mass in the new chapel he became very ill and collapsed immediately afterward.

He died in the mission house, lying in his dusty robe on a calfskin with an Indian blanket over him and his saddle for a pillow. Thus had he lain down to sleep many nights of his busy life. At the age of sixty-six, Padre Eusebio Francisco Kino ended his twenty-four years of tireless service in Pimería Alta. He was buried in the chapel he had just dedicated.

Fortunately, this devoted missionary did not live to know that in 1751 his beloved Pimas, aided by the Apaches, would revolt against the missionaries, soldiers and settlers. The Indians had endured too many abuses from the Spaniards, and too much hard work and discipline had been demanded from them by the Jesuit fathers with less understanding than Padre Kino. Some of the mission churches were sacked, and several priests murdered before the uprising was put down. It led to the establishment of a military post, or presidio, which was built at the Indian village of Tubac in 1752.

## Chapter X

## Captain de Anza and Fray Garcés

The small presidio of Tubac on the Santa Cruz River, founded in 1752, was the first settlement of Spanish people in Arizona. It was a military outpost with a company of soldiers stationed in the thick-walled barracks, prepared to pursue marauding Apaches or any other rebellious Indians at any time. There were small adobe houses for the families of the soldiers; crops were grown in fields near the river. It was a real little Spanish settlement.

The commander at Tubac, Captain Juan Batista de Anza, was a good man for the place. He was the son of a frontier soldier, and was well acquainted with the country and people. For Spain, he had a strong desire to see civilization pushed farther into the Indian country.

The missions of Guevavi, Tumacácori and San Xavier

del Bac had been badly damaged during the Indian up-
risings of 1751 and had never recovered their prosperity
under the few Jesuit fathers who followed Father Kino.
Then in 1767, King Carlos III of Spain quarreled with the
Company of Jesus and expelled all Jesuits from the Spanish
colonies. The missions in Sonora were handed over to the
Franciscan Order.

At San Xavier del Bac the Franciscan, Fray Francisco
Garcés, arrived to minister to the Indians. This man was
different from the severe, black-robed Jesuits. Clad in
the gray-brown robe of the Franciscans, Fray Garcés was
a stocky, square-built type of man of the greatest simplicity
and loving kindness. He came from peasant people in
Spain, and it was easy for him to understand these simple
farming Indians. Very soon he had won their love, and
they were glad to build a house for him. The church
built by Padre Kino had been partly destroyed in the rebellion, but was repaired sufficiently for services.

To the loving heart of Fray Garcés all these Indians
were his children, and there were hundreds more scattered
over Pimería Alta, the country he was anxious to explore.
He wanted to convert them all, and in addition his great
interest in exploration made it difficult for him to stay in
one place as a priest.

Indians from many tribes came to visit the Gray Robe
at San Xavier, to hear his good words and beg him to
visit their villages. Fray Garcés could not resist these
invitations. He saddled up his mule, filled the saddle
bags with jerked beef and trinkets, with tobacco so
cherished by the Indians and the stone pipe in which to
smoke it. Tobacco and strings of beads were his first
offerings to strange Indians.

Off he went with only Indians to guide him, wherever

they chose to take him. He slept on the ground or in their huts, ate their Indian food and squatted for hours beside the camp fires, smoking the pipe of peace and passing it around, while he learned the Indian languages. As one of the more formal fathers said of him, he was like an Indian himself. On the journeys he carried a cloth banner, with a painting of the Virgin and Child on one side, on the other side was shown a soul tormented by devils. These pictures pointed up his talks about the love of Jesus and Mary, contrasted with the misery of being a heathen.

Fray Garcés visited the Pima villages along the Gila and continued down stream to the Yuma village at the junction of the rivers. The Yuma chief at this time was a big, hawk-faced, intelligent Indian named Chief Palma, who became a good friend of the missionary.

Crowds of Yumas gathered around the campfires to listen to the magic words of the Old Man, as they called Fray Garcés. The Yumas were the most powerful tribe on the river. Chief Palma had the intelligence to realize that many more white men would come to the river, and it would be to his advantage to make friends with the Spaniards.

Fray Garcés was escorted to villages of other tribes. He crossed the Colorado lying on a small raft of reeds, propelled by swimming Indians. On foot he traveled from village to village on the California side, showing his banner and giving his message of peace. Everywhere the Indians followed him in throngs.

The expeditions of this traveling friar were known to Captain de Anza at Tubac. This missionary was a man after his own heart, one who wanted to discover the country and win peaceful cooperation from the Indians by his teaching. The two men became friends, visiting back and forth between Tubac and San Xavier. They had both read Padre Kino's accounts of his journeys and knew his famous map of Pimería Alta. They knew of his great dream to join the settlements in Sonora with those in California by a land route across the Colorado River.

At this time, late in the eighteenth century, the Spaniards had explored the coast of what they called Alta California by ship, starting small colonies at San Diego and Monterey. The Franciscans, under Father Junipero Serra, were beginning to build their famous chain of missions along the King's Highway. There was one mission post at San Diego and another at San Gabriel. The missionaries were having a struggle to teach their Indians how to grow enough food to supply them between the infrequent arrival of ships from Mexico to the port of San Diego.

Captain de Anza was convinced that Padre Kino's plan was practical. He made the long journey to Mexico City to propose an exploration to the Viceroy, and arrived at a propitious time. The Spanish government was paying attention once more to the northern settlements. New Mexico was settled and prosperous, missions and seaports were founded in California. The King of Spain and his Viceroy were aware of the fact that Russian and English ships were exploring the northern coast of California. It would be practical to establish Spanish rule in California without delay.

For these reasons the Viceroy listened to the captain's bold plan to work out a route to California and then take colonists to that province. For guide, Captain de Anza asked for the services of Fray Francisco Garcés, a man who knew the trails and had a way with Indians in the villages. When Fray Garcés learned of this request he was more than delighted to accompany his fellow explorer, the rugged captain from Tubac.

Permission was obtained from the superior of the Order for the father to be absent from his post for the long journey. The father at Tumacácori was assigned to look after affairs at San Xavier del Bac in his absence.

After many difficulties in assembling supplies and soldiers the expedition was gathered at Tubac in 1774. They set out on the great adventure with mounted soldiers, pack animals, and some food animals.

Captain de Anza and Fray Garcés led their men over the terrible Camino del Diablo, known to them both. It was hot summer weather, the few pools in the canyons were very low, and they suffered torments of thirst and heat. Finally they came through to the Gila and down the river to the Yuma settlement.

Chief Palma and his people received the Spanish company with joyful celebrations. The ambitious chief made it clear that he wanted Spanish soldiers with arms and horses to settle among them. He wanted Fray Garcés, the Old Man, to remain with them and build a mission.

The Indians showed Captain de Anza a shallow place at the crossing where they could ford the river on horseback and get their pack mules over. Chief Palma escorted the captain and friar to the top of a high bluff on the California side. Both men were impressed with the great sweep of river and country to be seen from this high place. Captain de Anza chose it as the ideal site for a presidio to guard the crossing, with Indian help. To Fray Garcés it was the perfect location for the mission he hoped to build. It was on top of this bluff that, in later times, Fort Yuma was built to protect the river crossing for emigrants.

Beyond the river De Anza's company was faced with the desolate region of shifting sand dunes and bone dry sand with never a water hole. The horses' feet sank deep in the dunes, the pack mules were bogged down, stinging wind and sand beat on men and animals. The captain sent most of the pack animals, with their drivers, back to the river, while the two explorers and some soldiers struggled on. They found a way through the desert of sand, discovered a pass in the mountains beyond, and came through to the valleys of California.

They arrived at mission San Gabriel exhausted but triumphant. They had made a trail, difficult though it was, and the fathers welcomed them with enthusiasm. They were happy over the prospect of a land route by which they might obtain supplies and colonists from the more settled province of Sonora.

Captain de Anza sent the friar back to the Yumas, while he traveled on to visit the small outpost of Monterey. Guided by a California Indian, Fray Garcés worked out a more effective route through the sand dunes. He remained with the Yumas until Captain de Anza returned, full of plans for the colony he would found in California.

Two years passed before Captain de Anza accomplished his purpose. With the Viceroy's approval, men, women and children to the number of two hundred and forty persons were gathered, pioneers who were willing to try life in California. Colonists, animals, and supplies were gathered at Tubac for the start of the expedition. Fray Garcés and another Franciscan, Father Eixarch, were to accompany the cavalcade to the Colorado, there to remain, preparing the Yumas for the mission to be built.

At the Yuma village the captain staged an impressive ceremony, when he presented Chief Palma with a fine officer's uniform and cape trimmed with gold braid, as well as a cane of office. He was formally appointed to be the King's representative on the river. What glory to give orders to his people and impress neighboring tribes in this gorgeous costume, backed up by Spaniards with guns and horses!

During several months of weary, dangerous travel and much suffering, the courageous company of pioneers made their way to San Gabriel, and on to the Bay of San Francisco. Captain de Anza had chosen this as a strategic site for a Spanish foothold. A mission and presidio were founded. In the year 1776, when in far away Philadelphia bells pealed to celebrate the signing of the Declaration of Independence and the birth of a new nation, a captain from Arizona founded Yerba Buena, which was to become the city of San Francisco.

Meanwhile the two fathers, Garcés and Eixarch, preached to the Yumas. Fray Garcés had another assignment as well. He had instructions from the Viceroy to visit tribes farther up the river, to seek out a route from California to New Mexico.

Through the most desolate desert and mountainous territory the dauntless missionary traveled from tribe to tribe, learning geography while he preached to the Indians. Everywhere he went he brought his message of love and peace, urging the tribes to cease warefare with each other.

From trader Indians Fray Garcés heard talk of canyons of the great Colorado River, and of the tribes farther east. He must explore this wilderness and find a route across it.

An agile trader of the Havasupai tribe escorted Fray Garcés and his mule through some of the Colorado canyons, and he scrambled down with the trader into the secret, fertile canyon of the Havasupais, where their de-

scendants still live.  He stood on the brink of the Grand
Canyon, marvelling at its mysterious depths.

The Havasupais talked of the Hopis who lived in stone
towns on their mesa tops.  Fray Garcés remembered that,
in the Indian rebellion of 1680, these Indians had murdered
their missionaries and had refused to have anything to do
with white men since then.  He must win these people.
He insisted on accompanying the trader of the Havasupais,
who was going on a trading trip to the Hopis, although the
Indian told him the people were hostile.

Leading his mule, Fray Garcés toiled up the steep
trail to a Hopi village, following the trader.  As usual, he
offered gifts and friendship to the clan elders who met him
with surly looks.  For the first time in his life Garcés
met Indians who refused his gifts, who would not talk to
him or listen to him.

They left him and his mule in the street all night
without food or water.  In the morning the elders, with
grim faces and beating drums, escorted the friar down the
trail to the desert plain below and told him to leave.

Fray Francisco Garcés had traced paths through the
vast wild territory for future Spanish pioneers.  He had
won the friendship of all Indians, but he had failed in his
mission to the Hopis.  Somehow, through toil and suffering, the disheartened missionary found his way back to the
Colorado and so, at last, home to San Xavier del Bac.

The administration of his military job at Tubac kept
Captain de Anza busy.  The fierce Apaches were increasingly troublesome to mission settlements and to Spanish
pioneers who were filtering into the valley from Sonora,
Mexico.  Prospectors were searching for rich ore in the
mountains; some farmers and cattlemen were venturing
into the Indian country.  The post at Tubac was too ex-

posed to attack. A stronger garrison was needed that could be more easily defended.

To the distress of the Tubac settlers the garrison was moved in 1776 to a walled town, built near the old Indian village of Tucson. The presidio was named Tucson, which had for inhabitants the soldiers and their families besides a few other settlers.

The captain and Fray Garcés did not forget the promised settlement of fort, mission, and colony at the Colorado crossing, but their pleas to the Viceroy to order this project were ignored. Captain de Anza took Chief Palma to Mexico City, dressed in his gold-braided uniform, to impress the Viceroy. The Indian made a sensation at the Viceroy's court. He was assured by the Viceroy that soldiers and missionaries would be given his people. When Chief Palma returned he boasted of his success and of the great things the Spaniards would do for the Yumas.

Promises were easy to make but difficult to fulfill. The Spanish government was absorbed in European problems; the Viceroy had troubles near at hand. He failed to realize the importance of the Colorado crossing. So time passed and nothing happened.

Then Captain de Anza was promoted to be governor of New Mexico and left the presidio in Arizona. This was a great loss to Fray Garcés and his hopes for the mission and colony. The Franciscans knew that the situation was becoming dangerous. Chief Palma was losing face among his people because the great things he promised had not come to pass. A rival Yuma chief taunted him, saying he had been deceived by the Spaniards.

At last, in 1779, the Viceroy appointed a pitifully small company of soldiers to escort a few colonists to the Colorado. Fray Garcés and several other Franciscans were appointed to build two missions. But, through the failure of the Spanish authorities to keep faith with the Yumas and through the arrogance of the soldiers and colonists, it was an enterprise that had little chance for success.

The Yumas were greatly disappointed with this miserable colony. This was not what had been promised them, and this Spanish captain had brought no gifts with him. Chief Palma was criticized. The Franciscans worked with all their strength to hold the friendship of the Yumas.

Fray Garcés built a small log church on the bluff where he had dreamed of having a fine mission. Down the river a few miles, fathers Diás and Moreno built another chapel, and there were settlers' houses around each mission.

The colonists insisted on planting their crops on the flat land beside the river where the Yumas had grown their corn and beans for centuries. Soldiers pastured their horses in groves of mesquite along the river, trampling the bushes from which the Indians harvested mesquite beans, important in their diet.

In vain the friars protested to the arrogant military captain about these abuses. They warned him that the resentment of the Indians was dangerous; it would lead to trouble. Their protests were met with indifference, and the colonists could not be persuaded to consider the Indians' rights. For a while Chief Palma worked with the missionaries to calm his people, but even he became uncooperative when he realized that his friend, the Old Man, could not win what the Indians wanted from the commander or his brutal soldiers.

Fray Garcés and his companions learned that hostile tribes of the river were planning to attack the Spaniards. They were persuading the Yumas to join them because of their hatred for the soldiers and colonists.

Then in 1781 the storm broke over the unfortunate settlement. Swarms of yelling Indians, Yumas and other tribes, attacked both settlements in a savage sweep of fury. Houses were ransacked and burned, all the men were beaten to death with the terrible war clubs. The women and children were carried off to Indian camps. Fray Garcés and his companion, Fray Barreneche, went among the murderous Indians on the bluff, trying to save their people from death. The Indians dragged them away and beat them brutally until they died, and the missionaries down the river were murdered in their chapel.

The smoke of burning buildings stained the sky above the river, while wild war dances and savage yells in the Indian villages celebrated the massacre.

In a moment of fury against all Spaniards the Yumas killed their best friend among the white men, Fray Francisco Garcés. The Spanish government, through delays and lack of understanding, lost the river crossing so important in the advancement of their colonies. Hostile Yumas controled the crossing for a long time to come, and the farsighted plan of Padre Kino, of Fray Garcés, and Captain de Anza came to naught.

## Chapter XI

### Changes for Arizona

For about twenty years there was comparative peace for the inhabitants of southern Arizona, thanks to a new policy towards the warring Apaches instituted by Viceroy Galvez. After battling the Indians with the full strength of Spanish troops, they were ready to talk peace. They were offered supplies of food and trade goods they wanted, handed out at intervals, so long as they did not attack pioneers or steal their stock.

The scheme worked fairly well most of the time. Cattle and horses grazed on the grassy plains; ranchers could tend their fields and live without fear of being murdered. The Indian workers of the mission settlements with their flocks and irrigated fields flourished under the Arizona sun. Tumacácori and San Xavier del Bac were the most

97

civilized settlements in the spacious Santa Cruz Valley.

Under the direction of the Franciscan fathers the two splendid churches that are now treasures of Arizona were built. There is little information about the architects and craftsmen who were responsible for the handsome buildings, though tradition states that the architects of San Xavier were two brothers named Gaona from Caborca, Mexico. The unfinished tower of San Xavier is supposed to have been left that way because Ignacio Gaona fell from the tower and was killed during the last months of its construction. Artistically skilled friars, with Indian helpers, are supposed to have designed and painted the delightful frescoes and decorations of the interior. No one knows what sculptors created the enchanting angels and the statues of saints.

The new church at San Xavier was begun in 1783 on a different site from Padre Kino's ruined church. It was placed near a small black hill, now crowned with a shrine, and was fourteen years in the building. Its beautiful interior was a place of worship for the mission Indians and all the settlers of the vicinity.

At Tumacácori the plans for church and mission buildings were more expansive than at San Xavier, and the church itself was more massive. There were difficulties in obtaining money and supplies for the work, but services were held in the half-finished church, and mission work went on in the buildings and gardens around it.

Mining had been going on in the southern mountains ever since the exciting discovery, early in the eighteenth century, of the Bolas de Plata, or Balls of Silver. Huge chunks of rich ore were found in a valley called Arissonac, a little south of the present Mexican border and west of Nogales. There was a wild mining boom, and many individuals carried off quantities of rich ore before the Spanish authorities clamped down on the site. An excellent silver mine was worked, mostly for the profit of the King of Spain.

That boom started prospectors northward. They combed over the mountains, staking claims and digging their own mine holes. Several good silver mines were in operation in the Santa Rita Mountains and those to the west of the Santa Cruz Valley. These explorations gave rise to a host of legends about rich veins of ore, found and then lost, that were passed on to later generations. An interesting theory prevails that after the name Arissonac became well-known the country that was formerly Pimería Alta received the name of Arizona.

Southern Arizona in those years was a sparsely inhabited, easy-going region of small ranchos, mines, mission settlements, and some large Spanish land grants. There was no central government, and the only towns were the village of Tubac and the walled presidio of Tucson. Few white men ventured into the Indian-infested regions north of the Gila River.

There were well-organized provinces on each side of primitive Arizona. These provinces, California and New Mexico, had their governors and civil officers in towns. In California the Franciscan missions were thriving settlements; there were towns and great cattle-raising haciendas of Spanish landowners. In New Mexico, as well, there were landowners of vast domains where cattle, sheep, and horses were raised. The province had many settlements and the capital town Santa Fé. Pueblo Indians lived in self-sufficient villages. These northern provinces had to take care of themselves and become self-supporting, for little attention was paid to them from Mexico or Spain. Government headquarters were too far away.

In Europe the Spanish monarchy was declining; the country was constantly engaged in wars. Spain had lost her grip on the possessions in North and South America. The provinces were ruled by harsh laws and irritating restrictions on trade with any country but Spain. In every province American-born Spaniards were seething with resentment, ready for revolt. They were inspired by the French arguments for liberty, by the successful revolution of the North American colonies against England, and the birth of a new nation, the United States.

From the year 1810 on through ten to fourteen years of war, the Spanish-Americans of South America, Central America, and Mexico fought to win their independence. In the end, Spain lost all these possessions. The American nations we know today in Latin America were set up on republican principles, inspired by France and the United States, but their constitutions did not bring liberty to the people. Competing generals and aristocrats ruled for many years.

Arizona, being part of the Viceroyalty of New Spain, or Mexico, was affected by the Mexican Revolution. When the patriot priest, Padre Miguel Hidalgo, rang his church bell in the village of Dolores and raised the cry of freedom on September 16, 1810, the war began. It continued for ten years. Garrisons on the frontier were greatly reduced or abandoned, for the military command in Mexico needed all available soldiers to fight the revolutionists.

This was good news for the Apaches. They swooped down from their mountain strongholds all along the frontiers of New Mexico, Arizona, and into Sonora. The white population was almost exterminated as ranches were burned, cattle driven off and helpless people murdered.

After the Mexicans had won freedom from Spain, and the Republic of Mexico was established, all the northern provinces belonged to that new nation. Arizona, as part of the province of New Mexico, was too sparsely inhabited and too far from Santa Fe to have any officials of its own.

It made little difference to the timid inhabitants of Tucson whether their commander and his soldiers were called Spaniards or Mexicans. If they could have some protection from Apaches as they tended their fields and animals, or traveled from place to place, it was satisfactory to them.

The inhabitants of the Santa Cruz Valley, however, were seriously affected by the antagonism of the new Mexican government to the religious orders. The Franciscan friars were ordered to leave their posts. Tumacácori and San Xavier del Bac were abandoned.

The great church at Tumacácori was never finished. After years of neglect, all the buildings fell into such ruin that it is difficult to imagine what the mission settlement was like in its time of prosperity. Passing travelers and soldiers camped in the roofless church. Treasure hunters dug holes in every likely place, searching for the legendary gold the fathers were supposed to have buried before they departed.

Fortunately, this historic place, Tumacácori, has been preserved as a National Monument. The buildings have been repaired and restored as much as possible from old records. In the museum, interesting dioramas give pictures of Spanish mission life. In one scene Padre Kino rides the trails with Indian attendants; in another there is a picture of early Spanish mining. Rebellious Indians are shown attacking a mission, and there are other vivid scenes.

One small display shows the interior of the church in all its glory, with the kneeling congregation of Indians and Spaniards attending Mass.

The exterior of San Xavier suffered great damage during the years of neglect, but the Indians who belonged to the mission lovingly tended the interior with its carvings, frescoes, and statues of saints. From father to son was handed the task of guarding the church from vandals, white or Indian. In the course of time, the Catholic Diocese of Tucson and the Sisters of St. Joseph administered to the people and began repairs. Eventually, the Franciscan Order returned to take charge of the church, and the fathers now minister to the Papago Indians and the Mexicans of the locality. The church has been restored with great care for authenticity, so that it stands in its desert setting in all its original beauty. The "White Dove of the Desert," as San Xavier is named, is a living reminder of the great work done by Spanish missionaries in long-ago Arizona. It is one of the historic treasures of the Southwest.

## Chapter XII

### Mountain Men Enter Arizona

Early in the nineteenth century, vigorous Americans of the young United States were surging westward over the prairies, along the rivers and over the mountains. There was boundless territory to be explored, and the vision of untold resources, as well as pride in their young nation, caused some aggressive men to evolve the doctrine of Manifest Destiny. That was the belief that North Americans were destined by superior race and energy to dominate the continent from ocean to ocean.

The advance guard of the westward-streaming pioneers was that hardy breed of hunters and fur trappers called the mountain men. They were of various nationalities — American, French-Canadian and others. To all of them the wilderness was an irresistible lure. They were

103

at home in the vast plains, the Rocky Mountains, the dark forests, and steep canyons throughout the great West.

In the early years of the nineteenth century, it was the vogue for men to wear tall hats of beaver fur, so popular in Europe and America. Strangely enough, that caused the development of the prosperous fur business in Canada and the United States. Trappers set forth into the mountains each season to trap beaver on the streams throughout the huge western territory. They were rough, primitive men, as expert as the Indians in wilderness life. Indians they understood; they would barter with them or fight them if necessary. Often the trappers took Indian women for temporary wives.

As soon as winter snows melted, groups of trappers for the fur companies, or "free trappers" who worked alone, would outfit themselves at some trading post. A pack animal was loaded with traps, powder and lead, sacks of flour, salt, coffee, tobacco, and sugar. In a leather pouch slung over his shoulder the trapper carried his "possibles": flint and steel for making fire, an awl for punching leather, a few other items. A flintlock gun, a hunting knife, and a small axe completed the supplies. Mounted on a lean horse, the mountain man was a well-known sight in the West with his long shaggy hair straggling out from under a fur cap, and his buckskin clothing shiny and greasy from many hand-wipings. Alone or in small groups, these men disappeared into the solitude of forests and mountains.

Late in the summer, the trappers emerged from their labors to trek with their loads of pelts to the spot appointed for the rendezvous, in some western valley. Here, trappers, traders, and Indians with their families assembled for a wild carnival of trading, gambling and drinking. The trappers traded their precious pelts for food, guns, liquor or, perhaps, Indian buffalo robes, moccasins, and dried buffalo meat. At the end of the riotous celebration, they were as poor as when they arrived. With just enough in the way of supplies to load their pack animals, off they went once more to the lonely life of the wilderness.

These men were intrepid explorers as well as trappers of beaver pelts. The lure of the unknown, a new river to investigate, another mountain to cross, led them on until they knew the unexplored West as well as the Indians who inhabited it. Many of the mountain men became guides for the pioneers on expeditions that set out to reach California in later years.

Taos and Santa Fe, although in Spanish and later Mexican territory, were favorite towns of the fur trappers who could sell their pelts to the officials and enjoy celebrations with the Spanish inhabitants. It was in Taos that young Kit Carson, the most famous of them all as trapper, scout, guide and soldier, began his career. Taos was home to him, for he had a Spanish wife and family. He knew the mountains and rivers of the West as well as any mountain man, but in addition he had qualities of character, intelligence and courage that made him one of the most famous men of his time in the exploration of the West. Kit Carson was one of the first of the mountain men to explore the Gila River from its head waters in the mountains of New Mexico.

The exploring trappers did not investigate the rivers of Arizona until the 1820's. The fur of beaver in these southern streams was not so good as that of the animals in colder country, but as the beaver supply became diminished in the more northern regions the trappers filtered into Arizona.

Some of them were working through northern Arizona

in the region of the Little Colorado and the San Francisco Peaks, hunting for furs and tracing out trails to California.   Old Bill Williams, one of the most skillful and
hardy of mountain men, a strange, solitary character, was
one of these explorers.  He is known to have been in the
region of the San Francisco Peaks, although no definite
record of his explorations has been preserved.  He was
known well enough among the early explorers to have
left his mark in the name of Bill Williams Mountain and
also a river by that name.  Antoine Leroux, a French trapper, was at home in northern Arizona, too, and became a
guide for American pioneers later on.

For most of the trappers who followed the beaver
in Arizona, the Gila River was the pathway.  From the
rough canyons and deep forests of its mountainous territory, they followed it down to the lowlands, fighting
Indians or trading with them and gathering a store of
pelts to sell back in New Mexico.  Some of these men
trapped on the tributaries of the Gila, the Verde, the Salt,
and San Francisco rivers.  Here Kit Carson began to acquire his great knowledge of the southwestern country
that made him such a famous guide.

Two of the most spectacular characters among these
mountain men were Sylvester and James Ohio Pattie, father
and son.  They were Kentuckians who had made themselves at home among the Spanish of Santa Fe, although
it was foreign territory.  Trappers from outside were not
very welcome, but they could get a license to trap in New
Mexico territory if the governor was in a good mood.
Many got away into the mountains without a license, but
that did not bother them.  They were out to get beaver
pelts, whether legally or otherwise.

The Patties got their license and started down the

Gila with a party of trappers. With a famous mountain man, Ewing Young, they explored the Gila, Salt, and Verde rivers, followed the south rim of the Grand Canyon and investigated the San Juan River. More is known of their adventures than those of other trappers because the son, James Ohio, kept a record of hair-raising adventures, written down in a journal in his own extravagant style. Later, this journal was edited by a newspaper man of Cincinnati, by name Timothy Flint, who published it with the title *The Personal Narrative of James Ohio Pattie,* a very popular book.

Although James Ohio embroidered his stories with many melodramatic details, they are basically true. They give a picture of Spanish life in New Mexico and of the trials of hunting beaver and fighting Indians in the wilderness, in the 1820's. On their last expedition, father and son followed the Gila to the Colorado and went down that stream to a place where they crossed into California. They managed to reach San Diego, where the Mexican governor clapped them into jail as interlopers. Sylvester, the father, died in jail, but James Ohio made his way back to the United States by way of Mexico.

Another mountain man who had a real part in the story of pioneer Arizona was Pauline Weaver. His real name was Paulino, but to his companions he became Pauline. On the frontier of Tennessee, he was trained in the ways of the wilderness by his father and came as a young man to St. Louis on the Mississippi. There he joined French and American trappers who frequented the place and became one of those who followed the beaver down the Gila.

He went on to California where he made friends with the Mexican governor who gave him a grant of land in San Gorgonio Pass in return for making a successful treaty with the Indians of that region. Here he made his home, but he continued to explore and trap the rivers of Arizona, or to pan for gold along the Colorado.

When gold mining and settlement began on the central plateau where Prescott was built, Pauline Weaver found his most important work as Army scout, as guide to prospectors, and as a friend to the Indians. His mother was a Cherokee Indian, and perhaps for this reason he had a deep understanding and liking for all Indians. He always worked as a peacemaker between natives and whites.

The tough mountain men, following their urge to explore and trap beaver, made known the mountains, rivers, and plains of the far West and Southwest. In Arizona, the best of them, Kit Carson and Pauline Weaver, were invaluable in their help to the pioneers who were soon to arrive.

Chapter XIII

War With Mexico

The men of Manifest Destiny, in their great ambition to extend the United States to the Pacific Coast, had their eyes on California in the 1830's and 1840's. In the years after Mexico had won independence from Spain, that country was constantly weakened by revolts of ambitious generals and other bad leaders. The Mexican government could not administer efficiently the distant provinces of New Mexico and California, and the officers they sent to the provinces were often inadequate. The people got along as best they could, continuing their Spanish way of life in towns and on large ranches.

Trade as well as territory attracted Americans. Already Yankee trading ships were scouting the California coast. They entered Monterey and San Diego harbors to trade their cargoes of manufactured goods for shipments of hides from the great cattle-raising haciendas. Occasionally, men from these ships managed to slip ashore and remain in the country. Bit by bit, American pioneers were making their way across northern Arizona and the California mountains to settle in towns or on farms.

Traders were following the trails of mountain men into Taos and Santa Fe. Their white-topped, heavy wagons, laden with trade goods, ground out deep ruts on the Santa Fe Trail. They were welcomed by the Spanish people, who delighted in the goods they brought and enjoyed making fiesta with the big, rough-spoken "Americanos." Through these men the people were already friendly with Americans before the inevitable war between the countries began.

The Mexican officials charged a high tariff on each wagon but made no attempt to stop the infiltration of American trade. A few traders took their wagons down the road along the Rio Grande to El Paso and on into Mexico to sell their goods. The most successful in this business was James McGoffin, a friendly, clever man. He made himself at home in Santa Fe and El Paso, acted like a citizen of the country and was popular with the people. His careful propaganda about the advantages of opening the country to Americans had great influence on leading men of Santa Fe.

It was in Texas that resentment and antagonism between Americans and Mexicans came to a head. Mexico had neither the energy nor the people to settle that great territory. There were the towns of El Paso and San Antonio, with a few other settlements and missions in that region of Texas. American pioneers from the south and east pushed into the nearly empty territory. They were allowed by the Mexican government to settle provided they became Mexican citizens and Catholics and did not import slaves.

Hundreds of Americans came in to take up farming land and start towns. They did not obey the law against slaves. They felt no loyalty for Mexico and resented laws and restrictions imposed by a government they considered alien to them.

In 1836 the American-Texans declared their independence from Mexico, and a short, bitter war was fought. General Santa Anna, then dictator of Mexico, brought troops and artillery to besiege the Texans, who had made a fort of the old Alamo Mission in San Antonio. The ruthless, destructive siege went on until the last defender was killed, and "Remember the Alamo" became a battle cry Texans have never forgotten.

General Sam Houston led the Texans in their campaign of vengeance for the Alamo and other atrocities until the Mexicans were defeated. General Santa Anna signed away Texas, which became for some years the Lone Star State.

When Texas decided to join the union of the United States in 1845, the Mexican government, having never acknowledged the independence of Texas, felt that it had been unjustly taken from them by the big neighbor to the north. This caused widespread resentment in addition to other suspicions over infiltration of Mexican territory. President Polk offered to buy the territory the United States wanted, including California and straight across to Texas, but the Mexican government refused.

The Texans declared their border with Mexico was the Rio Grande, while the Mexicans insisted it was the Nueces River farther north. That left a disputed region where "incidents" could easily occur. When President Polk supported the Texan claim and sent troops with General Zachary Taylor to protect this area, trouble soon began and there were skirmishes between General Taylor's soldiers and the Mexicans. In the surge of angry feeling that followed on both sides of the border, President Polk announced "War exists by act of Mexico." That was in 1846. The expansionists were pleased. Pioneers in the Middle West were eager to enlist in the army. Some thoughtful Americans, even some members of Congress, realized that the main object of the war was to obtain territory of a neighboring country, and considered it unjust.

It was inevitable that a strong, expanding nation would push aside a weak one to satisfy the urge for expansion. To the Mexicans the war meant loss of lands that had been explored by Spaniards and settled in parts by their own people. Bitterness towards the United States would endure for many years.

The huge territory of New Mexico, including Arizona, was not a battleground in the war. American government was set up in Santa Fe and other towns to provide a base for the Army of the West. This army was expected to march across the dangerous, half-empty territory of Arizona to aid in the conquest of California. United States naval ships were already off the Pacific Coast, prepared to enter and capture San Diego or Monterey as soon as they received word war had been declared. Colonel John C. Fremont, with a company of pioneers, had been in California organizing discontented American settlers, so it was expected that this company would be ready for action.

General Stephen Kearny assembled his Army of the West at Fort Leavenworth in Missouri. The troops marched over the Santa Fe Trail, accompanied by traders with wagons who wanted military protection. General Kearny had sent word to Governor Armijo of New Mexico requesting him to yield peaceably to the Americans and prevent war. As the army approached, Governor Armijo departed from the country after disbanding the militia, so there were not sufficient soldiers to defend Santa Fe.

The Army of the West marched into the city without firing a shot, to be welcomed by the acting governor and other officials. The flag of the United States was raised over the ancient Palace of the Governors. The people did not seem to be much disturbed by this change of government. For the most part, they accepted General Kearny's assurance that their rights, religion, and lands would be protected if they became citizens of the United States.

After civil government had been restored, General Kearny prepared to follow his orders to take troops to California. With three hundred dragoons mounted on mules, with wagons and two howitzers, the Army marched down the Rio Grande road. Before they turned westward they were met by a galloping horseman, who turned out to be the renowned Kit Carson. He had been in California with Colonel Fremont and was now ordered to carry dispatches to Washington at full speed, to announce that United States naval forces held the ports. Colonel Fremont and his company were in control of towns. California was won.

This was a startling blow for General Kearny, who was ordered to take an army to the conquest of California. He insisted that he must go on, and Kit Carson must accompany him as guide, since he had no man with him who knew the country. Carson protested that he was under orders to deliver the dispatches, but the General used his authority to order him to accompany the troops to California. Another mountain man, Fitzpatrick, was assigned to take over the dispatches and hurry off to Washington.

Kit Carson submitted reluctantly to General Kearny's order. The General sent the wagons and some of the dragoons back to Santa Fe, hoping to speed up the journey by traveling light. He must discover what was really happening.

The experienced frontiersman led the troops over very rough country to the Gila River in order to avoid Tucson and its Mexican garrison. When they reached the river there were canyons to pass through before they reached the lowlands. The heavy howitzers, supposed to be pulled by mules, were often pushed and pulled by both men and animals to get them through narrow rocky passes. Grass was scarce, and water was often unobtainable.

When the weary company reached the Pima villages along the river, they were more than thankful for the food given to them by the friendly Indians, who impressed the General and his men by their civilization and good farming. Men and animals had a rest before they continued to the Colorado and the crossing into California.

On the other side of the river they captured a Mexican rider who was carrying dispatches to Mexican authorities in Sonora. One of the letters he carried gave General Kearny a shock worse than the news brought by Kit Carson. The Mexican commander in California announced that American marines and sailors had been driven back to their ships at San Diego after attempting to march to Los Angeles. Santa Barbara and Los Angeles were in Mexican hands, and the country was in revolt against the

Americans in the northern districts as well as the south.

This was terrible news for the company of exhausted, ragged men who were expected to help in the conquest of California. They were brave soldiers, however, and by sheer grit they marched through the Colorado Desert to approach San Diego. Then they had a bitter fight with well-mounted Mexican cavalry and were marooned on a hill. They were almost without food and water, while the cavalry circled the hill, cutting off escape.

Kit Carson and young Lieutenant Beale offered to slip through the cavalry lines by night to carry word to Commander Stockton at San Diego of their desperate situation. With Carson's wilderness skill, the two men succeeded in getting through and reaching San Diego. A company of soldiers was sent to the rescue of the dragoons and, after driving off the Mexican cavalry, General Kearny's men marched to San Diego to join in the conquest of California.

A more momentous trek across forbidding Arizona was made by Lieutenant Colonel Philip St. George Cooke and the Mormon Battalion. General Kearny's journey was a military march, but Colonel Cooke was ordered to work out a wagon road from New Mexico to California for the passage of military supplies. It would be the first route for wheeled vehicles to cross southern Arizona.

The Mormons, at this time, were wandering westward with Brigham Young, seeking permanent settlement. They offered to enlist in the Army of the West, and President Polk accepted 500 men to make the march with Colonel Cooke. They were to enlist for a year and be mustered out in California, where they might take up farm land if they wished.

Many of the company had wives and children with

them, but they were sternly weeded out by the practical commander. Even then Colonel Cooke had a company of untrained volunteers, ignorant of military discipline, men who were not very skillful at managing animals and wagons in the wilderness.

Finally, in October 1846, the commander had assembled his wagons, supplies, mules and stock. His battalion was equipped and ready to march on the mighty trek to California.

General Kearny had sent two mountain men, Pauline Weaver and Antoine Leroux, to act as guides. Colonel Cooke did not think too much of them. Even though they did not know all the country to be crossed, they were skilled in finding pathways, grass, and water holes in primitive plains and mountains. The guides assured Colonel Cooke that wagons could not be taken over the route by which Kearny's army had proceeded, and they helped to seek out a more southern route.

After leaving the Rio Grande Valley, the Battalion crawled onward over the arid, cactus-covered plains of southern New Mexico and Arizona, up and down arroyos, through mountain passes where wheels had never before broken a trail. Often the soldiers had to help the mules drag the wagons through deep, sandy wastes or through rocky defiles by ropes attached to the wagons.

When the company reached the San Pedro River Valley, they met the most fantastic enemy imaginable — a herd of wild bulls! These animals, escaped from Apache raids on isolated ranches, had become as wild as buffalo. Instead of running from the wagons and mules, they attacked the train with ferocious fury. There was a wild tangle of men and animals and much gunfire until the soldiers drove off the bulls. Mules had been gored, men were injured, and a few were killed. Colonel Cooke re-organized his shattered battalion, and they moved on-ward toward Tucson. Although they were passing through Mexican territory, the few people they met paid no atten-tion to them.

As they approached the walled town a messenger from the Mexican commander rode out with a letter, urging the Battalion to bypass the town. In messages back and forth, Colonel Cooke refused to do this. He had no quarrel with the people of Sonora, he declared, but his company needed supplies.

The Mexican officer then moved out of the town with his soldiers and some of the inhabitants. Colonel Cooke camped his Battalion outside the walls where water and grass could be obtained. The men had strict orders to treat the people kindly and take nothing from them. In fact, they were treated with curiosity and hospitality from the easy-going Mexicans. Probably they found this visit from "gringo" soldiers a pleasant excitement. They supplied grain for the caravan and made no objection when a soldier tied a flag to a tent pole and climbed up to fasten it on the top of the town wall. The Stars and Stripes was the third banner to be raised over the old town where Spanish and Mexican flags had flown before.

As the company struggled on, constantly searching for grass and water for the animals, they were delighted to find the old trail along the Gila, a trail first made by Fathers Kino and Garcés and Captain de Anza. The Pima Indians welcomed and fed them as they had welcomed Spaniards and Mexicans in the past and Kearny's soldiers in that same year.

Colonel Cooke decided to float some of his supplies down the Gila River to the Colorado in order to lighten the loads in the wagons. Two wagon beds were lashed together over cottonwood logs and packed with flour, pork, corn for the mules, and some baggage. Lieutenant Stoneman, who knew river navigation, poled the barge down the shallow stream. He had trouble with sand bars and snags, but came through to the Colorado and crossed that river on the same barge. In cold wind and a driving dust storm the men, animals and wagons were forded across. After traveling through the sand dunes, the ragged, exhausted men, with worn-out mules and delapidated wagons, came through to San Diego.

Colonel Cooke was justly proud of this extraordinary journey. He wrote a detailed account, describing the route, the water holes or lack of them, difficult sections of the trail, the places where grass would be found, etc. This account was studied thoroughly by companies of emigrants who followed Cooke's Wagon Road to California.

When the men were mustered out in California their commander gave them a tribute of appreciation in his final speech. He reviewed their journey in these words: "History may be searched for an equal march of infantry. Nine-tenths of it has been through a wilderness where nothing but savages and wild beasts are found, or deserts where, for want of water, there is no living creature. There with almost hopeless labor we have dug wells which the future travelers will enjoy. Without a guide who had traversed them we have ventured into trackless prairies where water was not found for several marches. With crowbar and pick we have worked our way over mountains which seemed to defy aught but the wild goat, and hewed a chasm through living rock too narrow for our wagons."

He ended with a tribute to his Battalion. "Thus marching, half naked and half fed, we have discovered and made a road of great value to our country. Thus, volunteers, you have exhibited some of the high and essential quality of veterans."

The Mormon Battalion had indeed done a great service, for over the wheel ruts gouged out by their wagons, within a few years, came companies of emigrants bound for California. Later, stage coaches rolled over the same route. The railroad and modern highways follow approximately the direction of that first wagon trail.

Many of the Mormons who had left families behind made their way eventually to Salt Lake City, where Brigham Young had established the Mormon community.

In 1848 the war was over, and the Treaty of Guadalupe Hidalgo was signed on February 2. The Mexican people suffered the humiliation of having their capital, Mexico City, captured by General Winfield Scott's troops after General Santa Anna had fled into exile.

Peace between the countries was assured by the Treaty, but its terms were bitter for the Mexicans. The government was obliged to cede an enormous territory to the United States: New Mexico, California, Nevada, Utah, parts of Colorado and Wyoming, and Arizona north of the Gila River.

# PART III.
# ANGLO-AMERICANS TAKE OVER ARIZONA

## Chapter XIV

### The Gold Rush and the Gadsden Purchase

After the war with Mexico and the acquisition of so much territory, adventurous pioneers made for California by any route they could find. That great land was the principal goal, with its marvelous resources, with towns and seaports already established. It had been prepared for American settlement by such scouts as Fremont and various emigrants who settled there before the war.

In 1848 came the news that gold had been discovered in California. This news caused feverish excitement, spreading over the country like wildfire. By 1849 the rush to the gold fields became the greatest migration of people so far known in America, all determined to find fortune in the land of glittering gold. The 49'ers traveled by every possible route; by ship around Cape

Horn, or across the jungles of the Isthmus of Panama to take ship on the other side, or by trails across the country.

Many emigrants followed the Old Spanish Trail from New Mexico across northern Arizona to the Colorado. This travel, plus the need for the government to learn more about the country, led to the first expedition of United States Topographical Engineers, commanded by Captain Lorenzo Sitgreaves. He was ordered to develop a better route to California and study the possibilities of navigation on the rivers. Guided by the experienced mountain man Antoine Leroux, Captain Sitgreaves investigated the Zuñi and Little Colorado rivers. It was soon discovered that navigation on these peculiar western rivers was not promising.

The company explored the region of the San Francisco Peaks, mapping out an acceptable route, then made their way down the Colorado River banks to the junction with the Gila. That old-time crossing had become quite a thoroughfare due to the rush of emigrants to California. The desperate companies crossed by any means they could manage, sometimes building rough rafts, sometimes aided by the Yuma Indians. At first, these Indians were friendly until the horde of white men making demands on their services and food supplies became exasperating.

The first actual ferry at the crossing was built by Lieutenant Cave Couts and his soldiers. He had been sent by the Army with a company of dragoons to build a fort. He set up a small post on the hill where Fray Garcés had built his mission, on the California side. It was called Camp Calhoun. This was in 1849, during the first great rush of goldseekers. Lieutenant Couts and his soldiers built a large barge, with rope strung across the river by which to pull it over. By this means throngs of emigrants reached the California side. There Lieutenant Couts at his primitive fort was supposed to provide them with food before they faced the terrors of the Colorado River sand dunes.

Various desperados saw a chance to reap money from the emigrants by ferrying them across on rickety rafts, charging them high fees and often robbing them besides. The worst of these was a villainous character, John Glanton, who had been a professional Indian scalp hunter for the Mexican government. He seized a large ferry boat that was being run by some Indians and a few white men and killed most of the men. After operating the ferry for a while at outrageous prices, he made off to San Diego to bank the cash he had collected.

When Glanton, with a gang of roughnecks, returned to the ferry, the Indians pretended friendship and bided their time. The gang celebrated their winnings by going on a tremendous binge. When they were all sunk in a drunken stupor, the Yumas pounced on them with their terrible war clubs and beat them all to death. Then they gathered the bodies and burned them in the buildings. A few men of the gang, who had not been in the camp, escaped to San Diego with the story. A military company was sent to punish the Yumas, but they came off badly in a battle with the Indians, so they returned to San Diego.

There were other bloody battles between outlaw white men and Indians before a regular ferry, decently operated, was started by a sturdy German, L. F. J. Jaeger. His partners were Ben Hartshorn and Captain Johnson. They built a ferry service at Pilot's Knob, below the mouth of the Gila on the California side, in 1850.

While these men were building a stockade, five Yuma

head men came to parley with them, armed with bows and arrows. Captain Johnson and his companions held their guns ready while Chief Santiago spoke. When he asked what the white men were doing, Johnson replied, "We are going to stay here, build boats and ferry people across the river."

Santiago replied with dignity that white men would be permitted to come through to cross the river, but they could not settle on Indian land. Captain Johnson leveled his gun and remarked calmly that he and his men were going to stay. Faced with guns, the Indians departed. Santiago had stated the Indians' case clearly, but it did them no good, because white men took over the crossing from that time on.

When Fort Yuma was built on the hill in 1852, commanded by Major Heintzelman, there was protection for travelers. Hartshorn and Captain Johnson sold their shares in the ferry business, but Jaeger remained to develop the ferry in which Major Heintzelman had taken shares.

Jaeger was a strong, hard-headed man with an eye for business, a good builder and machinist. He learned to keep peace with the Indians and be fair to them. They called him Diego; the Mexican goldseekers called him Don Diego. During the years of his successful ferry business, he was known far and wide as Don Diego the Ferryman.

In the south, streams of emigrants followed the rough wagon road worked out by Colonel Cooke and his Mormon Battalion during the war. This region was still Mexican territory, for American Arizona, by the Treaty of Guadalupe Hidalgo, was north of the Gila River. The sparse population of the region, however, was indifferent to the nationality of people who crossed the country.

The only settlement where travelers could replace worn-out animals and buy food was the walled town of Tucson. The Mexican inhabitants were friendly and quite willing to make a little money by selling supplies to the emigrants.

From Tucson the emigrants followed Cooke's Road to the old trail along the Gila and down that river to the Colorado. After Jaeger's ferry was in operation animals, wagons, and people were taken across at a fairly reasonable price.

The tremendous westward surge of pioneers to the land of gold brought to a head the question of a railroad across the country. There was talk of surveying a route at the 35th parallel of latitude, which would follow more or less the trail south of the San Francisco Peaks. Even more popular was the plan to follow Cooke's Wagon Road, to survey a rail route from Texas to California. But this southern section still belonged to Mexico.

The railroad plans increased the dissatisfaction over the Treaty of Guadalupe Hidalgo. The expansionists, the men of Manifest Destiny, declared that the United States should have acquired more Mexican territory. They had always wanted the province of Sonora and Baja California included in the deal. Thus the United States would have had a port on the Gulf of California and a route for a railroad. Controversy raged in Congress between the slavery and non-slavery elements over this issue. The northerners did not want more southern territory for fear more slave states would be the result.

Besides the territorial question in the Treaty, there was a provision that United States troops should police the Mexican border. They were supposed to keep Indians from raiding into Mexico, and it was provided that Mexicans should be recompensed for damage from these raids. It was a provision impossible to carry through, causing anger on both sides of the border.

Things were not going well in Mexico. The people were suffering under the presidential dictatorship of General Santa Anna, who had once more seized power in the country. His extravagant spending had almost depleted the national treasury.

At this time, President Franklin Pierce yielded to the clamor for more Mexican territory and sent James Gadsden, as Minister from the United States, to negotiate a treaty for a new boundary line. The atmosphere in Mexico City was extremely uncomfortable for an official from the United States, because people hated their northern neighbor and resented their own dictator as well.

James Gadsden tried to buy Sonora and Baja California, but much as the Mexican dictator wanted the money, he did not quite dare to give away so much of the national territory to the hated Yankees. General Santa Anna finally agreed to a new boundary line that would give the United States the Mesilla and Mimbres valleys in New Mexico, and southern Arizona from the Gila River to the present Mexican border. The price was to be $15,000,000, but the penny-pinching Congress thought it was too much, and bargained over it until General Santa Anna agreed to sell for $10,000,000.

It was a bad deal for Mexico. Liberals of the country were furious, and before two years had passed these elements in government had ousted the dictator and sent him once more into exile.

The treaty, usually called the Gadsden Purchase, was written in 1853 but not ratified by the United States Congress until 1854. The United States gained a route for a railroad and a large slice of Mexican territory, most of it in southern Arizona. The treaty gave Americans the right of navigation on the Colorado River through Mexican territory, and also freed the government from the promise to control the border Indians.

Arizona, north of the Gila River, was already part of the territory of New Mexico in the United States, and the southern land was now added to it. The northern boundary was drawn straight across from the northern counties of New Mexico to the California line. The western boundary was the Colorado River, and a boundary commission was sent to work out a new southern boundary. The line was fixed to run from the west bank of the Rio Grande just above El Paso to Nogales, then to a point about twenty miles below the Gila. The Gadsden Treaty had placed the point six miles above the mouth of the river, but Congress, for some reason, changed it to the present twenty miles below the Gila junction with the Colorado. It is generally assumed that the territory gained by the Gadsden Purchase was about 45,000 square miles, but the latest reckoning in 1940 makes it 29,640.

There were orations in Congress against the Gadsden Purchase by senators who did not think it a good bargain, despite acquiring a rail route. It was not worth while to pay so much for this land that one senator called, "Desolate, desert and God-forsaken." Kit Carson stated that "a wolf could not make a living from it."

Arizona was still a poor relation in the huge territory designated as New Mexico. The governor was situated in far-away Santa Fe, and the nearest civic officer was in Mesilla. It was impossible to maintain government at such a distance. Lonely Arizona had no law except what communities made for themselves, and in

1854 Tucson was the only town. Tubac was a deserted village; there were a few tiny settlements such as Calabasas, but no settlements in the north. Some Mexican ranchers and a few Americans were raising cattle and crops in the Santa Cruz Valley, while prospectors were investigating the mineral wealth of the mountains.

It made little difference to the inhabitants of Tucson when the Mexican garrison returned to Sonora, in 1856, to be replaced by a company of United States Dragoons, who marched in to set up camp in the town and raise the Stars and Stripes once more over the Old Pueblo. The few American pioneers were delighted and most of the people were rather pleased, for the energy and vigor of Americans were beginning to make an impression. There were a few American shopkeepers; one of them was Solomon Warner, the best merchant in town.

The dusty, sunny lanes were often crowded with mule pack trains, bringing goods from Sonora for the small shops. Mexican carretas, with solid wooden wheels that creaked as they turned, crawled into town with Mexican specialties. Sometimes emigrant wagons paused in the town to renew their supplies and rest from the hardships of the trail. A few enterprising traders, from Albuquerque in New Mexico, drove ox-drawn carts of merchandise across the desert plains to try their luck in the new American town, Tucson. They found good business and some set up shop in the small place.

The Mexicans liked the new arrivals, and some of their girls married American pioneers. The people continued their happy-go-lucky way of life, tending their fields by the river, keeping their shops, and enjoying the fiestas. The population grew as both American and Mexican families moved in, some of whom built houses outside the walls.  While tending their fields, farmers kept sharp watch for Apaches, who often raided close to the town.  Respectable members of the community were disturbed by the violent fights and general lawlessness of undesirable characters from Texas and California, who thought this town without lawmakers was an easy mark.

The new spirit of American enterprise was felt also at the Colorado River crossing.  Jaeger was successfully running his ferry, and Fort Yuma was a permanent post. James Gadsden thought he had done well when, in his Treaty, he provided for free commerce on the Colorado and Gila rivers for both Mexicans and Americans.  Those who lived in the country laughed at the idea of commerce on the two unpredictable rivers that could change suddenly from fierce floods to shallows and sand bars. But navigation of the Colorado had been studied for some time.  The problem of supplies for the fort and ferry settlement, brought overland from California, was extremely difficult.  Schooners from San Francisco sailed around the peninsula of Baja California and up the Gulf of California to the mouth of the Colorado with supplies and building materials.  The goods were transferred to barges, which were poled and hauled up river to the Fort.  Sometimes Indians attacked the boatmen and wrecked the cargo, or, if they escaped Indians, the barges were frequently stuck on sand bars.

Then in 1852, a schooner arrived at the river's mouth, carrying lumber and an engine for a small steamer.  The little ship was assembled at the head of the Gulf and christened the *Uncle Sam*.  Proudly it chugged up the river with streamers of black smoke coming from its funnel, its paddle wheels kicking up foamy water, its whistle shrieking.  Indians were frightened to death at this strange object. They might well be frightened, for the beginning of steam navigation on the river meant the end of their control. They could fight men on land but not puffing monsters on the water.

Two years later a larger steamer, the *General Jessup,* went into service on the river. Captain Johnson, who had been a partner of Jaeger's, had established a navigation company. Freight and passengers were unloaded from the schooners at the head of the Gulf to be transferred to Fort Yuma by steamer. Often extra freight was pulled on barges behind the steamer.

Now that there was river traffic, disappointed gold-seekers from California began to filter in, exploring the river banks, panning for gold. The richness of placer gold in the sands soon led to a new gold rush, this time to the Colorado and Gila rivers.

Arizona, now a territorial part of the United States, was beginning a new phase of its story, when American pioneers would develop and settle its wide-open spaces.

Chapter XV

Camels and Steamboats

The beautiful northern region of Arizona, with its mountains, forests and plains, attracted the attention of the United States government after the war with Mexico. It was important to work out transportation to California for the Army and for pioneers, and to provide military protection for people coming into the territory.

Captain Sitgreaves had explored a route in 1851 to help emigrants bound for the California gold fields. Then when Colonel Sumner became governor of New Mexico after the war, he began Army operations from there. The Navajo Indians were making a great deal of trouble, raiding the farms of New Mexico settlers and Pueblo Indians to steal livestock and sometimes to take captives as well. These Indians were of the same race as the

Apaches who were such a menace to settlers in the southern sections of Arizona and New Mexico. Like the Apaches, they were nomadic people and proud warriors. Fort Defiance was the first military post in Arizona. It was built in 1852 on the eastern edge of Navajo country to control the Indians and to be headquarters for Army operations.

In 1853, the government ordered another expedition of Army engineers to survey a route for a railroad along the 35th parallel. Lieutenant A. W. Whipple was in command. From the Zuñi pueblo he and his engineers went west, explored some of the Little Colorado River Valley and, with the snowy crown of San Francisco Peaks for guide, they continued to the gorge now called Canyon Diablo. From there they took a course farther south than that surveyed by Captain Sitgreaves.

The rugged country was being sketched out for transportation purposes. Distances to be crossed were immense in this primitive country. There were always difficulties in finding fodder for the animals and water for man and beast. During the 1850's, much discussion was going on in Washington about improving methods of transportation, and this led to the introduction of a new animal into Arizona — the camel.

While Jefferson Davis was Secretary of War, in 1853, he became convinced of the value of camels for transportation in the "desert" Southwest. They were beasts accustomed to traveling over arid land; they could carry heavy loads; they needed little water and were easier to feed than mules and horses. Although Secretary Davis did not succeed in getting Congress to appropriate money for camel purchase, his successor in office accomplished it. Congress allotted $30,000 for the purpose of buying camels in the countries of the Mediterranean. Major Wayne, a firm believer in camels, was sent to buy a herd. On a Navy ship, he visited ports of Tunis, Egypt, and Syria, and finally collected a herd of the desert animals. Accompanied by native drivers, the reluctant camels were shoved aboard ship in two loads and transported to Indianola, a Texas port on the Gulf of Mexico. From there they were driven to a camel camp near San Antonio.

In 1857 the government was ready to try out Operation Camel. At the same time the Army wanted a wagon road surveyed from Fort Defiance to California. This double job was assigned to an energetic young officer, Lieutenant Edward Fitzgerald Beale. He was a Californian who had served in the Mexican War and in the Navy, a man who had enthusiasm for the great West and its possibilities. He was ready for any undertaking.

With orders to assemble a Camel Corps, Lieutenant Beale and an escort of soldiers arrived at the camel camp at San Antonio. Some of the native camel drivers refused to set out on such a trek and returned to their countries. Among those who remained were Hadji Ali, whose name was soon Americanized to Hi Jolly, and Greek George. The native drivers were invaluable because the American packers did not know how to load camels, so there were many sore backs among the animals. Nor did these men know how to make camels obey orders and had to depend on the native drivers to speak to the beasts in a language they understood. The Army wagon mules and the soldiers' horses went wild with fright at the first sight and smell of the strange beasts, but they soon became used to them.

The caravan traveled slowly over Texas to New Mexico. Horsemen, mule-drawn covered wagons, and the procession of ungainly, humped creatures created a fantastic sight. The chiming of camel bells announced the approach of the caravan. As they passed through New Mexico, the Spanish villagers came out in crowds to see the strange animals. It was a traveling show for them.

Lieutenant Beale never lost enthusiasm for his camels. He wrote of their docility and patience, their acceptance of heavy loads, their preference for browsing on greasewood and other desert shrubs instead of needing corn and grass like the horses and mules. In a country where there was daily search for water holes, it was another point in their favor that they needed little water.

From Fort Defiance the expedition set out on the real task — that of finding a good route to the Colorado River for wagons and military companies. Through the difficult, anxious days on the trail the Lieutenant kept a careful record of everything they learned about the country — the character of the terrain, the Indians they encountered. The hardships, the constant search for water, fodder and firewood did not discourage him. With courage and ingenuity he led his caravan onward, following the maps of Sitgreaves and Whipple to a certain extent. Often it was necessary to work out a different route, one that wagons could follow. The company had to find a way around Canyon Diablo and struggle through rocky passes. So well did Lieutenant Beale describe the route in his journal that men of later times have been able to follow it. Faint ruts and scratches of wheel tracks on rock can still be seen.

Lieutenant Beale studied the country with a keen, appreciative eye. Enthusiastically he wrote of the mountains, the pine forests, and lovely valleys. Especially he praised what is now Fort Valley, northwest of Flagstaff, where they camped to enjoy the grass and the bubbling spring, named for Antoine Leroux. This spring was a landmark for many later travelers.

After struggling through various mountain ranges the company came at last, in October, to the top of a high hill, from which point they saw the river lying below them in the distance. The Lieutenant wrote in his journal: "Only those who have toiled so far, with life, reputation, everything staked upon the result, can imagine the feelings with which I looked down from the height of this mountain upon the cottonwoods and shining surface of the river far below us."

As they traveled toward the river they came into Mohave Indian country, and the friendly, half-naked people swarmed about them, full of curiosity. They were eager to trade their corn, beans and melons for any bit of clothing the soldiers would part with. The camels must have made a sensation, especially when the drivers persuaded the beasts to swim across the river. The Lieutenant forded his whole company across the Colorado at a point some miles north of the modern town of Needles, California. On his recommendation the Army built Fort Mohave in 1859, on the Arizona side.

Following orders, Lieutenant Beale, with Hi Jolly and Greek George in charge, took his camel caravan to his ranch at Fort Tejon to spend the winter. Sometimes on the trip the Lieutenant had ridden a big dromedary that was trained for riding. Now he trained a team of camels to be driven with a surrey, and when he made trips into Los Angeles with his remarkable team the camels caused a near riot.

In January, Lieutenant Beale returned to the river with a military escort and a few camels. He had orders to go back over the trail to test it for winter travel. As he assembled his men, horses, and camels on the river bank, he was startled to hear the blast of a steamer's whistle, and the *General Jessup* appeared. Captain Johnson had stopped to take on wood when he saw the caravan approaching. He was delighted to welcome the Lieutenant, and there were mutual congratulations, while the steamer ferried Beale's company across the river.

The meeting was a strange scene in the wilderness, a scene the Lieutenant recorded in his journal: the wild-looking Indians, the weird camels, the soldiers — and a steamer in the river! Beale understood the threat of steamboat traffic to the Indians when he wrote, "The steam whistle of the *General Jessup* sounded the death knell of the river race." Steamboats and increased travel by white men did indeed mean the end of control of the river by Yumas or Mohaves.

A flat-topped stone monument at Kingman honors the achievement of Lieutenant Beale. A procession of metal camels, soldiers, and covered wagons streams across the top. He had put through an exploration exceedingly valuable for the future of the region and had proved the worth of camel transportation. It must have disappointed Lieutenant Beale that the Camel Corps, as planned for military use, was never operated. The United States was deeply concerned over approaching war with the southern states, so interest was lost in western transportation. The camels were cared for at Fort Tejon for a while. Some were used to carry freight, and some were used by the Army. Later they were taken to San Francisco and sold at auction to circuses or for ranch work.

Camels were never accepted by westerners, who thought mules, horses, and burros were the proper animals to carry loads. Mule drivers and packers hated the sight of them; horses and mules stampeded if they were approached by camels. In the end they were set free to roam in the deserts and canyons of Arizona and California. For years camels would be seen at times, looming up in the night to frighten prospectors or travelers. They were hunted by Indians and shot at by white men until they gradually drifted into oblivion. Who knows, there may yet be camels in remote canyons or desert spaces!

The brave camel experiment, an odd and legendary chapter in the frontier history of the Southwest, came to an end.

Greek George was killed in a brawl, but Hi Jolly spent a long life in California. After giving up the care and feeding of camels, he worked for the Army occasionally or turned to prospecting. He died near Quartzite, Arizona, where a commemorative stone, topped by a metal camel, was set up to honor the cheerful little camel driver.

Another transportation problem for the Army was the navigation of the Colorado River above Fort Yuma. To be sure, Captain Johnson had two small steamers, the *General Jessup* and *Colorado No. 1*, puffing up river from the mouth to Fort Yuma and some distance beyond, carrying freight and passengers. This experienced river man was also studying the question of navigation on the upper river. He had petitioned the government to help in his plan to explore for the head of navigation, but had received no reply.

The Army was quite concerned, however, with the problem of transporting military supplies and troops up river to join the wagon route Lieutenant Beale had surveyed. When Captain Johnson was finally asked what he would charge to take military men to the head of navigation, the government thought his price too high.

Instead, a young officer, Lieutenant Joseph C. Ives, was assigned to the task. He was to oversee the building of a small steamer and to make the exploration. His small boat, with an iron hull, was built in a Philadelphia shipyard. The long journey by which it was shipped in sections did not improve it. After the sections had been transported by rail across the Isthmus of Panama, they were shipped to San Francisco. Then a schooner transported them to the mouth of the Colorado River. Lieutenant Ives and his artisans were aboard.

When Lieutenant Ives asked Captain Johnson for a pilot to navigate his small craft, the captain agreed to find one for him, but he went on with his own plans to be the first navigator on the upper river.

While Lieutenant Ives and his men struggled through many weeks with the difficulties of assembling their iron craft on the mud banks of the Colorado, Captain Johnson wasted no time. He fitted out the *General Jessup* for an exploring trip up the river.

Captain Johnson, who knew very well the sand bars and changing channels of the river, successfully navigated the *General Jessup* to a point about seventy-five miles above the place where Lieutenant Beale and his camels had crossed the river. It was on his return trip that he saw Beale's company and stopped to ferry them across. However, he did not return in triumph to Yuma. The steamboat hit a rock that tore a hole in the boiler, and she sank some miles before reaching the Fort. The craft had to be rescued by the men of the companion steamer, who patched her up to return to service. At any rate, Captain Johnson had the satisfaction of knowing that he had been the first to navigate the upper Colorado River.

On Christmas Day, 1857, Lieutenant Ives' small steamboat, christened the *Explorer,* was ready to go. Steam was raised in the boiler and she set off successfully. The people at Jaeger's Ferry and the Fort watched this new craft come puffing past, flag flying, clouds of black smoke streaming from the stack, a great surge of spray kicked up by her rear paddle wheel. The *Explorer* was an odd little craft, only about 50 feet long, with a narrow iron hull, a tiny deck at the prow, and small cabin at the rear. The engine and boiler were exposed in the open center of the boat.

Thanks to skillful navigating by the borrowed pilot, the little craft made a trip up river to the entrance of Black Canyon. When they tried to go farther the steamboat got stuck on sandbars, and when pulled off those it was nearly wrecked in the rapids. Lieutenant Ives' report to the Army was rather discouraging. He described the difficulties of navigation and estimated the great expense of operating a steamer on the upper river. The Army was glad to sell the *Explorer* to Captain Johnson, who used it for a while to transport wood on the Gila. Eventually it broke down and drifted into a side channel, where the rusted hulk lay for years.

The two trips up river had proved that the Colorado was navigable at least as far as Fort Mohave, where Beale had crossed. Captain Johnson put more steamers into service for the use of the Army or for prospectors hunting gold. Several small gold camps grew up along the shores, and river navigation was helpful to pioneers entering Arizona.

## Chapter XVI

### Mines, Pioneers, Indians

After the Gadsden Purchase the old Spanish land of southern Arizona was open to American pioneers, and they lost no time in taking advantage of it. Some came to raise cattle on the grassy plains, some to open shops in Tucson. It was known that Spanish and Mexican mines had been worked in this region, therefore prospecting was the greatest attraction.

Two men who explored the mining possibilities were to have a good deal of influence in the next phase of the Arizona story. Charles D. Poston, a Kentuckian, was a man of exuberant enthusiasm, a mining engineer, and a born promoter. His companion, Herman Ehrenberg, was also a good prospector and a topographical engineer. He had been in the Southwest for some time.

These two men, with several other prospectors, had been on an exploring trip in the Santa Cruz Valley in 1854. They had tested ores in the Santa Rita Mountains and the Cerro Colorado and had investigated old Spanish mines. While exploring they had camped in empty houses of deserted Tubac.

On their way back to San Francisco by way of the Colorado River they arrived with their pack animals at the crossing where Don Diego Jaeger was prospering with his ferry business. They were broke, and Don Diego demanded $25 to ferry them and their animals across the river. He had his establishment on the California side and a landing on the Arizona bank.

Poston and Ehrenberg retired to their camp among the mesquite bushes to consider the problem of how they would cross the river with no money for the ferry. Charles Poston came up with a clever idea. Soon the men had set up their surveying instruments among the bushes and rocks. They ran lines and drove stakes in rows.

This was too much for Don Diego's curiosity, he had to find out what they were up to. When he questioned Poston that promoter replied cheerfully, "There is going to be a city here and we are surveying lots." He told Don Diego that, with the river traffic and business from the mines they were going to open, this would be a big place. When the ferryman asked the name of this mythical town Charles Poston said, on the spur of the moment, "Arizona City."

Don Diego was so impressed that he asked to buy a lot, and the men graciously agreed, he could have one for $25. They proceeded to lay out a fine piece of property on the river. They also surveyed lots for themselves and made a record of each. When Don Diego gave Poston the money he pocketed it, and soon paid out the identical $25 for passage of his party across the river on the ferry.

This tale was one of Charles Poston's favorite humorous stories, but it must have had foundation in fact. When the prospectors reached San Diego, Poston filed the plan for the non-existent city and the lots that had been surveyed. The claims held good when Arizona City finally became a crude settlement on the river bank. It took a long time to grow, but eventually the settlement became the city of Yuma.

Charles Poston went East to raise money for a mine company. His promoter's skill and enthusiastic arguments won capital. In 1856 he returned to the Southwest as the manager of the Sonora Exploring and Mining Company. Herman Ehrenberg was one of the officers and Major Heintzelman of Fort Yuma was the president.

In San Antonio, Texas, Poston assembled a hardy group of frontiersmen and some mining engineers, with wagons and supplies, for the long trek over Cooke's Wagon Road to Tucson and then to Tubac. The weed-grown, tumbledown village was chosen as headquarters for the company. The Sonora Exploring and Mining Company bought the large Mexican ranch at Arivaca, whose owner was probably glad to leave the region haunted by murderous Apaches. They bought Mexican silver claims in the Santa Rita Mountains, to the east of the Santa Cruz River, and other claims in the Cerro Colorado to the west.

This enterprise, started with such energy and confidence, inspired Mexican miners and their families to trek to Tubac for jobs in the mines. Mexican ranchers who had abandoned their farms because of Indian raids returned, and American pioneers moved in. Colonel Douglas had a mine near Sopori; Patagonia Mine near the border was discovered by Mexicans who sold it to Captain R. S.

Ewell and Colonel Douglas, who in turn sold it to Lieutenant Sylvester Mowry from Fort Yuma. This mine, later called the Mowry Mine, proved to have rich silver and lead ores and was famous for some years.

In the beginning the Americans had to use the old Spanish arrastra for crushing ore and the primitive Spanish methods for smelting. The arrastra was a round floor of hard-packed earth surrounded by a low rock wall. A long rotating pole attached to a post in the center of the floor was also attached by chains to big boulders. The chunks of ore were dumped on the floor. The pole was then hooked to the collar of a mule or burro, and the animal walked round and round, dragging the boulders over the ore until it was crushed.

In the course of time, mine machinery, ordered from the East, was shipped by steamer to a landing at Kansas City, then brought overland by ox cart or wagon to Tubac. Also, some machinery was shipped to the port of Guaymas in Sonora on the Gulf of California, thence by cart to its destination. With sufficient machinery the mine work stepped up in efficiency and success. Many mines were opened in the Cerro Colorado region, the richest being the large Heintzelman silver mine. Another company, the Santa Rita Mine Company, was organized to develop the old Salero silver mine in those mountains.

Within two years Tubac was a thriving village with cultivated fields and fruit trees extending to the river banks. At that period the Santa Cruz was a stream of running water. Groves of noble cottonwoods that shaded the banks were domes of green in summer, of copper-gold in autumn. There were cattle in the pastures, horses and mules in the corrals.

Outside the walls of Tucson, also, the inhabitants

grew crops in fields irrigated from the river. The old town was becoming more lively as American pioneers opened shops to serve the needs of the miners in food, dry goods, hay and grain for the animals.

In and out of both towns crawled strings of pack mules or loaded wagons, bringing all sorts of goods from the port of Guaymas. Freight wagons transported loads of ore to Guaymas, to be shipped to San Francisco for testing.

No one has so well described the happy life at Tubac as Charles Poston himself, for he was the moving spirit of the whole enterprise. He was the only representative of law and order in the region, having been appointed Deputy Clerk of Tubac by a distant officer of New Mexico Territory. Since there was no priest for the village, Poston cheerfully married, baptized, and read burial services when called upon. They all loved him. He settled quarrels and administered justice when miners became engaged in brawls.

The Mexican families added warmth and gayety to the settlement of mining men, especially the light-hearted girls from Sonora who had come to the village in the hope of finding husbands among the miners. There were lively weekend gatherings when the miners and overseers returned to the village from the mine camps. Fiestas, with singing, flirting, and the dancing of fandangos, were held in the plaza. The favorite gambling game was monte, at which the girls were expert.

For some time the medium of exchange was in the form of small silver bars from the mines. As the working population increased, this currency was cumbersome. An amusing form of paper money was printed. These "boletas", as they were called, were a boon to Mexican workers

for most of them could not read.  A pasteboard with the
picture of a pig was worth 12½ cents, a calf 25 cents, a
rooster 50 cents, a horse one dollar, a bull five dollars, and
a lion ten dollars.  These boletas of Tubac were used for
payment of weekly wages on ranches and at the mines.

The large building, which had been the Mexican
barracks and fort in the old days, was remodeled for headquarters of the mine officers.  In the large dining hall, the
engineers and others were fed well from local produce of
the fields and game brought in by hunters.  Here, too, the
company entertained guests.  Many were distinguished
friends of Charles Poston from distant cities, who endured
the hardships of travel to see what this mine company was
doing in the Arizona wilderness.  The mine officers were
highly educated men of world-wide experience, so the con-
versations during their social evenings were on an intellectual level.  Horace Grosvenor and Raphael Pumpelly
were two of the talented men who came to serve as superintendents or engineers at the mines.

The people of the valley rejoiced when in 1857 a
stage line came through twice monthly, on a route from
San Antonio to San Diego.  This line soon won the nickname of "Jackass Mail" because, after crossing the Colorado to California, the unfortunate passengers had to leave
the coaches to ride mules over the sand dunes.

The next year, 1858, transportation and mail service
was really improved.  The Butterfield Overland Mail was
organized with a government contract to carry mail from
St. Louis, Missouri, to San Francisco.  The journey was to
be made each way in twenty-five days.  Stage stations of
adobe buildings were built at intervals along the route.
The station keeper tended a herd of horses or mules for
change of teams, and provided fodder for the animals as

well as food of some sort for the exhausted passengers.

It was a great day for the inhabitants of Tucson when the first six-horse team and swaying coach thundered into the dusty lanes. Now Arizona was in contact with East and West once a week. More people came to Tucson to start business; more visitors came to the mines. It took hardihood to survive that journey by coach. Passengers were crowded into the interior or crouched on top, clutching the sides for safety. The driver must make time to keep the rigid schedule, so he drove his team at a gallop. The coach jounced and jumped over rough trails and rocky passes, over arroyos and dry river beds, until the passengers were more dead than alive.

An escort of soldiers accompanied the stages through Apache country. These Indians responded to the building of settlements and increased transportation with ever more ferocious raids. They lurked among the boulders of Apache Pass, waiting a chance to attack the stages. The ranchers and mine companies were frequently robbed of their animals. After repeated urgent requests for military protection, the government assigned several companies of dragoons and their commander to set up an Army post some miles east of Tubac. Fort Buchanan was only a group of adobe buildings without even a stockade for protection, but the people felt some degree of safety to have soldiers nearby.

The wild warriors of the mountains were the only cloud on the booming prosperity of the region. That threat was disregarded by Charlest Poston and Sylvester Mowry in their enthusiastic descriptions of the beautiful country and the great possibilities for development with mines and agriculture. They were Arizona's first boosters.

The mine companies were also anxious to publicize

their interprises and to give the local inhabitants some news. They supported a newspaper, the first in Arizona. A Washington hand-press was bought in the East and shipped to the port of Guaymas. From there it was brought by wagon to Tubac. On March 3, 1859, the first edition of *The Weekly Arizonian* appeared. The editor, Edward Cross, expressed the settlers' indignation because they were left without law or government by the neglect of Congress. In addition, there were items about cattle deals, Apache raids, and mine advancement. Each week the people of Tubac and Tucson eagerly awaited their newspaper.

It was not only the big silver mines of the south that were attracting people to Arizona. Prospectors from California, hunting for gold dust and nuggets, were washing the sands along the Colorado and Gila. Then rich "pay dirt" was discovered by Jacob Snively on the Gila, about twenty miles above the Colorado. Arizona had its first gold rush and its first wild mining town, as hordes of prospectors hurried to the sands and hills of the Gila. The "dust" was so rich that men were taking out five dollars a day from a few pans of sand. Later, many miners made as much as $125 a day. Gila City, as it was called, was soon booming with gambling halls, saloons, and countless huts of feverish miners who were digging out the sands and washing them in rockers in the river. The easy gold was soon exhausted. As the miners did not have machinery for digging the gold in the hills, the roaring mine camp became a ghost town.

Prospectors were sampling the gravels and river banks along the Colorado above the ferry settlement, discovering gold and starting mine camps. Two accomplished frontiersmen, Herman Ehrenburg and Pauline Weaver, led prospectors to discoveries of rich placer gold in gulches back of the river, at a place they named La Paz. In no time, La Paz was a booming settlement.

In the years from 1856 to 1861 it seemed that southern Arizona was at last emerging from an undeveloped wilderness to a prosperous pioneer section of the country. The Apaches were determined that this should not happen. The eastern mountains, from the Chiricahuas and Dragoons to the Superstitions, were the haunts of many Apache clans, all fierce enemies of white men. This country was their homeland, and with all their ruthless skill as warriors they fought to hold it.

Cochise, the strong, intelligent chief of the Chiricahuas, and Mangas Coloradas of the New Mexico bands were the only Indian leaders who realized it was impossible to drive all white men from the country. It was best to learn to get along with them. Under Cochise' leadership the Chiricahuas did not attack Americans, although they made deadly raids into Mexican territory.

Resentment grew among the ranchers of Sonora because the Americans did not prevent these raids. In retaliation many crossed the border to steal stock from Americans. On the trails in Sonora many bandits attacked pack trains bringing supplies from Guaymas. Lawless Mexicans filtered into Arizona to set the Mexican miners against their employers. Some hot-headed characters among the American settlers made matters worse by attacking Mexicans on ranches and driving them back across the border. Ranches were short of workers; most of the Mexican miners could not be trusted. The clouds of danger grew darker.

The ignorant act of young Lieutenant Bascom, fresh from West Point, was responsible for changing wise

Cochise from a cooperative Indian to a bitter enemy of all white men.  The lieutenant was sent from Fort Buchanan with soldiers to seek news at Apache Pass of a boy and some stock that had been stolen by Indians.  Cochise and several of his relatives were at Apache Pass.  They were friendly with the stage station keeper who bought wood from them.

At Lieutenant Bascom's request the station keeper, Wallace, asked Cochise to meet the young soldier at his tent for an interview.  In all confidence, since they were on friendly terms with Americans, Cochise and his relatives went to the lieutenant's tent.  Lieutenant Bascom, knowing nothing about Indians, questioned Cochise severely about the stolen boy and cattle, implying that his warriors were responsible.  Cochise assured him this was not so, but he would try to find the boy and cattle and see that they were returned.  At this statement the arrogant officer accused Cochise of lying and arrested him and his companions.  They would be held as hostages until the boy and stock were returned.

In a fury, Cochise leaped up, slit the tent canvas with his knife and escaped.  That night Apaches attacked a stage coach and captured several passengers.  The next day Cochise seized the station keeper, Wallace, although he liked him.  Displaying his captives before the lieutenant's tent, Cochise demanded his relatives in exchange for the Americans.  Stupidly, the officer refused, whereupon Cochise killed his captives, and in retaliation Lieutenant Bascom hung the Indian's relatives.

From that time on, Cochise vowed destruction to all white men and their works.  There was no safety anywhere except within the walls of Tucson.  Some ranchers took refuge in the town, others escaped to Mexico.  Ranch

houses were burned by the Indians, travelers were murdered, the mine camps were attacked and all the mules
and horses run off.

The final blow came when, in 1861, the commander
of Fort Buchanan was ordered to burn all supplies and
march his men to New Mexico. The Civil War had begun, which was a shock to isolated Arizonans, and fighting was going on in New Mexico between Union troops
and Texas Confederates.

In addition to this desertion, the Butterfield stages
were withdrawn by order of the government. The war
and Apache raids made the route too unsafe. Arizona
was completely cut off from the rest of the country.

The withdrawal of the soldiers convinced the Apaches
that they were victorious over the white men, that they
had driven most of them from the country; they were
determined to exterminate those who remained. Horace
Grosvenor was ambushed on a road and murdered. Other
men and drivers of wagons were killed. Lawless Mexicans helped the destruction by killing Charles Poston's
brother John, who was superintendent at the Heintzelman mine.

The mine officers decided that it was impossible to
continue work at the mines with both Indians and Mexicans threatening them. The mines must be abandoned
until the war was over. Stores and machinery were packed
in the barracks at Tubac. The officers thought there was
little chance of saving their goods, for they felt sure that
Mexicans would carry off anything the Indians might
leave. Then Charles Poston, Raphael Pumpelly and others
set out on mule back to reach Guaymas and a ship for
San Francisco.

The remaining inhabitants of Tubac were besieged

by whooping Indians, but they were able to hold out until they were rescued by a troop of mounted men from Tucson. Tubac was burned by the Indians and looted by Mexican bandits.

The dark clouds of disaster completely overwhelmed the glowing picture of prosperous mines and ranches in southern Arizona.

Chapter XVII

Arizona in the Civil War

During those prosperous years, from 1854 to 1861, the American settlers had become increasingly indignant over the neglect of their interests and needs by Congress and the national administration. They pleaded for military protection and received only the small number of troops at Fort Buchanan. There was no law enforcement and no government for the people of mines and settlements in this distant part of the territory of New Mexico. Officials in Santa Fe were too far distant to pay attention to this newly acquired Gadsden Purchase.

There had been bills before Congress in favor of making the land of the Gadsden Purchase and the area north of the Gila River into a territory separate from New Mexico, but they had failed in spite of the fact

153

that President Buchanan had recommended the plan. The citizens of Tucson held meetings of protest. At one time they organized an assembly to administer laws until a territorial government was established.

It is not surprising, then, that some Americans in Tucson were so discouraged with the national government that they thought their best chance for law and order was to join the Confederacy. In addition, there were plenty of southern sympathizers in the town to urge that this be done.

The year 1861 was a crucial year for the inhabitants of Tucson, who were the only townspeople of southern Arizona in that dark time. After the Butterfield stages and the troops were withdrawn, a convention was held at which the leading Americans declared they were ready to join the Confederacy. They elected Granville Oury as delegate to the Confederate Congress that was to meet in Richmond, Virginia. Other leaders in the resolution were Sylvester Mowry and Captain R. S. Ewell.

The Texas Confederate troops were having success in New Mexico, and it was part of the Confederate plan to gain control of the Gadsden Purchase lands. That would give them a route to California, a base for possible acquisition of Sonora, and a port on the Gulf of California. At Mesilla, New Mexico, the officer in command of that region, Lieutenant Colonel John R. Baylor, proclaimed a Territory of Arizona. It was to consist of the sections of Arizona and New Mexico south of the 34th parallel. On February 14, 1862, President Jefferson Davis of the Confederate States of America confirmed Baylor's announcement by proclaiming the Confederate Territory of Arizona.

Soon after, Captain Sherod Hunter, with a mounted company of Texans, marched into Tucson and took possession in the name of the Confederacy. Another flag was raised above the walls, following those of Spain, Mexico, and the United States. The Mexican people and their forebears had seen many companies of soldiers come and go, and most of them made no choice between Union and Confederate.

Captain Hunter and his men were rather a rough lot, but they did not interfere with the Mexican people. They were chiefly concerned with the problem of collecting food for the troops. The Captain ordered Union men to work for the Confederacy or get out, and most of them did leave for Mexico temporarily, including the good merchant, Solomon Warner, and a popular Mexican merchant, Estéban Ochoa.

Confederate occupation did not last long. Union volunteers in California were forming the California Volunteers, or California Column, a company of 1,800 men. They were to march first to Yuma to relieve that Union garrison. Their advance scouts in Arizona met some of Captain Hunter's men at the Pima villages, where both sides were trying to collect flour and corn from the Indians. Following this encounter, a troop of the California Volunteers marched to meet Hunter's men, and a brief battle was fought at Picacho Peak, the only battle of the war in Arizona. It was not decisive for either side, but Captain Hunter learned from the encounter that Union troops were advancing into Arizona. He thought best to remove his small company from Tucson, and they retreated toward the Rio Grande, taking along some southern sympathizers.

On May 20, 1862, the advance guard of the California Column entered Tucson, and the Stars and Stripes once more flew over the old town, this time permanently. In June, General Carleton, commander of the California

Volunteers, arrived to set things in order. Arizona's brief experience of the war was over.

Meanwhile, another territorial bill for Arizona had been introduced in Congress. Charles Poston, after leaving the mines, had gone East and was in Washington to work for its passage. General Carleton must have been confident that Arizona would win a separate territorial status, for his first act was a proclamation setting up the Territory of Arizona. He announced that it was his duty to represent the authority of the United States over the people of Arizona "until such time as the President of the United States shall otherwise direct."

The citizens of Tucson were asked to take the oath of allegiance to the United States or to leave, and some leading men were arrested, among them Sylvester Mowry. He was known to be pro-Confederate and was accused of having aided Captain Hunter with supplies and lead for bullets from his Patagonia mine. He was tried, but no traitorous activities were proved against him. It was a time of violent feelings, and in spite of the lack of evidence Mowry was sent to prison for six months at Yuma, and his mine was confiscated.

The Apaches, who thought they had conquered the white men, were enraged to see companies of soldiers marching back and forth across the country. Whether the uniforms were blue or gray, they attacked indiscriminately. The Indians were the greatest menace to peace and progress as military government, after the war, strove to establish order.

Cochise and Mangas Coloradas gathered their warriors among the rocks and hills of Apache Pass to prevent military convoys from going through. When an advance guard of California Volunteers, escorting a wagon train, entered the Pass the Indians fell upon them with fury. A bloody battle raged. But the soldiers had howitzers, and shells from these guns, bursting among the rocks, slaughtered the Indians. Many were wounded or killed, and the Indians could not prevent the wagons from going through.

The battle in Apache Pass pointed up the importance of protecting this strategic place for the passage of the Army or travelers. In that same year, 1862, General Carleton ordered the building of a military camp in the pass, overlooking an important spring. That was the beginning of old Fort Bowie. From that post, for many years to come, soldiers would escort wagon trains, stage coaches, or travelers through this Apache-haunted region.

Next, General Carleton turned his attention to protection for miners in the central plateau region near present-day Prescott and Wickenburg. Captain Walker, an old trapper and scout for troops, had led a group of miners from various parts of the country to hunt for mineral riches in the region of mountains and streams, inhabited only by Indians. Among the hills the company built themselves a log stockade and fort as protection. From this stronghold they explored and prospected in every direction, sampling ore and trapping beaver as well. They worked placer gold with success at Lynx Creek. After them came the Peeples Party, guided by Pauline Weaver. These prospectors had great luck. They found a basin and hill where gold nuggets were strewn over the ground in such quantities that they scooped them up in tin cups. Further exploration showed good veins of gold, and the party named their claim Rich Hill. They also found gold at Weaver Gulch and Antelope Creek. The hills and streams of this pleasant plateau country, swarming with miners, seemed to General Carleton the most valuable section of the territory. A military camp was set up to protect miners and future settlers from Indians.

In the north, the Navajos were as great a menace to settlements in New Mexico as the Apaches were in the central and southern parts of the country. These nomadic people were skilled at adopting things they wanted from other inhabitants. From Pueblo Indians, whose flocks they stole, they learned to be sheepherders, and their women learned weaving from captive Pueblos. The men became expert horsemen, riding the horses they stole from ranchers. To the proud warriors, horses were a symbol of wealth, so they vied with each other to collect great herds that ran wild in their country. As the tribe grew in numbers and power, they spread westward from New Mexico into the vast land of canyons, mesas, and desert plains in northern Arizona, a land they made their own.

When the Civil War began, most of the troops were withdrawn from Santa Fe and Fort Defiance. Like their cousins the Apaches, the Navajos thought they had a chance to drive all white men from the country. They terrorized the countryside with their raids.

After General Carleton took command of the whole vast territory of New Mexico and Arizona, he and his officers determined that these Indian wars must cease. Stern orders were issued that Apaches and Navajos were to be relentlessly pursued, the warriors killed, women and children captured.

Some older Navajo leaders wanted to make peace, for they understood that the tribe could not conquer the Americans, they must learn to live with them. However, they could not control the warriors. While the women and elders lived in the remote canyons, the women herding sheep and tending crops, the warriors swooped on settlers in fierce raids. Then they retreated with their loot to hiding places in their desert land where soldiers could not reach them. The Mescalero Apaches in southern New Mexico were equally troublesome.

General Carleton and his advisers decided that these warring Indians must be removed from their native haunts and settled on a reservation, where they could be taught to support themselves by farming. A flat area in southeastern New Mexico was chosen, near the Pecos River. It was poor scrubby land, the only trees a grove of cottonwoods called Bosque Redondo. The reservation was to be managed from a small adobe military post called Fort Sumner. Here the wild people of mountains and canyons were expected to settle down and become farmers. The Mescalero Apaches surrendered and were placed on the reservation.

General Carleton then issued an order for the Navajos to surrender. They were desperate because they were being constantly hunted by soldiers and were half-starved from destruction of their crops and sheep. Some hundreds came into Fort Defiance and were sent on to Fort Sumner. Thousands more retreated to the innermost reaches of their land, the steep-walled gorges of Canyon de Chelly.

In 1863, General Carleton ordered Kit Carson, who was then a colonel of New Mexican volunteers, to take his soldiers and gather in the rebellious Indians. As the troops pursued the Indians deeper into their country, Kit Carson adopted a "scorched earth" policy. Wherever the troops found corn or wheat fields they were destroyed. Peach trees, grown in sheltered canyons, were chopped down, and sheep were killed. Winter began, but the soldiers pushed on through cold and snow, fighting Indians on mesa tops and in canyons. Lack of food and bitter cold forced hundreds to surrender, but many hid in remote canyons and were never found.

Men, women and children were herded together. A soldier escort marched them over exhausting miles in winter cold to Fort Sumner. This agonizing episode in their history remains a bitter memory in the minds of older Navajos.

From 1863 to 1868, the exiled Navajo people lived in misery at Fort Sumner. They were weakened by illness, by hunger when crops failed, and by longing for their desert homeland. The Mescalero Apaches and the Navajos resented each other. The whole experiment was a failure due to complete lack of understanding of the Indians by Army officers and to the stubborn refusal of the Navajos to be made over into farmers.

At last the Army and the United States Government gave up the scheme to force Navajos to live like white men. A treaty was made with the tribe, and people were allowed to return home. They were given rations, some sheep to start their flocks, tools, and seeds for planting.

These independent, hardworking folk settled down in their beloved desert land, now set aside as their reservation, to build up their own way of life. Flocks of sheep were tended by women and children, horses were raised by men, small crops were cultivated. The women became expert weavers of blankets, using the wool of their sheep and vegetable dyes. From Mexican silversmiths the men had learned silver craft. They made buttons, bracelets and necklaces, ornaments for bridles and saddles. These could be traded for food at the trading posts, as well as used for personal adornment. Many hard years were before them, but the Navajos were started on a new path.

While the Army was bringing some order into the scattered sections of Arizona, the population was increasing. Energetic men were extracting minerals, raising crops and cattle, and starting business in the few towns. The pioneer people were looking forward to the next big step forward in their history — a territorial government of their own.

# PART IV.
# TERRITORIAL ARIZONA

Chapter XVIII

A Territory at Last!

On December 29, 1863, a remarkable company assembled at the tiny settlement of Navajo Springs, in the snowy chill of a northern Arizona winter. They were the appointed officers of the new Territory of Arizona. The Organic Act had been signed by President Lincoln on February 25, 1863.

The officers had traveled by ambulance, a military covered wagon, over a rough trail from Santa Fe with a military escort. When they passed the boundary between New Mexico and the new Territory, they paused for an inauguration ceremony.

The Chief Justice swore in the new officers, champagne was produced, and the health of Arizona Territory was proposed. The President's proclamation was read, after which Secretary McCormick raised the flag and made a short speech. Governor John N. Goodwin spoke of his hopes for the new Territory, his words being translated into Spanish for the benefit of the New Mexican soldiers. The ceremony must have seemed strange and crude to the new officers from the settled eastern states. Here they stood in the wilderness to inaugurate territorial government, with no citizens of Arizona to greet them.

The Organic Act was the culmination of a long, persistent fight by Americans of Arizona and their eastern friends to win separation from New Mexico and a territorial government of their own.

The lawmakers, in 1863, were influenced by the importance of establishing new federal territories between the Confederate South and the Pacific Coast. Friends of Arizona had emphasized the need of the neglected settlers for a stable government. Also, there were politicians, some just completing their terms in Congress, who were looking for new posts. They might be willing to try their luck in a wilderness territory, rumored to be rich in mineral resources.

Charles Poston, who believed enthusiastically in the future of the land, had been in Washington since 1862, using his persuasions to help in the passage of the territorial bill. In his reminiscences, Poston told one of his impish tales of how he clinched the deal by inviting the available politicians to an oyster supper in Washington. When they were mellowed with good food and drink he persuaded them that his favorite region, Arizona, had a great future which they might help to develop. Whether this story is legend or fact, it was true that Charles Poston worked for Arizona among the politicians with determination and skill. His work for the Territory won him the title "Father of Arizona."

President Lincoln had appointed John A. Gurley as governor, but he died before the expedition started for the West. The final list of appointments was as follows: Governor, John N. Goodwin, Maine; Secretary, Richard C. McCormick, New York; Chief Justice, Almon Gage, New York; Associate Justices, William T. Howell, Michigan, and Joseph P. Allyn, Connecticut; District Attorney, John Titus, Pennsylvania; Territorial Marshal, Milton P. Duffield, California; Superintendent of Indian Affairs, Charles Poston, Kentucky and Arizona.

Arizona's first government was composed of men from many states, and the American pioneers who were energetic citizens of the new Territory had also come to Arizona from various parts of the country.

The officers, while at Santa Fe, had not been sure of their destination but had thought they should proceed to Tucson. General Carleton, military commander of the Union forces in New Mexico, advised them to make their goal the central Arizona plateau where a military post, Fort Whipple, had just been established. It was a region where profitable gold mines were already in production. The troops were to watch over the mines and other enterprises of the settlers. The General spoke with enthusiasm of the forests, plains and hills, the mineral-rich mountains, the excellent climate and great possibilities for development.

On this advice, the company moved on from Navajo Springs to join the soldiers at Fort Whipple, which was then in Chino Valley. They were pleased with the country and cheered by the evidences of pioneer settlement in the mining camps and the valley.

Here at the Fort the officers spent the winter months, while plans were made for the organization of government.  Governor Goodwin toured the region with a soldier escort to get acquainted with the settlers.  Secretary McCormick designed the seal for the Territory.  The first design showed a deer, flanked by saguaro and pine, with the San Francisco Peaks in the background.  The words *Ditat Deus*, God Enriches, were added.  Later, a design with a different theme was worked out to show the all-important miner.  He was drawn leaning on pick and shovel, with a wheelbarrow beside him and mountains in the background.  In 1877, after some argument and objections to the wheelbarrow, this design was chosen, minus the wheelbarrow, for the official seal of Arizona Territory.

It had been supposed by the Americans in Tucson that their community, the only real town, would of course be chosen for the capital.  There was much opposition to this from some Arizonans and from officials in Washington who resented the southern sympathies of many men in Tucson.  La Paz, a gold mining camp, was so prosperous that its citizens put in a plea to have the capital, and other small mining towns added their bid.  General Carleton, however, advised the officers to choose the region near Fort Whipple, in the center of the Territory.  Here they could build a capital city that would be all American, with no Confederate sympathies and no Mexican influence.

In May, 1864, it was decided to found the capital on Granite Creek, where new gold strikes were causing excitement.  Fort Whipple was moved to a site near the prospective town.  Homesteaders in log cabins were there already, but their claims were settled, and town lots were laid out and sold at auction for the first family homes.

Then the question was asked, what should be the name for the future capital of Arizona Territory? There was lively discussion on the question. Secretary McCormick, a rather bookish man, proposed that the town be named in honor of William Hickling Prescott, author of the book *The Conquest of Mexico,* a best seller of the period. In fact, the educated explorers of that time, such as the engineers of government surveys, were convinced that Montezuma's people, the Aztecs, had built the Indian ruins they discovered in many places. Perhaps that belief led to the inappropriate name given to the cliff dwelling in Verde Valley, Montezuma's Castle, and to other uses of the names Aztec and Montezuma.

So the small settlement of log and plank houses on Granite Creek received the name Prescott, in honor of a literary man who wrote about Indian civilizations conquered by Spaniards. The first houses were built of mud-plastered logs. One of these was a boarding house for miners, run by a hearty woman with the odd name of Virgin Mary. Later, this log house was called Old Fort Misery and was a hangout for all the rough characters from the mines.

A stout, two-storied house of hewn logs was built for Governor Goodwin and Secretary McCormick, on land they had acquired. It had six rooms and a kitchen on the ground floor, with a large sleeping room above. Here the Governor and Secretary lived. That Governor's Mansion, still intact and standing in the grounds of the Sharlot Hall Museum, is a cherished historic shrine.

There had been no government appropriation for a public building, but Secretary McCormick was authorized to rent quarters for the sessions of the Territorial

Legislature.   Since there was no available building, a citizen, Van C. Smith, offered to erect a building for business purposes that he would rent to the territorial government.   A large structure of hewn logs was built on Gurley Street with rooms spacious enough for the assembly and the council.   The first three sessions of the Legislature met there, and the structure acquired the title of Old Capitol Building, which it retained even after the Legislature moved to Tucson, then back to Prescott to the new City Hall.   The old building later housed business firms and a saloon.

In May, 1864, Governor Goodwin called an election for members of the Legislature.   Charles Poston was elected delegate to the National Congress on a platform that called for support of the Union.   Judges were assigned to their posts: Howell to Tucson, Allyn to La Paz, Turner to Prescott.   Four counties were laid out by the Legislature, named for Indian tribes that inhabited the areas.   They were: Mohave, with county seat at Mohave City; Yuma, with county seat at La Paz; Pima, covering the territory of the Gadsden Purchase in southern Arizona, with Tucson as county seat; Yavapai, north of the Gila, covering about half the Territory, with county seat at Prescott.

Pioneers began to flock into the new capital to run shops, sell produce, and engage in mining.   It was a source of pride that their village was the seat of government. Some men brought their wives, which helped to give the rough little settlement the character of a community.   One lady, a Mrs. Ehle, is credited with bringing to Prescott the first chickens, the first cat, and a hive of honey bees. The men were hunters.   They brought in elk, deer and antelope from the plains to supplement the food supply. Prescott soon became a busy pioneer settlement, set in a charming valley with rounded, forested hills near by and mountains in the background.

A party of farmers investigated the prospects for growing crops in the Verde Valley with irrigation from the river, and did very well at it. They were soon feeding their families and selling their surplus in Prescott.

The elected members of the Legislature went to work with a will at each session to put through laws for the improvement of their separate districts. At every session there was a battle over the location of the capital; Tucsonans claimed their right as citizens of the oldest town to have the capital. In 1867 they won, and Tucson was the seat of government for ten years.

At Tucson, after holding a few legislative sessions in inadequate quarters, a long adobe building at Ochoa Street and Stone Avenue was rented from the big freighting company of Tully & Ochoa. The building had two large rooms for the sessions of the assembly and council and a few small, dark rooms besides. Across the street Tully & Ochoa had their merchandise store and the corral for their mules.

In 1877, Prescott won back the capital and the Legislature was quartered in the new City Hall. Prescott remained the seat of government until 1889, when the new town, Phoenix, was chosen as the permanent site of the wandering capital. The bill for removal of the capital was approved and signed by Governor Zulick on January 6, 1889, and the entire legislative body moved to Phoenix to continue the session on the fourth of February. The members traveled by Pullman cars on the railroad, in which citizens took such pride, by way of Los Angeles, and spent a couple of days enjoying that city before proceeding to Phoenix. It was indeed a roundabout way to travel from Prescott to Phoenix, and it was rumored that the citizens of Phoenix had raised a fund to pay all expenses of the removal of the Legislature.

Arizona territorial government was carried on in temporary quarters in Phoenix until the new City Hall was completed. There were fine rooms for the officers, large halls for the two branches of the Legislature, and a territorial library.

During the twenty-five years in which territorial government rotated from log or adobe structures to City Halls at Prescott and at Phoenix, vigorous Arizonans built up their primitive land with towns, cattle ranches, mining, and agriculture.

## Chapter XIX

### Pioneers in Northern Arizona

The great red river, the Colorado, was the goal of explorers in the mid-nineteenth century after the Civil War. Energetic nation-builders turned their attention to the little-known region north of the San Francisco Peaks in Arizona, in southern Utah and in Colorado, the territory through which flowed the great river and its tributaries.

Exciting gold rushes and silver discoveries had brought prosperous mining camps and towns to the Rocky Mountain region of Colorado, but westward there was a wilderness explored by only a few groups. The Mormons were moving southward from their headquarters at Salt Lake City to found settlements. Mountain men, hunting beaver, had managed to get into some canyons of the

171

Colorado, and a few daring prospectors had climbed down the walls in search of gold.

The course of the great river was known. Two tributaries, the Green River in Wyoming and the Grand River, coming from its headwaters in the Rockies, joined to make the main stream of the Colorado. As the river cut through the high plateaus of Utah and Arizona, other tributaries, the San Juan, the Little Colorado and smaller rivers, entered the main stream. After the Gila River had added its waters, the mighty Colorado reached the Gulf of California. The deep, awesome canyons, through which the stream carved its way for hundreds of miles in Utah and Arizona, were mysterious and unexplored to men of the 1860's.

The Colorado was in use from its mouth to the head of navigation in Black Canyon, which is now under the waters of Lake Mead. When Lieutenant Ives and his tiny steamer, *The Explorer,* reached the end of river exploration in 1858 he ordered his crew to take the boat to Yuma. Then he left the river and saw some of the canyons on his way to Fort Defiance. Father Garcés, in his remarkable journey through wilderness country, had climbed down into the canyon home of the Havasupais.

Explorers, who had stood on the rim of the awe-inspiring gash in the earth called Grand Canyon, had wondered how to get down to the river, how to follow its course through the canyons. To accomplish this was the great adventure of the mid-nineteenth century.

In September, 1867, a raft floated out of the canyons at the Mormon settlement at Callville, near the head of navigation. The man clinging to the makeshift raft was rescued by settlers, a man who was ragged, starving, sun-blackened, and incoherent. When he recovered from exhaustion he declared he had come through the Grand Canyon gorges. He and a companion had taken to the river to escape Indians, he said, on a raft made by tying logs together with a lariat. His companion had drowned. This man's name was James White, a prospector. Although the Mormons fed and tended him, they did not believe his story. It was too incredible, and he was so obviously half-crazy from his experiences that nobody thought there was truth in his tale.

In the East, scientists and empire-builders were talking of the Colorado. This river system, flowing through six states, could surely be used for transportation in the region about to be developed. Some dreamers, with no knowledge of the fantastically wild country, believed a railroad could be built in the canyons to reach the lower river and steamboat traffic.

The man who was to undertake the momentous adventure of exploring and studying the course of the great red river was in the West in the summer of 1868. He was Major John Wesley Powell, a veteran of the Civil War, in which he had lost an arm. That did not interfere with his plans or his energetic enthusiasm.

Major Powell was a naturalist and teacher of geology. He had studied and taught in colleges of Illinois and had become curator of the museum at Illinois State Normal University. He brought a group of alert students to the country west of the Rockies to collect specimens for natural history and geology. In the course of this work, he pursued his interest in the Colorado River and its tributaries. He was determined to attempt the daring journey through the canyons, starting on the Green River in Wyoming.

At the town of Green River he gathered a small

group of frontiersmen, mostly mountain men and prospectors. While they remained in camp, Major Powell returned to the East to raise funds and have boats built for the river journey. Although he did not succeed in getting government sponsorship for his project, President Grant gave him an order to collect rations from any Army post. To buy instruments and tools, the Major scraped together funds by donations from various scientific institutions. Four heavy wooden boats were built, strong enough to withstand rapids and rocks, with watertight compartments fore and aft to hold important instruments and records. These boats were shipped to Green River on the railroad that had just been completed through Wyoming.

In the spring, Major Powell was on hand at Green River with everything prepared for the adventure. On May 24, 1869, ten men in four boats were launched on the river, a flag flying at the bow of the leading boat, in which Major Powell went ahead to scout for channels and rocks. Townspeople assembled on the shore to cheer them on their way.

The men rowed the boats except when the current carried them, and used the oars to avoid the dangerous rocks. These men were fearless characters who thought the work of running rapids an exciting game of strength and skill. Rough water and rocks gave them good training, as they proceeded down the river through Utah. Each night they found some place to camp on shore. Major Powell kept a daily record of their experiences, putting down observations on geological formations, and on currents and rapids of the stream.

At times, when the cliffs could be scaled, the one-armed Major and some of his men climbed to the top to survey the country. They saw the strange arid miles of southern Utah, a land of many-colored eroded cliffs, buttes and mesas. When the Green River carried them into the main stream of the Colorado, the weary voyagers found a place on shore where they could camp and rest while they repaired their battered boats.

After launching the boats in the main stream, the increasing current rushed them through deep canyons where raging waters made a constant roar of sound. As they were swept or struggled through one gorge after another, the alert leader observed and made records, naming canyons as they passed through.

For days their boats slipped through the winding course of a deep gorge of rare beauty, with inviting side canyons, narrow and confined. In some places lovely patches of verdure were nourished by small falls coming down the cliffs. Here and there on ledges they found ruins of ancient Indian shelters and some broken pottery. Major Powell gave the name Glen Canyon to this long gorge because of its beauty.

Soon the San Juan River joined the Colorado. After sweeping on some distance, the voyagers came to a feasible crossing with shallow water and large rocks. This they recognized as the Crossing of the Fathers, or Vado de los Padres, known in the history of Spanish exploration. In 1776, Fathers Escalante and Dominguez had made a journey through the wilderness from New Mexico, traveling until they reached the Virgin River. They had to turn back, and while seeking for a better route they found this crossing. Indians must have known it a long time, the Powell party decided, judging from the trail they found. After the stream had carried them into Arizona, the explorers come to the mouth of the Paria River and observed that the Colorado might be forded here.

The river rushed them on between the smooth, lofty walls of Marble Canyon, so named by Major Powell. Later, they reached the junction with the Little Colorado River that added its muddy waters to the silt-laden red river. They rested here and counted over their stores of food, which were running low. The worst of the journey was before them — the Big Canyon itself.

The spirits of the most adventurous were subdued as they slid between the towering walls and entered the dark granite gorges in the deepest part of the Grand Canyon. The river roared in constant rapids and falls; they were trapped between the confining walls. Sometimes they managed to portage their boats around falls, or they tied ropes to the boats and guided them through the raging waters while they climbed along the cliffs. When the vertical walls left no foothold, it was necessary to run the boats through rapids. They were upset many times, their boats caught in whirlpools, or battered against the rocks. Somehow they came through and were sped on their way.

They found a sandy shore to camp on, where a clear running creek entered the river. It was such a relief after the muddy, dangerous waters they had encountered that they named it Bright Angel Creek.

Then once more they were swept between dark granite walls, as the river looped back and forth. The roar of waters warned them of the worst falls they had yet to encounter. There was no room on shore to portage the boats, yet to launch themselves into the fierce rapids seemed certain destruction.

Several men of the party had reached the limit of their endurance. They conferred with Major Powell, arguing that the only escape was to try to climb the cliffs to the country above. Their leader could not agree to leave the river when he had so nearly accomplished his dream of completely exploring the canyons. Three men decided to leave; the others stood by their leader. The men were given guns, but they refused to take any of the scanty rations. There were sober farewells as the three started their climb to the top.

One by one the other men launched their boats into the foaming rapids ahead of them. Miraculously they came through, after being submerged and beaten on the rocks. They struggled on until on August 29, 1869, after emerging from the canyons, they came to the mouth of the Virgin River. Some Indians and Mormons, fishing in a quiet spot, were startled when they saw the exhausted adventurers. From May until August these men had been imprisoned in the canyons. They had no food left except some moldy flour, a bit of coffee, and a few dried apples.

The Mormons took them to the nearest settlement and cared for them until they recovered sufficiently to return to civilization. These friendly settlers told them that reports had been circulated that the whole party had been lost in the canyons. Later, Powell and his companions learned that the three men who had left them had reached the top of the cliffs only to be killed by Indians, who thought they were miners.

It may be that James White, on his raft, was the first man to float through the gorges of the Grand Canyon, though he nearly died of it. Later, study by historians led them to believe his story was true.

Nevertheless, Major John Wesley Powell and his companions were undoubtedly the first to explore the hundreds of miles of the Colorado canyons. Major Powell was the first to report on geological structure of the walls, to map the falls, rapids and tributary streams. The news of his dramatic exploit startled the country, and he became a national hero, honored by scientists and the government. He wrote the story of his journey, published first in a magazine and later in book form. To his great satisfaction, the government appropriated $10,000 for another journey through the canyons in 1870. This was a larger expedition with stronger, more efficient boats, and a geologist along to give a full report on the structure of the canyons.

Major Powell did not make the entire second trip with this group. He left them in order to continue the various enterprises his eager spirit was developing. He was responsible for the organization of the U. S. Geological Survey, and headed its work in the West for some time. Scientists, writers, and artists, inspired by his reports, hurried west to write, paint, and study the marvels of nature revealed in and about the canyons.

In recent years skilled boatmen have conquered the fierce river in the canyons by means of specially designed boats. The trip from the San Juan River, through the gorges of the Grand Canyon, is one of the most thrilling of river expeditions for adventurous people who love the wilderness.

During his wanderings in Arizona and Utah, Major Powell became interested in the Indian tribes. He was appointed Indian Commissioner to work with Utes, Paiutes, Havasupais, Navajos, and Hopis. In this work he met Jacob Hamblin, the Mormon pioneer who is often called the Apostle in Buckskin. He was one of the most important characters of pioneer times in Arizona, a sturdy explorer, a man devoted to the Mormon interests and the Indians. To this single-minded, good-hearted man the Indians were souls to be converted to the Mormon faith, and helped to a better way of life. Besides preaching to the Indians, the Mormon Church gave him the task of finding sites for new settlements.

Major Powell, who liked Hamblin, sat with him through many pow-wows with Indian groups. They treated the Indians as human beings with certain rights in their own territory. In turn, the Indians respected and trusted these men. They were accustomed to being treated as savage creatures by the pioneers, to be fought with or thrust aside. Jacob Hamblin persuaded many of them to stop their attacks on white men.

Jacob Hamblin began his pioneer work in Arizona in 1857. He came down the Paria River to the Colorado and decided this was a good place for a ferry which would permit pioneers from Utah to cross over on their way to the Little Colorado River. Several times he tried without success to pole a barge across the river, but he finally succeeded in running a ferry barge that could carry a couple of wagons and teams at one time. At this crossing the dauntless Mormons brought wagons down over the cliffs by ropes, crossed the river, and worked out a wagon road to their settlements along the Little Colorado.

A trading post and small settlement was later built at the crossing that was named Lee's Ferry, because it was the hiding place for a fanatical Mormon, John Lee. With others, he had been involved at Mountain Meadow in an Indian attack and massacre of an emigrant party crossing Utah. He ran a ferry until the United States Marshals caught up with him. He was executed for his participation in the Mountain Meadows Massacre.

The Mormons brought their wagons through desolate country to the flat land along the Little Colorado. It was an arid region, subject to droughts or flash floods from the treacherous river. They went to work on the construction of a dam made of brush and rocks, and then dug irrigation ditches to their fields. They called their settlement St. Joseph, which was later changed to Joseph City. Many times floods washed out their dam, but they worked on from year to year until they had a permanent structure.

Other groups settled around the shallow body of water called Mormon Lake. At that time, the changeable lake was a swampy meadow where their cows could graze. Men of three settlements combined to build up a dairy, and for some time they made good profits from the sale of butter and cheese.

In 1876, people in New England were becoming excited about northern Arizona from the accounts of lecturers and writers, who were enthusiastic in their descriptions of a country of which they had little actual knowledge. A large group of men, the American Colonization Company, formed an expedition to make a settlement in Arizona. They traveled by train to New Mexico, the end of the line, where they bought wagons, teams, and supplies for the westward trek. When they reached the valley of the Little Colorado they were dismayed to find the Mormon colony hard at work. They were suspicious of Mormons and did not want to settle near them.

An advance scouting group moved on farther in search of a good site. They camped at a small spring just south of the San Francisco Peaks. It was June, and the weather was delightful. To amuse themselves, while waiting for the remainder of the company to catch up, they stripped a pine tree and hung an American flag on it for a signal. When the other group arrived, they all celebrated the Fourth of July with patriotic gusto around Old Glory on the pine tree staff.

These pioneers, called the Boston Party, soon moved on to Prescott, having heard that mechanics were wanted in that small place. Old Spring, and the pine tree flag pole near it, remained a landmark on the trail, a stopping place for all weary travelers over Beale's Wagon Road. The camp at the flagstaff, as it was called, gave the name Flagstaff to the future town.

Often, in times of drought, the Mormon farmers had to haul water from Leroux Spring, north of the pine tree flag pole. To establish a claim to the water, John Young built a log cabin at the site and started a Mormon Cattle Company in the valley so rich in grass. He was the son of Brigham Young, the Mormon leader. A high-walled stockade of logs was built for protection against Indians that was named Fort Moroni for the Mormon angel. John Young successfully raised cattle in this valley until the railroad-building reached the area. Then he went into the business of supplying ties for the tracks. He sold his cattle to the Arizona Cattle Company, and before long the cowboys had cut down the stockade to use the logs for firewood. This was the beginning of cattle-raising in fertile Fort Valley.

Jacob Hamblin made friends with the difficult Hopis, who permitted him to start a Mormon settlement named Moencopi. Chief Tuba of Oraibi was his friend and helped him start other settlements. Tuba City was built by Mormons and named for the Hopi chief. In later years, when the Indian population had increased so greatly that more reservation land was needed, the Indian Service bought Tuba City and Moencopi from the Mormons.

Some of these industrious farmers went on to the upper valley of the Little Colorado to found towns and farms. In 1880, land for the settlement of St. Johns was bought from Solomon Barth, a New Mexico sheepherder, for a herd of cows. To pay part of this debt David Udall, leader of the settlement, drove his herd from the Mormon settlement at Pipe Springs on the border of Utah to Lee's Ferry. In the bitter cold winter the Colorado was frozen solid at this crossing. David Udall drove his cows across on the ice, then proceeded by the Mormon wagon road to St. Johns.

These dedicated people — sober, industrious, and willing to endure any amount of hardship to establish their farms and missions — were valuable pioneers. They were civilizers of the fine lumbering and farming country in the plateau region of the Little Colorado.

## Chapter XX

## Gold, Silver, Copper

Arizona's mountains and streams were first explored by the trappers of beaver, the mountain men. They were followed by another hardy breed of men, the prospectors. These explorers were led on by gleams of gold in the gravel of stream beds, or by veins of rich metal cropping out on rocky ledges. Alone in the silent mountains except for their laden burros, the prospectors followed their dream of the " big strike." They turned up at settlements with bags of "dust" or of gold nuggets, to trade them for supplies as they continued their search for gold on their claims. Or they brought samples of ore to assay stations, hoping that signs of gold or silver in the rocks indicated worthwhile veins of minerals.

The least rumor of a "big strike" sent eager men to

stake claims, expecting to make a fortune. Out of the discoveries, disappointments and dangers of the prospectors' search grew the tales of lost mines that have lured men for years in Arizona.

The prize story of mysterious gold is that of the Lost Dutchman Mine in the Superstition Mountains. Many and varied are the tales told of the cold, unfriendly German, Jacob Walz. He would appear at intervals in Tucson, Florence, or Phoenix with a sack of fabulous gold nuggets. After cashing in on his riches he would go on a big spree, then vanish once more. He slipped away by night, wrapping his burro's hooves in cloth to leave no trail, and all efforts to follow him were unsuccessful.

Rumors grew about the wealth he had found somewhere in the Superstition Mountains, near the sharp peak called the Weaver's Needle. It was said that he and his partner had killed the men they found digging into a rich ledge, after which Jacob Walz had cold-bloodedly disposed of his partner as well. When he was dying, the "Dutchman" tried to tell his girl friend how to find the gold that had served them well, but his talk was incoherent. All attempts to follow the trail he had tried to describe were unsuccessful.

Over the years, legends have grown up about the Lost Dutchman Mine. Countless men have gone into the wild mountains in search of it. Some have never returned; others claimed they had been mysteriously shot at. No one has found a trace of the lost gold, but men are still hunting for it.

In the 1860's, this excitement of gold hunting made every man a potential prospector. Near the little town of Prescott successful mines were being worked. Prospectors swarmed like ants along the banks of the Hassayampa River.   Here came Henry Wickenburg, a Prussian, who had come to America and joined frontiersmen in California and at Yuma.   For years he had dreamed of finding a fortune, but he could hardly believe his luck when, quite by accident, he discovered the gleaming nuggets that led him to rich veins of gold.   Some say that as he wandered he saw a vulture circling low, and its shadow was cast on the ground where he found the nuggets, so he named his mine the Vulture.   Others say his burro ran away, and as he picked up rocks to throw at him, he saw they were gold-bearing quartz.

Wickenburg staked his claim and dug into the ledge, discovering valuable ore.   He had no mill, no money to buy one, and his mine was twelve miles from water.   Laboriously he carted his ore to the river bank, where he built an old-fashioned arrastra to crush it.   When this method became too difficult he sold ore at the mine to any man who wished to buy it, and these prospectors built more arrastras at the river.

Like many another prospector, Wickenburg did not have the money to develop a deep mine, so in the course of time he sold his claim to an eastern corporation, but did not obtain all the money.   The discoverer of the Vulture lived alone in an adobe hut near the river while the rough mining town of Wickenburg, named for him, grew up around him.   The Vulture produced millions of dollars worth of gold under various owners as shafts were sunk ever deeper.   A stamp mill was built at the mine, and others at the river.   An eye witness said that what was once a hill looked like an immense hole in the ground, so many tons of rock had been dug out.   Eventually, the miners struck a great fault in the rocks and the valuable gold vein was lost.   It has never been found but old-timers often declare that the great Vulture will some time produce gold once more for modern miners.

Arizona began to attract attention from the outside world after news of its mineral-rich mountains spread abroad. Prospectors, mining men, and promoters came in increasing numbers. Placer gold gave out along the Colorado; however, several deep mines were worked in the Castle Dome region and around Mineral Park in the Mohave country. Gold was still the leading mineral but silver and copper were also mined. Stamp mills were built at various places and ore was shipped from river ports by steamer to San Francisco. La Paz remained a busy gold town until about 1870, when the capricious river changed its channel, leaving the settlement with no outlet on the stream. The town was marooned and slowly died, until only a few crumbling adobe ruins remained.

Prescott and Wickenburg were town centers for the many mines in the region around them. Northeast of Prescott, Mingus Mountain and other black hills were investigated. Claims were staked and mine shafts dug by groups of men. They found silver and copper, but at that time the processing of copper ore was difficult, and the problem of transportation from the mountains to any shipping point was almost insurmountable. However, the mines that would later produce wealth, such as the United Verde, were under way.

Silver bonanzas brought a rush of eager men to explore the wild, craggy Pinal Mountains to the east of the desert valleys. When General Stoneman was in charge of Army posts in Arizona he had established a base camp and built a zigzag trail up the face of the mountains to the plateaus. He built Camp Pinal and Pickett Post Camp to keep watch on the Apaches who haunted the mountains.

One day a soldier named Sullivan, while resting from work on the road, picked up some heavy black metallic lumps. When they were pounded they flattened out instead of breaking. Sullivan stowed them away. After he left the Army he worked for a rancher named Mason in the valley near Florence. He showed the "black stuff" to the ranchers, then he disappeared and was not seen for years. Meanwhile, the ranchers were curious about these black lumps, but other discoveries distracted them.

Some men found good silver in the mountain ledges, and the Silver Queen Mine was started. Then, across the mountain, prospectors discovered a globe-shaped boulder of almost pure silver — and the rush began. Miners hurried to stake claims and sink shafts along a ridge that proved to be a rich mineral belt. A mining camp named Globe, from the silver boulder, sprang up along the tree-shaded banks of Pinal Creek.

In 1875, the rancher Mason and four companions made a search for more of the "black stuff" that the soldier Sullivan had showed them. With burros, they went up to the Globe mines to take out some ore for study. On the return trip they were attacked by Apaches and one man was killed. His companions carried him up the trail to bury him in one of the great stone ovens the soldiers had once used to bake bread. Continuing down the trail, a refractory burro led them to their bonanza by running off to outcroppings near the trail. Copeland, who chased the animal, broke off some pieces of rock and suddenly gave a yell.

"I've struck it!" he cried. "It's good enough for me."

He had the black metallic lumps they had been looking for.

Overjoyed, the companions hurried to Florence to lay in supplies, then returned to their claims. On March 22, 1875, they laid out the location of their mine. So was born the Silver King, the richest silver mine of early territorial days.

The discovery caused the wildest excitement in the valley. The farming settlement of Florence was almost depopulated, as every able-bodied man hurried off to work at the Silver King. Before long two of the partners sold their shares, and the others joined with promoters who organized the Silver King Mining Company. The mine was quite near the modern town of Superior.

Ore was packed over the mountains on burros from the mine to the mill at Picket Post, five miles away. The pack trains also carried loads of wood to be burned for fuel in the smelter. Men and animals wore a deep track along Mineral Creek. From the modern highway to Superior, travelers may see traces of the old trail if they know where to look.

Deep shafts were sunk that produced silver in various forms, some of it very pure. The boastful owners of the mine minted silver into dollars, which they gave away as souvenirs. In later years, when the railroad had reached the Colorado, ore was transported by freight wagons to the river and shipped to reduction plants.

One day a shabby old man appeared at the booming Silver King Mine, showing great interest and asking questions. He was the one-time soldier, Sullivan, who had first found "the black stuff."

A great copper mine, the Old Dominion, was developed at Globe in the 1870's and brought great prosperity. When the Lewisohn Brothers of New York bought control and built up the best machinery for ore processing, the Old Dominion became the pride of the region. The houses and stores of Globe were set along the road that led up to the hoists, the slag heaps, and mounds of colored tailings around the mine buildings that dominated the town.

In the 1870's and 1880's, news of Arizona's wealth of silver and copper brought miners of many nationalities to work in the mines. Mexicans, with a natural flair for the work, came from wherever they were living in the Territory to settle with their families in each new mine camp. Hardrock miners came from Europe to dig the deep shafts and tunnels of the great mines. Italians, Slavs and Cornishmen, the "Cousin Jacks," were part of every mining community. Each group brought with them their language and customs, giving the population an international flavor.

The mountains were gradually giving up their riches. Prospectors and mine promoters continued their search to the mountainous region of the Gila River near the New Mexico border. There they found a mountain with seemingly inexhaustible bodies of rich copper ore. The famous Longfellow Mines, hewed out of the mountainside in deep shafts and tunnels, brought miners from near and far, especially Mexicans, to work in this expanding camp. The mill and smelter were built on a flat piece of land where the San Francisco River makes a big bend at the foot of the mountain. Here the town of Clifton grew up to house miners and storekeepers. Mexicans' wooden shacks clung like birds' nests to the slopes of the mountains near the shafts. Later on, the Longfellow Mines developed into the great Morenci, an open pit copper mine that is still producing.

To the town of Clifton, in 1876, came Isadore Solomon with his wife and brother. He bought an old store built by a former trader on the road through the mine region. He and his brother set up charcoal burning pits to reduce the wood of the mesquite thickets in the valley. The charcoal was used in the adobe smelter in Clifton. Solomon's store and trading post expanded as a supply center for the whole region. When a small settlement grew up around it, the name naturally became Solomonville in honor of this important pioneer and his family.

More copper-rich mountains were discovered in the late 1870's when miners began to explore the Mule Mountains and the canyon known as Mule Gulch in southeastern Arizona. The first prospectors, looking for silver, were disgusted when they found "copper stain." Next, an Army scout, John Dunn, found some good samples of copper ore but could not work the claim himself. He sent another prospector with a "grub stake" to explore the claim. This George Warren was a keen prospector, and what he found looked so good that he staked several claims, naming the region Warren Mining District. Several small mines were being worked when a gentleman from the East arrived, looking for copper prospects. He was Dr. James Douglas. The Phelps Dodge Company, then a small eastern firm, sent him to buy good copper claims in Arizona.

Dr. Douglas understood minerals, although he was not a mining man. He bought property in Mule Gulch near the small Copper Queen, which was being worked by another company. When the Phelps Dodge claim was being developed a great body of rich copper ore was discovered on the line between the two companies. Instead of fighting each other, the rival companies combined their claims as the Copper Queen Consolidated Mining Company. This procedure was followed later with other rival claims in Bisbee and its environs.

The Copper Queen has always been one of the romantic mines of Arizona, a bonanza of copper that created a town clinging to the walls of the steep canyon. It was the first mine of a large number owned and operated by the Phelps Dodge Company in Bisbee, Warren and beyond. Hardrock miners hollowed the Copper Queen deeper and deeper into the wall of the canyon to extract a wealth of minerals. The town lived by the prosperity that came from the Copper Queen. When the rich ores were exhausted, the old Copper Queen excavation in the canyon wall became one of the sights of the town, called the "Glory Hole."

Bisbee was at first a raw camp of prospectors, miners, burros, saloons and dance halls; a roistering camp that boasted of its wild doings. As it became a company town, the officers brought their families to live in neat, small houses on the canyon sides, reached by winding trails or flights of steps. Brewery Gulch was the haunt of miners in search of entertainment, but the more civilized people worked to create a stable community. Copper was taking first place as a source of mineral wealth. Hidden stores of silver, however, were yet to be discovered.

The last great silver bonanza burst upon the attention of Arizonans in 1877. The great discovery was made by the most confirmed prospector of them all, Ed Schieffelin, who was the romanic idea of a prospector personified. He was a very tall man with long curly black hair and beard, wearing patched old clothes and a slouch hat. To him the search for minerals, the excitement of the big strike were the consuming interest. After claims were worked, Ed Schieffelin generally lost interest and went on to find more gold or silver in other lonely canyons.

He was working at the Silver King when he heard about the riches of gold and silver in southern Arizona. He hitched a ride with some soldiers on their way to the new Fort Huachuca on the Mexican border. Miners were digging on claims in the San Pedro Valley north of the Mule Mountains, and here Schieffelin did some prospecting. The miners avoided the wind-swept plateau as a dangerous haunt of Apaches, but Schieffelin took his burro, his grub stake, pick and shovel, and made off to explore the ledges. Companions told him he would find nothing but his tombstone, for Apaches would kill him, but Schieffelin was a cautious prospector. He camped under shelter of ledges and slipped from place to place unseen.

He found good "silver float" and traced it to a ledge. There he hacked with his pick, digging out rich ore. He took samples of it north to the Signal Mine, where his brother Al was working, to have it assayed by their friend Richard Gird. It looked good; so the three returned by wagon to the ledge and tested the ore once more. "Now I have found my tombstone," Ed gloated, and named his claim the Tombstone. The brothers took ore samples to show Governor Safford in Tucson, for he had once done some mining. The Governor thought it was rich ore and persuaded a prosperous citizen named Vosburg to stake the brothers to $300 worth of supplies. They returned to their claim and continued to search for other veins of silver.

Hundreds of prospectors hurried out from Tucson to camp on the hillsides and stake claims. The Schieffelins developed the Tough Nut and Lucky Cuss mines, which were richer than the original Tombstone. Mining camps sprang up on the plateau, mine corporations were formed, and the Schieffelin interests were bought for $1,000,000. The brothers left Tombstone before it became the most important town in Arizona, but riches did not make the dreaming prospector Ed happy. He could not adapt himself to the civilized life of towns, so wandered north for further prospecting, this time in Alaska. When he died he was alone in a cabin in Oregon.

His will directed that he should be buried in his old prospector's clothes with his canteen and pick, on the ledge where he had discovered the silver of his Tombstone. There he lies in the place where he was most happy, with a cemented rock monument over his grave.

Ajo, the small town of Mexican inhabitants in the southwestern part of Arizona, was known for a long time to have rich copper deposits. The valuable copper was not utilized until the New Cornelia Mine was developed by John C. Greenway. The mine was eventually sold to the Phelps Dodge Company.

Before the close of the nineteenth century, mining of silver and copper had become big business, operated mostly by wealthy corporations with the finances and experienced mining men to follow the ore bodies deep into the mountains. These companies, operating with the most up-to-date machinery, mills, and smelters, extracted all the minerals from the ore.

The United Verde Copper Mines, controlled chiefly by Senator Clark of Nevada, were tunneled and blasted into the heart of Mingus Mountain. The mines produced a wealth of copper. Jerome, the town clinging to the mountainside in tiers of houses, competed with Bisbee and Tombstone as a wild, tough, and extravagant community.

Silver, gold, and copper — mines of colorful names such as Silver King, Copper Queen, Old Dominion, Lucky Cuss,

Tough Nut, Contention — brought prosperity and population to the Territory of Arizona.

The needs of the mines led to the making of roads through mountainous country and to plans for railroads. Pioneers came to serve the mine towns and other communities as blacksmiths, wagon and harness makers, teamsters, storekeepers. Farmers raised crops to feed the communities; ranchers raised cattle, horses and mules for the needs of the people.

While the mining camps went their roaring way, building reputations for gambling, gun fights and general lawlessness, other pioneers were establishing businesses and working for law and order in settled communities.

## Chapter XXI

### Farmers in the River Valleys

On the heels of men seeking gold and silver came
pioneers who were looking for good land to farm crops
and raise cattle. The small town of Prescott, capital of
the new Territory, was a market for foodstuffs, and the
Verde River to the east was ideal farmland. This river,
lined with cottonwoods and willows, provided moisture
for grassy fields, and irrigation ditches could be led to
the plantings of grain or vegetables. Above the fertile valley rose ramparts of gorgeous cliffs colored rose, orange,
and pale gray, a part of the Mogollon Rim.

It was an excellent spot for farmers but it had one
drawback — the ever-present Indians. Settlers on the central plateau were almost as much plagued by Apaches
as the people to the south. The Indians had a secure

retreat in the craggy cliffs of the Mogollon Rim, from which they could descend on the farms. Settlers in the Verde Valley built stockades of stone on their land for protection, hoping to harvest their crops and sell their cattle before Apaches stole the products of their hard labor. Camp Verde was built on high land above the river to protect the farmers.

Besides Tonto and Pinal Apaches, other Indians had their ancestral homelands in the region — the Yavapais and Hualapais. They resented the invasion of their hunting grounds by white men as much as did other Indians.

In this dangerous pioneer period Pauline Weaver, the guide and prospector, was the peacemaker between red man and white. He was the friend of all Indians and they trusted him. In councils between aggressive Indians, the Army, or settlers, both sides would listen to him.

His usefulness as an arbitrator came to an end after some rebellious Apaches saw him with a company of soldiers he was guiding to a camp where there had been trouble. In revenge, these Indians pursued him on a trail and shot arrows into him from ambush, leaving him severely wounded. He managed to reach Fort Whipple, where he was cared for. From that time he became a regular scout for the Army. Weaver was getting old, his wound troubled him, and he spent his last few years living quietly in his cabin by the river. Legend has it that a young Apache woman, whom he had often befriended, took care of him and brought him food. When he died it was this girl, Aha-sa-yamo, who wrapped the old scout in his blanket for burial.

Camp Verde and Camp McDowell, another post at the junction of the Verde and Salt, kept watch on the Apaches until Indian troubles died down and farmers could pursue their work and harvest the crops in safety.

It was not long before men with farming on their minds discovered the possibilities of the Salt River Valley. Centuries before, in prehistoric times, the Hohokam Indians had found the desert valley a good place to develop farming. The climate was hot and dry, but the land was productive when water was brought to it — and the river was there. The ruins of the Hohokam settlements and irrigation canals attracted the attention of white pioneers when they arrived, looking for farm land.

The first man to make a camp at the site of future Phoenix was a trader from Camp McDowell, who supplied the cavalry horses with fodder. This man, John Y. T. Smith, set up tents for a "hay camp" along the river, where grass grew thick and long around the remains of Indian canals. He had laborers cutting and drying the hay harvest.

The camp was near the road by which men traveled back and forth across the valley, from the mines along the Hassayampa and at Wickenburg, to the Verde River. Casual passersby stopped to visit with the hay camp men. One of the visitors was Jack Swilling, who was prospecting on the Hassayampa. He was an accomplished pioneer in many ways, a man of ideas.

Jack Swilling studied the grass-grown ruins of the ancient canals near the camp. If one of these was dug out, he figured, the lay of the land would make it possible to run water from the river through a canal to water acres of farm land. His enthusiasm for his ditch aroused interest among his companions at Wickenburg, and they formed the Swilling Irrigation Canal Company in 1867. With a group of men Jack Swilling came back to the hay camp to dig out a large canal from the ancient one, which soon became known as "Swilling's Ditch." Supplies for the work were hauled fifty-four miles from Wickenburg by eight-mule teams.

In no time at all farmers were building temporary huts and digging ditches from the canal to the fields they planted. Within a year crops were harvested and several farmers had houses built. Soon a small settlement of adobe houses sprang up along the canal and irrigation ditches.

The first woman in the settlement, Mrs. Adeline Gray, arrived with her husband in 1868. The Grays were traveling by mule-drawn wagon from Arkansas, with California as their destination. When they saw this green spot along the river in the desert valley they stopped to make camp and rest and to watch the activities of the farmers. Like many others who have fallen in love with the warm sun and bright skies of Arizona, they stayed. Columbus Gray took up land; they prepared their fields and irrigation ditches and built an adobe farm house. During her lifetime, Mrs. Adeline Gray saw this tiny settlement of farmers change into a modern city, with an airport adjacent to their land!

Thomas Hunter, one of the old pioneer settlers, reminisced about the early days. He remembered watching Indian women come into the mesquite thickets of the valley to gather wood, while their warriors stood guard with bows at the top of a ridge. The women filled the tall, three-pronged baskets they carried on their backs and marched in procession over the ridge. Thomas Hunter allowed Indian women to enter his grain fields to gather the fat worms that infested the crop. He was rid of a pest, and the Indians considered the worms a delicacy to eat raw or cooked.

All sorts of odd characters wandered into the new settlements in that pioneer period. One of them was a drifting Englishman, Darrell Duppa, whose enthusiasm and vigorous ideas were a big stimulus to the farmers. He was supposed to belong to a titled family in England; however, the best information obtained on his family was that they were landed gentry, not titled.

Darrel Duppa was a well-educated man with a background of classical literature. He studied with interest the crumbling walls of ancient Indian settlements and the grass-grown remains of their canals. Enthusiastically he proclaimed: "Our city shall rise on the ashes of the ancient civilization as the phoenix bird of Arabia rose from the flames to new life." That is the legend of how Phoenix acquired its name, though some old-timers dispute the claim that Darrell Duppa thought of it.

Little new Phoenix soon had a dusty "Main Street" lined with a few stores, saloons, a bakery, and a hotel of sorts. As pioneers built their houses, they planted trees along the sandy lanes for shade from the glaring sun. Hancock's store was the first town building. It was a combined store, courthouse, justice office, and butcher shop. The proprietor killed a beef, quartered it and hung it up outside the store. Customers cut off what they wanted with their own knives and paid at the rate of 25 to 36 cents a pound. One beef a week generally supplied the demand.

Indians of the countryside were curious about the new settlements, but the pioneers were not hampered by attacks. The original inhabitants, Pimas and Maricopas, were peaceable farmers on their irrigated land. The Pimas had known white men for centuries as Spanish and American explorers passed their villages along the Gila on their way to the Colorado. These Indians went on with their usual occupations, willing to cooperate with white men when necessary.

Darrell Duppa continued his praise of the "city," which was laid out in lots in 1871. He proclaimed it would become the garden of Arizona and would win the capital because it was in the center of the territory and was progressing so fast.

After a year the new "city" had a postmaster, Jack Swilling, who served outlying settlements with a pony express mail. He developed his canal and built the next big ditch, the Tempe Canal, at a place where trails crossed the Salt River.

Here, too, the classically educated Englishman had his say about a name. In his explorations he climbed a tall butte near the river, looking out over a valley thickly grown with mesquite. To him it looked like the Vale of Tempe in Greece, and so he named it. When a settlement was formed, Tempe was the name finally accepted for it.

To this favored spot came Charles Trumbull Hayden in the early 1870's. He was from Connecticut, but had traveled westward to St. Louis and then to Santa Fe. He prospered, but moved on to Tucson as a passenger on the first Butterfield stage. There he acquired a government contract to supply Army camps and built up a freighting business. Soon he became Judge Hayden, appointed as the first probate judge at Tucson under the laws of New Mexico.

When he heard about Swilling's Ditch, Judge Hayden came to investigate, and soon moved to the tiny settlement of Tempe. He saw how trails of travel from Prescott to Tucson crossed the river near the butte. Here a ferry was needed. Before long Judge Hayden had it operating to aid transportation across the river. Hayden's Ferry was in operation until the railroad tracks and a bridge across the river made it unnecessary.

He took stock in the Tempe Canal Company, using its water to turn the wheel of the grist mill he built. Farmers came from miles around to have their grain ground. The enterprise developed into the largest in the Territory, and even today Hayden Flour Mills is an important asset to Tempe.

Mormon farmers came to this fertile valley, so excellent for agriculture; they laid out their farm plots, dug their ditches, and built their homes. This settlement was named Mesa. From the very beginning it was an orderly, prosperous farming community.

In the 1870's and 1880's white pioneers had learned from studying the ancient Indian canals how to bring water to the valleys of fertile soil, to create a verdant region of food crops and beauty. The plains of desert vegetation were contrasted here and there around the ranches with fields of wheat, barley, and alfalfa that were blocks of green in early summer, of gold at harvest time. There were a few orange groves; some of them were planted by an energetic pioneer named W. J. Murphy.

Florence, Tempe, and Mesa were growing farm communities. All the settlements in the great valley were desert towns, subject to blazing heat much of the year. Settlers sought refuge from the sun's glare by lining their streets with shade trees, and ditches of running water under the trees gave a hint of coolness. The low houses were built of adobe for the most part, although brick was also used. In the heat of summer most people slept outdoors, on porches or on the flat roofs of adobe houses.

There were no house coolers in those days to make life comfortable for the inhabitants.

In Phoenix one enterprising citizen started a small factory to manufacture ice. People shook their heads over this scheme. Did this man think he could make real ice while the temperature soared to 100 degrees in the shade and eggs hatched into chickens on the way to market? Nevertheless, the daring man did succeed. In his first year he peddled chunks of ice on a wheelbarrow from door to door. The next year ice was delivered by hand cart, and the business was well established.

Aside from the few who had this luxury, the inhabitants of towns and ranches depended on the desert cooler to keep food. This contraption was a wooden-framed cupboard covered with burlap. Over it was hung a pot of water so arranged that a small, constant drip fell on the burlap. Breezes blowing through the wet cloth kept the interior cool.

Irrigated farming was not easy. The desert climate had extreme changes. There were severe droughts when everything withered and dust covered streets and houses. After summer cloudbursts or after spring runoffs from the mountains, there were flash floods that washed away the dams of brush and rock in the river.

In the old Gadsden Purchase section of Arizona, Apaches were a menace to the growth of farms and ranches, which were succeeding bit by bit. Tucson was the business center for the countryside. It was the only real town, a busy place, where people of two nationalities mingled in building a community. Tucson was still on the main southern route from east to west. Travelers to California made a well-beaten road of the old trail along the Gila River to the Colorado. Gila Bend became a small but lively settlement. It was a trading post, a stage station, and a source of supplies for that part of the country.

The southern settlements did not have the irrigation that permitted trees and gardens, such as those of the Salt River Valley. To be sure, the land between Tucson and the Santa Cruz River was a place of refreshing greenery, of growing crops and fields irrigated from the river. The Santa Cruz at that time was a flowing stream. There was so much moisture that there were actually two shallow lakes between Tucson and Sentinel Peak, surrounded with lush grass and shrubs.

In the towns and other small settlements, people depended on the thick-walled adobe houses to keep out sun and heat. The floors, of packed earth or brick, were swept and sprinkled every night for coolness. Although the shut-up houses faced dusty streets, many families had walled areas in the rear with flagged walks and flowers growing in pots.

Pioneers with courage and ambition were making a settled territory of Arizona. People came in by various kinds of wagons over the roads in the north and south, or by river steamer on the Colorado. The needs of pioneers soon developed improved transportation to reach the scattered settlements in the young Territory.

## Chapter XXII

### From Stage Coach to Railroad

In 1870, when people were coming into Arizona to prospect or work in mines or on farms, there was not a single stage line in the Territory. Inhabitants had to depend on horseback, mule or burro pack trains, or horse-drawn wagons of various kinds.

Local stage lines soon began operating to serve the mining camps or farming towns. Rattling over roads that were little more than rutted, dusty trails, they carried mail and passengers from Tucson to Phoenix, from there to Prescott, and from the Colorado River ports — Yuma, Ehrenberg — to valley settlements and mines in the mountains.

The journeys were far from pleasant. Passengers were bruised and jolted in swaying coaches, their faces and clothing plastered with dust. At the crude stage stations on the routes they found neither comfort nor decent food. However, people in such pioneer country took hardship and discomfort as a matter of course.

Each new settlement or older town had its post office, and others besides Jack Swilling carried mail on horseback to villages. In Tucson the government officer in charge of mails was Thomas Jeffords, a six-foot, athletic man with such red hair and beard that the Indians called him Red Whiskers.

Tom Jeffords had been in the Southwest long enough to know something about Apaches. As an Indian trader he had acquired some knowledge of their language and customs. He did not share the hatred for Apaches so prevalent among the settlers.

His mail carriers had the route between Tucson and Fort Bowie in Apache Pass, serving small settlements on the way. Apache Pass was a special haunt of the Chiricahuas who, under their powerful chief Cochise, were the greatest menace to the safety of people in southern Arizona. The lonely express riders were a favorite target, to be shot from ambush. So many of Jeffords' men were killed that they seldom lived to collect their wages.

Thomas Jeffords believed that the only way to stop the murders was to appeal to Cochise himself. He knew the story of how this intelligent chief had become a bitter enemy of Americans through the tragic episode with Lieutenant Bascom at Apache Pass in 1861, but he felt sure that Cochise could be reasoned with. He must seek out the chief in his mountain camp, and he must go alone to show he came on an errand of peace.

On horseback, Tom Jeffords rode the many miles to the mountains. When he reached the Indian camp he dismounted among the startled women of the rancheria, unbuckled his cartridge belt and gave it with his gun to a squaw. He walked up to the proud chief Cochise and sat down beside him. For some time there were no words between them. Jeffords understood that such was the Indian custom. Presently he began to talk, slowly, in terms the chief could understand. He said he knew that Cochise was a man who believed in straight dealing, so he had come to discuss some agreement whereby the mail carriers would not be molested. Cochise considered his arguments. He recognized a brave man, and he was one who respected truth and frankness. The two men talked for some time, and Jeffords won by his courageous appeal. Cochise promised that his warriors would not attack Jeffords' mail carriers, and the promise was kept; although other mail riders and travelers on lonely roads were still in danger.

That was the beginning of a most unusual friendship between Indian and white man. Jeffords admired and respected the proud chief with the face of an eagle and relied on the Indian's loyalty to promises. The two men became blood brothers in the Indian fashion. Cochise' bands continued to war against Americans, but that did not interfere with the friendly relationship between Cochise and Jeffords. In the end, this friendship was a chief factor in accomplishing peace between the Chiricahua bands of Apaches and white men.

Indians were not the only hazard for stage coach travelers across the lonely country. Arizona had a collection of highwaymen and outlaws of all sorts, both Mexican and American, some of whom came from outside the territory to reap profit in a region that had little law enforcement. The sheriffs of counties had their hands full in their attempts to capture the outlaws.

Many stage coaches not only carried mail but Wells Fargo Company messengers who were transporting boxes of payroll money to the mine camps. The highwaymen had ways of discovering when payroll money was carried, and these stages were their favorite victims.

More often than not the robbers got away with their loot, for the stages passed through mile upon mile of empty country with arroyos, canyons, or mesquite thickets to provide hideouts. Passengers became resigned to having their pockets rifled of money or valuables and were thankful when they reached their destination without a bullet wound.

Sometimes men of the settlements took the administration of justice out of the hands of sheriffs. At Globe there was a big sycamore called "the hanging tree" where the self-appointed vigilance committee sometimes strung up outlaws.

Stages to Globe offered a particularly rich haul because of the large amounts of payroll money they often carried for the mines. At one time several men of the town, lured by the thought of easy money, planned to hold up the payroll stage and blame the attack on Apaches. Their plans went wrong, because a skirmish of gunfire took place in which the payroll messenger was killed. As they were leaving the scene the robbers met the town doctor and shot him to protect themselves. Before he died he named the men whose boot tracks, leaving the scene of the attack, also betrayed them. They were arrested, given a trial before the local judge, and two were condemned to die. They were handed over to the citizens' committee. While the church bell tolled, the men were marched to the "hanging tree." There the committee looped the ropes over their necks and strung them up.

Murder, by members of their own community, was more than the citizens would tolerate.

Over all the roads traveled the great freight wagons drawn by ten and twenty mule teams. They transported goods and supplies from Colorado River ports to towns or mines, or loads of ore from the mines to the nearest rail terminal in New Mexico or Texas, or to a river port. Freighting companies such as Tully & Ochoa and Samaniega in Tucson had a tremendous business serving mines and towns. In the center of Tucson the harness and wagon shops, the blacksmith shops, and big corrals for mules of the freight companies added to the clamor and odorous dust of the streets.

The freight wagons from the mines carried enormous loads of ore. Two or three wagons were hitched together, pulled by many pairs of mules. The driver rode the near wheeler mule. From his seat in the saddle he managed all the animals by a single jerk line, attached to the near leader. The mules understood the jerks, short or long, and were thus guided. It took great skill to handle all this, for in addition to the jerk line the driver manipulated the brakes of the wagons by another rope. This system was particularly difficult when the heavy wagons snaked down twisting mountain trails.

These freight drivers were tough customers, coarse and picturesque in language, bold and hardy enough to handle any situation. They took pride in their fine mules. Often the animals plodded along to the music of chiming bells that their masters had attached to the collars of their harness.

The Army, guardian of safety for the settlers, had many posts in the Territory. The needs of these posts for transportation of troops and convoys of supplies led to the development of roads. Soldiers marched to their destinations from New Mexico, or came from San Francisco by boat to the Colorado River. Steamers transported these troops to their port of debarkation, to continue their journey by wagon or horseback.

Steamboat traffic was important in bringing people and supplies into Arizona. The boats were loaded for the trip up river at Puerto Ysabel, a desolate place of mud and water at the mouth of the Colorado.

Army wives, in the 1870's, were sometimes traveling with their husbands to the larger forts. One of these ladies was Martha Summerhayes, whose husband was a lieutenant assigned to Arizona in 1874. She wrote a vivid account of her experiences which was published in 1908 in a book called *Vanished Arizona.*

They came by ship from San Francisco around the peninsula of Lower California to Puerto Ysabel, where they boarded the steamer *Gila.* The *Gila,* a wood-burner, puffed its way up the river to Ehrenberg, the busy river port founded by Herman Ehrenberg, and then on up the river to Fort Mohave. This was the place where Lieutenant Beale and his camels had made their crossing. Here the military contingent and the barge load of enlisted personnel, towed behind the steamer, disembarked. From there the company traveled in wagons hitched to teams of fat Army mules which could trot as fast as carriage horses.

At night they camped in tents along the route. They enjoyed the cool night air of the desert and the opportunity to shake off the dust that covered them thickly during the day. From the desert country the convoy proceeded to the pines and hills of Prescott and Fort Whipple. There they found a well-equipped post and sociable life among the officers and their wives, in comfortable quarters.

Later, Martha Summerhayes and another Army wife endured the exhausting journey by ambulance, or covered wagon, over the rugged military road through the mountains to Fort Apache, on the Apache Indian Reservation.

When Lieutenant Summerhayes and his wife left Arizona, in 1878, the tracks of the Southern Pacific Railroad had been built to the Colorado on the California side. After crossing the river the Summerhayes traveled to San Francisco in comparative comfort "on the cars."

Dos Palmas, a station on the Southern Pacific in California, became the starting point for a line of California-Arizona stages that crossed the river by ferry at Ehrenberg and proceeded, by way of Wickenburg and Prescott, to New Mexico. Passengers changed at Prescott for stages to Phoenix or Tucson.

That was an improvement in transportation, but there were constant demands and appeals to Congress by politicians and leading citizens for transcontinental rail service. Railroads were greatly needed to help the territory develop its resources.

Railroad building was big business in California, Texas, and the Middle West in the latter part of the nineteenth century. Financiers and promoters of rival railroads were planning new lines. They were petitioning Congress for funds and for land grants along the right of way.

Congress chartered the Atlantic & Pacific to build from Springfield, Missouri, to Albuquerque, New Mexico, and from that point across Arizona at the 35th parallel. That was approximately the route surveyed by Lieutenant Beale for his wagon road from Fort Defiance to the Colorado.

In the south, the Texas & Pacific Company was chartered to build from the Texas town of Marshall to San Diego. Rival organizations in California were competing to build across Arizona, and there were controversies in courts and in Congress to obtain concessions. The Texas & Pacific lost to the Southern Pacific when that line was permitted by Congress to build across the military reservation at Fort Yuma to reach the river.

The Southern Pacific tracks reached the Colorado on May 23, 1877. The company then secured the charter to build through Arizona. A railroad bridge was constructed across the river near Yuma and track-laying proceeded rapidly. The line followed to a certain extent the route of the old Cooke's Wagon Road at the 32nd parallel. In 1879, track-laying reached Gila Bend and then Maricopa, thirty-five miles south of Phoenix. Every mile of track from there to Tucson was cheered with enthusiasm by the citizens of the "ancient and honorable pueblo," as Charles Poston called the town.

On March 20, 1880, the first train steamed into Tucson. The small wood-burning engine, puffing clouds of black smoke from its funnel-shaped smoke stack, drew small wooden cars. The train pulled into the station where elated citizens were gathered to welcome it. They were proud, for their community had progressed all the way from a Spanish adobe village to a thriving American town with railroad service!

Cannon roared, the Sixth Cavalry band from Fort Lowell trumpeted triumphantly, adding joyful racket to the hysterical yells of the populace. Officials of the railroad, who arrived on the train, were treated to a banquet by the leading citizens.

Champagne fizzed as toasts were drunk, led by Charles Poston, the "Father of Arizona." All day and night the celebration continued with dancing, shouting, and drinking. The Mayor sent a telegram to the President of the United States, others to several important people. The legend persists that one telegram was addressed to the Pope at the Vatican in Rome. It may be pure folklore, but the story goes that Charles Poston helped the Mayor compose it, announcing to the Pope that Tucson, founded by Spanish Catholics three centuries ago, now had a railroad. While trains were still a novelty, it was a favorite pastime for Tucsonans to gather at the station to see the trains come chugging in.

Tracks were built on towards New Mexico, and railroad workers formed camps that became the towns of Benson, Willcox, and Bowie. The line was pushed through New Mexico to meet the Santa Fe at Deming.

The Atlantic & Pacific Company made slower progress in the north, due to the mountainous country and greater extremes of weather than in the south. At the close of 1881, tracks had reached Winslow, a rough railroad camp, as were each of the settlements when they became the end of the line. Winslow, Holbrook, Williams, Ashfork, Seligman, Flagstaff, Kingman — each of these towns began as dreary, brawling construction camps, consisting of stark wooden houses, the railroad station, and the water tank. By degrees each one became a small town with homes and businesses.

John Young, who had a cattle business in Fort Valley, and other pioneers of the region went into the lumbering industry by cutting timber for ties and buildings. Sawmills and lumber mills were built, logging camps were set up, and Arizona's lumber industry was on its way to becoming an important resource.

The Atlantic & Pacific was bought by the Atchison,

Topeka & Santa Fe Railroad.  Tracks reached the Colorado River in 1883.  Then work was halted while controversy went on between officials of the powerful Southern Pacific and those of the Santa Fe as to the route the Santa Fe might build from the Colorado to San Diego. When it was settled, the Santa Fe had a route to the Pacific Coast.

Arizona was then connected with the East and the Pacific Coast by two transcontinental railroads: one along the 35th parallel, the other across the 32nd parallel, routes that railroad builders had always planned.  Transcontinental rail service was first provided in 1869 by the joining of the Central Pacific from the West and the Union Pacific from the East.  The Southern Pacific came next when it had joined the Santa Fe in New Mexico to reach Chicago.

The Southern Pacific did not enter Phoenix during the first years of its operation.  Passengers left the train at Maricopa junction and went by stage to Phoenix until 1887, when a branch line was built to the capital city. The Santa Fe soon built a branch line from Ashfork to Phoenix, thus improving north-south traffic in the Territory.  Local lines were planned to serve other sections of Arizona.  By the end of the nineteenth century there was a rather complete network of rail lines.

Railroad shipping brought increased prosperity to mine districts and towns, but diminished the business of the huge freight wagons drawn by mules.  People could now travel by rail, as well as stage, to some towns.  The steamboat traffic on the Colorado came to an end when a railroad bridge was built across the river at Yuma.  No longer was the Colorado enlivened by the puffing river boats, streaming black smoke, dragging barges behind them. No longer were the small ports busy with the loading and unloading of cargo. The steamboats were sold, or rotted away in side channels at Puerto Ysabel. The river ports — Ehrenberg, La Paz, Hardyville, Callville — deteriorated into clusters of ruined buildings, a memory of the past.

## Chapter XXIII

## Cattle Kings and Cowboys

Since the era of Spanish settlement, when Father Eusebio Francisco Kino stocked his missions with cattle and horses, Arizona's southern range lands have been used by grazing livestock. Spanish and Mexican ranchers brought more animals, and managed part of the time to save their herds from marauding Apaches.

Pete Kitchen was probably the first American rancher in Arizona. A man of tough courage and iron will, he was so fearless and such a good shot that Apaches learned to keep their distance. They could not dislodge him from his ranch, called the Potrero, a few miles north of the Mexican border.

His solid adobe ranch house was perched on a hill above a valuable spring. From the flat roof, where some

217

of his men were always on guard, a wide sweep of country was visible. A volley of rifle fire chased off any Indians who approached. Pete Kitchen's laborers worked in the fields with rifles handy, ready for action.

This pioneer raised not only cattle but hogs and fodder crops. The Kitchen hams, bacon, and lard were known from Tucson to Silver City, New Mexico. When the mining companies and ranchers abandoned the country under the twin disasters of Apache attacks and the Civil War, this iron-hard rancher remained. He was on hand to welcome the pioneers who came into the Gadsden Purchase country after the war.

During the years when Texas cattlemen were driving their huge herds of longhorns north to railroad towns, Arizona ranges were ignored. However, when homesteaders began to settle on the plains and barbed wire fences interfered with the miles of free range, the trail drives were pushed farther west. Texas cattlemen moved first into New Mexico, where John Chisum became lord of thousands of acres and thousands of head of cattle. He drove herds to Albuquerque, Tucson, and Prescott where he found a good market. He also profited by selling cattle to government contractors to feed Indians on reservations.

Some Texans turned their attention to the southeastern corner of Arizona, in Cochise County, where long grassy valleys lay between mountain ranges. According to tales of pioneers, the rolling range lands of southern Arizona at that time were thick with tall grass that came to a horse's belly. There was fodder, too, in the brushy hills and canyons of the mountains, but fear of Apaches discouraged ranchers from risking their stock in the country.

One Texan, John Slaughter, was not afraid to try it. He had been an Indian fighter and a trail boss, driving herds through dangerous country, and had grown rich from the cattle business. When Ed Schieffelin made his great discovery of silver at Tombstone, Slaughter happened to be there. A rush of prospectors and settlers were coming to the region, so he saw a future market for beef.

Two years later he was driving a herd into this untried region when he came up with another outfit proceeding in the same direction. Amazon Howell, his wife, and daughter Viola were taking a herd into the southern Arizona country. The two outfits threw in together for the trip and settled near each other in the San Pedro Valley. On the way, a romance of the trail developed between Slaughter and the attractive Viola. They were married, but Viola did not settle down to the usual hard life of the pioneer woman. She was a real "cowgirl" who had grown up spending her days in the saddle while she helped her father with his herd. She rode with her husband over their ranges, or accompanied him when he was buying cattle. She was also an efficient home manager and hostess, directing many servants after the Slaughter cattle empire had become famous.

Respectable ranchers were not the only people attracted to Cochise County by the booming growth of Tombstone. All sorts of riffraff, outlaws who had been ousted from other places by law officers, found the canyons and arroyos of the Chiricahua Mountains perfect hideouts for their enterprise of stealing cattle in Mexico to sell in Arizona. The rustlers, called "cowboys" by the settlers, had their retreats in the mountains where they were safe from interference. They had only to build corrals in canyons where there was water, to hold the animals they stole in Mexico and drove through Skeleton Canyon to their hideouts. There they changed the brands. Markets were found for their stolen animals in Tombstone, Tucson and other towns.

The rustlers had their headquarters at Galeyville, a small lawless mining camp on the slope of the Chirica-huas, and on certain ranches whose owners were in league with them on their deals. One of these was the Clanton Ranch in the San Pedro Valley and another was the Mc-Lowery outfit in Sulphur Spring Valley.

Cochise County earned the reputation of being a dangerous place for settlers in the 1880's. From the bad men who held up stage coach travelers to the reckless deeds of rustlers, this region added to the Wild West folklore of Arizona. There were feuds between the Clantons, suspected of rustling, and the Earps of Tombstone, who held various law and order offices. This feud came to a climax in the famous gunfight at the O.K. Corral. Then there were the daring exploits of Johnny Ringo and "Curly Bill" Brocius, leaders of the rustlers.

In the bars and gambling halls of the rip-snorting camps, Galeyville and Charleston, rustlers and other outlaws let off steam and spent their ill-gotten money, dominating the scene with their six-shooters.

Local ranchers were aware of the rustlers' activities, but did not interfere until the outlaws began to steal cattle and horses from Cochise County ranchers. Then there was an outcry for the sheriff and his posse to put an end to this lawless business.

John Slaughter, whose neighbors believed he was the only man with the nerve and shooting skill to deal with the gangs, was appointed sheriff of Cochise County. His reputation was known, as well as his relentless skill with a gun. When he announced, "Rustlers, get out or be killed," the outlaws knew he meant it. Faced with his gun, they surrendered or fled. After four years of hard, dangerous work, Slaughter and his posse had made the region a safe place for peaceful settlers and cattle ranchers to live.

John Slaughter bought the huge old Mexican land grant, the San Bernardino, with countless acres on both sides of the border. Thousands of head of cattle grazed in Mexico as well as Arizona. His vaqueros, Mexican or American, were expert at handling cattle or driving off rustlers.

The Slaughters lived in the style of the Mexican haciendas, in a great house of Spanish architecture surrounded with trees and flowers, with artesian wells supplying plenty of water. San Bernardino was famous through the region for its herds, for the Slaughters' elegant style of living, and their hospitality. Every passing traveler stopped to visit and be entertained — Army officers, mining men, cattle ranchers, or Mexican friends.

Once the lawless rustlers were under control, other cattle kings became owners of tremendous spreads in the beautiful San Simon and Sulphur Spring valleys. At that time the whole region was public domain, thousands of acres of free range with no fences. Two great outfits were the Chiricahua Cattle Company, called the "Cherry Cows" by the cowpunchers, and the San Simon Cattle Company.

Another famous cattleman was William C. Greene, a combination of promoter and hardened frontiersman. Within a few years he acquired a huge cattle outfit on both sides of the border. In Mexico he built the whole town of Cananea to serve the needs of the copper mine of fabulously rich ore that he developed.

The free use of the ranges was soon hampered by the settlers who came in under the government's Homestead Act. This law allowed each settler a quarter section of land in the public domain for a nominal payment after five years of occupancy. The farmers, or "nesters" as the cattlemen called them, moved from the western plains into southern Arizona and then to the more northern cattle ranges. There was conflict between "nesters" and cattlemen wherever the farmers settled.

In the early days of cattle-raising in Arizona the herds were mostly Texas or Mexican longhorns. These animals were wild, lean and tough, with a tremendous spread of horns. They could support themselves on desert vegetation, fight off predatory animals, and endure long trail drives, but this kind of life did not produce tender beef. As railroad shipping points for sending cattle to market became more accessible, the ranchers realized they would profit if they developed a better type of animal.

Henry C. Hooker was one of the first cattlemen to improve his stock with purebred animals. At Carson City, Nevada, he began to make money as a contractor, selling beef for Army camps. From that enterprise Henry Hooker built up a herd of 15,000 head at the great ranch he established at Sierra Bonita in Sulphur Spring Valley. He improved his stock by importing Hereford and other fine bulls. Some ranchers followed his example and before many years had passed the brown-coated, white-faced Herefords were grazing on thousands of acres.

Hooker's ranch became a productive empire, with cattle and horses, hay fields, crops, a dairy herd, and poultry. He set up a modern windmill and water tank for the cattle and piped water to the house. As the valleys came into use for cattle-raising and farmers' crops, the lanky windmills with the turning fans, like giant sunflowers, became an Arizona landmark.

Another efficient rancher in the Sulphur Spring Valley was Brannick Riggs. He set out from Texas with his family and a herd of cattle, bound for California. When he reached the Chiricahuas the family liked the country so much he decided to stay. Near the mountains he built his home ranch, called Riggs Settlement. It became a family center as sons and daughters grew up, married, and started their own farming and ranching near by. They were hard-working, honest pioneers, an asset to the region. Some members of the family still live in the valley.

Two Englishmen, the Vail brothers, with their friend Hislop, came to Tucson by exhausting stage journeys to look over land and buy a cattle ranch. They went out on horseback or in buggies with ranchers who wanted to sell. The Englishmen soon learned to fit in with the hard life of a pioneer country. They slept on the ground in blankets or in rude bunk houses with cowboys, as they looked for good grass and water. The Vails bought a great spread east of the Santa Rita Mountains and founded their business with a herd of 5,000 cattle. Over the years this profitable Empire Ranch, as they named it, grew and prospered. Their cattle and the Vail family became important in the growth of southern Arizona.

After the Southern Pacific Railroad came through, providing shipping stations at Tucson, Benson, Willcox, and Bowie, settlers moved in wherever they could find reliable water and grass. They stocked their ranges with cattle and sheep, finding a market for beef and mutton at mining camps and Army forts. A Mormon colony built a farming settlement called St. David near Benson. The farmers dug artesian wells to provide water for their dairy cattle and for their farm fields.

Cattle ranches, large and small, were developed in the Gila River Valley and in the tall grass country of Chino Valley on the Prescott plateau. In the north, one of the largest outfits was the Aztec Land and Cattle Company, called the Hashknife because of the shape of their brand. Managers and foremen of these owners grazed 60,000 head of cattle on their range. It extended from Mormon Lake to the east of Holbrook; from the Little Colorado south to the Mogollon Rim. It was rough country for the cowboys, as cattle hid in mountain canyons and had to be rounded up, which took days of work among rocks and thickets. On the plains, Mormon canals and ditches were a hazard in herding cattle.

The northern country had been sheep range from the time Navajos and Hopis began depending on their flocks for most of their livelihood, and when Mormon farmers brought in sheep. Large outfits, such as the Daggs brothers, had thousands of their woolies competing with cattle for grass and water.

In Arizona, as in other parts of the West, there was warfare when sheepmen and cattlemen tried to feed their animals on the same broad ranges. The cattlemen believed they had a prior right to use the grazing lands. They were convinced that sheep ruined the grass by too close cropping, and that their sharp hoofs cut the soil and destroyed grass roots.

The tough, individualistic cowpuncher on horseback, riding miles over the range to watch cattle, scorned the solitary sheepherder who went on foot, alone for weeks at a time with hundreds of bleating woolies. Wherever sheepherders and cowpunchers met in the course of their work there was trouble; their enmity created violence.

Reckless cowboys thought it a fine joke to invade a sheepherder's night camp, yelling and shooting to frighten the sheep, peppering the cooking pots with shot, scattering the supper fire. At one time a band of rowdy cowpunchers raided a sheep camp along the Little Colorado River. They tied up the herders, and with guns popping they drove the terrified sheep into the shallow water where they died, bogged down in quicksand.

The cattlemen, making their own laws of the range, set limits to the territory where sheep might graze, but the sheepherders refused to recognize these limits. They fought back in any way they could. Ranch houses and lonely range camps were burned, cattle were killed, and occasionally cowpunchers were shot. Some sheepherders would shoot at any horseman wearing a hat.

The real war between sheepmen and cattlemen came to a head when sheep owners of the San Francisco Mountain country sent flocks down through the Tonto Basin below the Mogollon Rim, for winter feeding in Pleasant Valley. The cattlemen had made a rule that sheep could not come below the Mogollon Rim. The conflict centered about the enmity of two families: the cattle-raising Grahams and the Tewksburys who supported the sheep interests. The two families were Texans who had formerly been friends, but had quarreled to the point where they hated each other. This bitter feud added to the terrors of the sheep versus cattle war. When herders brought their flocks into the cattle ranges, the ranchers, supported by wild cowpunchers of the Hashknife outfit, drove off the sheep and often killed the herders. In retaliation the Tewksburys caught three cowpunchers and hanged them on trees. Grahams shot Tewksburys, who in turn shot

Grahams, whenever their paths crossed. This crazy conflict was known as the Tonto Basin or Pleasant Valley War.

At last, only one male Graham was left alive. This Tom Graham gave up and moved to Tempe, where he took up farming. He made the mistake of boasting that the Tewksburys were afraid to attack him. Soon after, while driving a wagon load of grain to town, he was shot from ambush. Before he died Tom Graham named Ed Tewksbury and John Rhodes as the killers.

The two men were arrested and tried before a local judge. In the courtroom the widow of Tom Graham drew a revolver to shoot John Rhodes, but the hammer jammed and the gun was taken from her. John Rhodes was acquitted, and eventually the case against Ed Tewksbury was dropped.

The bloody feud came to an end after most of the leaders were killed, but trouble between sheepmen and cattlemen was not really ironed out until the Tonto National Forest was created in 1905. The Forest Service laid down rules for grazing and for the conservation of ranges that both industries learned to respect. The forest rangers prepared a sheep drive through Tonto Forest, and between those limits the herders might bring their flocks from the north for winter feeding in the Salt River Valley.

Sheepmen and cattlemen learned to respect one another's rights and to obey the laws for conservation of the over-grazed ranges. Nowadays, each winter the sheepherders, who are mostly Mexican or Basque, bring the flocks down from the north by the sheep drive for winter feeding. In the same valley cattle are fattened in alfalfa pastures.

The old days of the free open range and huge cattle spreads are gone forever, but ranchers came to appreciate the value of barbed wire fences to keep their herds under control and to establish ownership. Modern cowboys are not the hard riding, hard living, gun-toting fellows of the old days. Those men were marvelous horsemen and ropers; their work was hard and lonely, with occasional wild sprees for diversion in the nearest town. There was nothing fancy about their dress — great leather chaps and high-heeled boots, cartridge belt and gun holster around their waists, slouch hats, and bandana kerchiefs for protection against dust.

The skills with horses and cattle that were developed by those men are just as valuable to the cowboy of today. And out of local competitions among cowboys in roping, bulldogging, and bronc riding grew the popular western sport of the rodeo, where professionals compete in the oldtime skills.

## Chapter XXIV

### The Army and the Apaches

When pioneers moved westward into frontier regions the Army played an important role in developing roads and protecting settlers. So it was in Arizona. Military camps and forts were dotted over the country, most of them consisting of adobe barracks and storehouses. Fort Whipple was built with a strong log stockade constructed in a square around the parade ground. Fort Bowie, situated in Apache Pass to protect travelers and a vital water supply, was one of the most important posts during the Apache wars. It was a large place, with barracks and officers quarters, well-arranged for defense.

Life was primitive and lonely for the soldiers. Aside from military drill and camp chores, their main task was to chase marauding Indians, for the forts were intended to protect settlers, wagon trains, and military convoys.

Army officers and their men, trained to orthodox military tactics, learned by hard experience to adopt some of the wilderness skills of the Indians. Those warriors could move over rough territory without a sound, never showing themselves from the cover of rocky canyons, boulders or thickets. From their lofty lookouts they could watch every movement of travelers or companies of soldiers on the roads, and the various bands were in communication by their code of smoke signals, sent up from mountain peaks.

The Indians of the Southwest naturally resented the invasion of their homelands by white men, and many tribes fought fiercely to drive out the invaders. Peaceful tribes, such as the Pimas, the Papagos, and the Pueblo tribes of New Mexico, learned to live on their lands with only occasional revolts against the white men.

The greatest menace to settlements in New Mexico and Arizona came from the powerful, antagonistic nation of the Apaches, composed of many groups and clans. Their homeland was ideal for such nomadic hunters and warriors. Range after range of steep, rugged mountains with inaccessible peaks and canyons provided strongholds from which warriors descended to capture stock, to burn, and kill. At home in every inch of their country, the Indians made speedy retreats into the mountains where soldiers could not reach them.

Hatred was mutual between the Apaches, who were trying to drive white men from their land, and the settlers, whose stock was stolen, houses burned, and people killed. "The only good Indian is a dead one," was a common phrase among settlers. Extermination, in their opinion, was the only solution.

Peace pacts that were fair to Indians and whites alike were often ruined by the actions of bad white men and bad Indians. In the rough life of pioneer settlements there were all too many brutal, lawless characters who employed trickery, cruelty, and broken promises in dealing with Indians. Also, there were unruly Indian warriors, with a fiery hatred for all white men, who could not be controlled by their leaders. Regardless of peace pacts, they would steal and murder at every opportunity. Other Indian bands, who were hunted from place to place and had lost their supply of game, often stole livestock in desperation because their people were hungry. They had no deer meat, no skins for blankets and moccasins.

Although ruthless in warfare, there were proud chiefs among the Apaches who were keenly intelligent. They possessed a code of their own for straight speaking and regard for promises. One by one, as terms of agreements were broken, these leaders lost faith in white men's promises.

The two most outstanding Apache chiefs were Mangas Coloradas, who controlled the New Mexico bands of Apaches, and Cochise of the Chiricahua bands in Arizona. At first these two wise leaders tried to guide their followers to peaceful cooperation with Americans. They understood that it was impossible to drive all white men from their country. It was best to make agreements whereby the Indians might keep their hunting grounds in return for refraining from attacks on settlers and their livestock. Years of bloody conflict might have been avoided if Americans had not lost the cooperation of these chiefs through the stupidity or treachery of individuals.

Cochise became a bitter enemy of Americans after his relatives had been arrested and killed by Lieutenant Bascom in Apache Pass. Mangas Coloradas with his bands went on the warpath after he had met with brutal treatment and broken promises from reckless individuals. Mangas was arrested by soldiers sent out to capture him. On the excuse that he was trying to escape, he was shot in the back by a guard.

The government was no help to harried Army officers, since the Indian Bureau and other agencies changed their policies from year to year. The men in far-away Washington did not understand the Indians or the real situation in Arizona. The newspapers of Tucson and Prescott railed against the weakness of the government and the inefficiency of the Army, thus expressing the feeling of the people. What the settlers wanted was safety, protection, and extermination of the "red devils."

In 1870 the Department of Arizona was created at Fort Whipple with General Stoneman in command. He followed the policy of settling friendly Indians on reservations, but kept his troops on the move after rebellious bands. He built military roads into the mountains and set some of the soldiers to building better barracks at the forts.

Many people accused General Stoneman and his officers of being too soft with Indians. In Tucson, special criticism was directed at Lieutenant Whitman at Camp Grant. This small military post was built on the San Pedro River at the entrance to Aravaipa Creek, because the trails of Indian travel crossed near there.

A band of peaceful Apaches had formerly camped and grown corn on the sandy land near the creek, but had fled to the mountains when Camp Grant was built, because they feared the soldiers would take their land.

Early in 1871, Chief Eskiminzin came in with some of his men to ask Lieutenant Whitman if they might return to their camp ground. They were half starved in the mountains and without food or blankets. The Lieutenant felt sorry for the people, who were evidently in bad condition. He permitted the Indians to camp on the land until he received permission from General Stoneman to make that their reservation. The post supplied them with rations and blankets.

Eskiminzin promised that his people would be obedient and peaceful, and the promise was kept. The families built their wickiups of stakes and grass and planted their fields. The experiment was so successful that other groups of Apaches came in until there were three hundred in the camp. Every few days Lieutenant Whitman counted them and issued rations. He and Eskiminzin liked and trusted each other. This Indian chief was a strong, sensible character, ready to cooperate in every way. Ranchers in the neighborhood seemed to have no fear of these Indians.

All went well until unruly bands of Indians, who were on the loose in the southern region, outraged citizens by stealing stock and making a raid on Tubac. There was fury among the people. All Indians were alike to them and they were convinced that Apaches from Camp Grant had made the raids. These Indians were fed and protected by the Army, they said, and in return they stole livestock and killed people, then took shelter at Camp Grant. In vain Lieutenant Whitman and Eskiminzin swore that their Indians had not been involved in the raids.

Mass meetings were held in Tucson. William S. Oury and a committee took their case to General Stoneman.

When they received no satisfaction, this group determined to organize a punitive expedition themselves. W. S. Oury and five other Americans, Jesus Elias and forty-eight Mexicans, with a group of ninety-two Papago Indians made up the company that started for Camp Grant. They had a wagonload of guns and ammunition and traveled in small groups to escape attention.

Marching by night, they reached a bluff above the Apache camp at daybreak, April 30, 1871. Most of the Indian men were away hunting in the hills when these reckless, cruel men attacked the camp of sleeping Indians. Women and children were beaten by Papago clubs, shot and knifed by Americans and Mexicans until the place was a bloody shambles. In half an hour the massacre was over. The killers set fire to the camp, then sneaked away into the hills, well satisfied with their work. The Camp Grant Massacre is the blackest episode in the record of American dealings with Apaches.

When news of this outrage reached the East, people were aroused. President Grant wrote the governor of Arizona that the whole Territory would be put under martial law unless those who took part in the massacre were indicted and tried by a federal judge in Tucson. The trial was held, but the jury acquitted the men without hesitation. No Arizonan at that time would give a verdict against fellow Americans for killing Apaches, even in such a brutal way.

Storms of controversy filled the newspapers. Lieutenant Whitman had all kinds of abuse heaped upon him while he remained in the Territory. General Stoneman was recalled by President Grant and General Crook sent in his place. Eskiminzin and the remaining families of his band were sent to the San Carlos Indian Reservation.

President Grant at this time tried a Peace Policy. Vincent Colyer, a Quaker, was sent to New Mexico and Arizona with powers to locate Indians on reservations under officers of the Indian Bureau. During 1871, he established Fort Apache Reservation in the White Mountains and found reservations for other willing tribes, so that about half the Indians who had been warring on white men were settled on these areas of land. The President approved his work, but he soon returned to the East.

The next peacemaker to be sent was General O. O. Howard, a friend of Indians, more tolerant and experienced than Vincent Colyer. The main object of his mission was to secure a peace pact with the Chiricahua Apaches and their chief, Cochise, the most aggressive band of all. No representative of the government had succeeded in meeting Cochise, who hated all Americans except his red-whiskered friend, Thomas Jeffords. The chief remained concealed in his mountain stronghold. He was kept informed of everything that was happening by Indian runners and smoke signals.

General Howard sought out the tall, rangy frontiersman, Tom Jeffords, who was then acting as scout for a troop of cavalry. He appealed to this friend of Cochise to arrange a meeting to discuss peace. Jeffords asked the General if he was willing to go with him alone to the Indian camp. When General Howard consented, Jeffords proceeded to plan with Chie and Ponce, two young Apache chiefs.

When Cochise had agreed to meet the General, if Jeffords vouched for him, the Indians led the small party into the depths of the Dragoon Mountains to the secret entrance to the stronghold. General Howard was impressed with the wild beauty and secrecy of the place, a small hidden valley with trees and a stream, surrounded by towering cliffs of red and buff sandstone.

The white men were directed to make camp under a tree, to await the coming of Cochise. In the morning the chief rode in, accompanied by relatives. He greeted his friend Jeffords affectionately and took the General's hand.

Cochise was growing old at this time; there was gray in the long hair that fell to his shoulders, but he was still a stalwart brown figure of a man, full of dignity. He sat down with Howard and Jeffords on blankets, and the conference began. It went on for several days.

The Apache chief refused to accept the reservation on the Rio Grande proposed by General Howard. His people must stay in their own country, he said, in the Chiricahua and Dragoon mountains with the valleys around them. He also demanded that his friend Jeffords be appointed as agent for the reservation. This Jeffords did not want, but he agreed in order to help the peace pact. Cochise then said he would call in his warriors, for he could not make peace without consulting them.

The warriors came in, to dance and sing all night around a huge bonfire. They sang to the spirits, asking their advice, and listened to orations by Cochise. When all was settled the white men were invited to join the council.

Cochise said solemnly to General Howard, "Hereafter the white man and the Indian are to drink of the same water, eat of the same bread, and be at peace."

The peace pact was confirmed by the military authorities and was respected by the Chiricahuas so long as the old chief lived. When he was dying Cochise made his sons, Tahzay and Natchez, swear to keep the peace.

Cochise was buried by his people somewhere in the stronghold. No white man but Thomas Jeffords knew the place, and he never revealed it. Cochise Stronghold, that beautiful retreat in the Dragoons, is now a county park, a memorial to a great Indian and a happy place for American families to picnic.

Many rebellious warriors, led by the young chief Geronimo, would not follow the peace imposed by the sons of Cochise. They escaped into the Sierra Madre Mountains in Mexico, and from there they continued their deadly raids against Mexicans and Americans.

In addition, conditions were bad on the reservations, due to the actions of greedy contractors and traders who cheated both the government and the Indians. There were traders who sold whiskey illegally to reservation Indians. Then the Indians got crazily drunk and went on a rampage, shooting and killing. Those who were not captured by soldiers fled to the Sierra Madres to join the outlaws.

Among the agents on reservations a few men stand out from the unworthy or inefficient ones. Thomas Jeffords did much for the Chiricahuas during the short time he was agent on their reservation. His work came to an end when some warriors broke away to go on the warpath and the reservation was closed down. Natchez, Tahzay, and their peaceful people were sent to San Carlos Reservation.

John Clum, the agent at San Carlos, led his Indians far along the path to self-support and orderly living during the four years of his work. He was a young man of great independence and positive ideas. In his opinion the Apaches had not had a fair deal. He was convinced that they would respond intelligently to friendly plans.

John Clum had a prejudice against the Army tactics with Indians, believing the administration of reservations should be handled by civilians.

This agent organized a company of Apache police and a court where reservation offenses could be tried by Apaches, with himself as presiding officer. The Army men were horrified at this scheme. But it worked. His Apache police and other Indians learned about self-government and discipline, and his band of police scouts became famous.

At Fort Apache, General Crook also had a band of Apache police under the famous scout, Al Sieber. During the troubled years of Indian war, the companies of Apache police worked on the reservations, and with the Army, against renegades of their own people. They were intelligent, loyal, and brave.

General Crook, the stern, just soldier, believed in a campaign of ruthless pursuit combined with fair dealing to the Indians who surrendered. When he took the command he talked to peaceful groups of Apaches, telling them "he did not speak with a forked tongue," the Apache phrase for false statements. Good Indians would be cared for on reservations and taught to help themselves. Bad Indians would be pursued until they were killed or surrendered. He asked his listeners to pass on this statement to their wild brothers. The Gray Fox, as the Indians called him, won respect and fear in his campaigns.

From about 1874 to 1886 the ruthless renegades, Geronimo and his band, were eternal trouble-makers. Geronimo was clever; he soon learned to get the better of inefficient agents on reservations. At intervals between raids, these Indians would turn up at the Reservation at Ojo Caliente in New Mexico, pretending they were ready to settle down. They would draw rations and blankets, stay a while, then slip away to their mountains.

In 1877, John Clum was ordered by the Indian Commissioner to march with his Apache scouts to Ojo Caliente to arrest the outlaws, who were known to be visiting there. Geronimo and his followers reluctantly assembled to meet John Clum at his demand, but they were in a hostile mood and unwilling to return to the Apache Reservation. John Clum suceeded in arresting them, with the exception of Geronimo, by the aid of his Indian scouts. Geronimo was finally taken prisoner and kept a captive in leg irons.

After his triumphant return to San Carlos, John Clum notified the authorities in Tucson that he would send Geronimo and his companions to jail in Tucson, to be held for trial. If that had been done the Indian wars might have ended then and there. Instead, the order came from Washington to release Geronimo and the others to live on the Reservation and receive rations.

John Clum was disgusted with the stupidity of the Indian Bureau in releasing the outlaw after he was safely in hand. He also resented the placing of a company of troops on the Reservation. He resigned his post and went to live in Tucson.

Geronimo soon gathered a band of rebellious Indians and persuaded Natchez to join them. They escaped from the Reservation to continue their raiding from the Sierra Madres in Mexico. By arrangement with the Mexican government, United States troops were permitted to pursue the outlaws into Mexico, as both American and Mexican officers were trying to capture them. The Indians were chased so relentlessly that Geronimo finally agreed to meet General Crook at the Canyon de los Embudos to discuss surrender and terms for their future existence.

Geronimo and Natchez made difficulties over the terms, but General Crook was nearing success when a passing trader sold whiskey to the Indians. In a rampageous mood Geronimo, Natchez and thirty-four Chiricahuas ran away into the mountains. The remainder of the band were conducted by soldiers to Fort Bowie. From there they were put on a train under military guard to be sent to Fort Marion in Florida.

General Crook was so severely criticized by the government for his failure to capture Geronimo that he resigned his command and General Nelson A. Miles was sent in his place. The outlaws were pursued by both Mexican and American troops until they were hungry and exhausted from the relentless chase.

In July, 1886, General Miles discussed the situation with friendly Chiricahuas at Fort Apache. He decided to send two Apache scouts, accompanied by Lieutenant Gatewood and a small group of soldiers, to seek out Geronimo and persuade him to meet the General to discuss surrender.

It was a difficult, dangerous task for the young officer. After making contact with a camp of American soldiers in Mexico, he set out with his Indian scouts and a few soldiers to find the Indian camp. After several days of scrambling through the most difficult canyons and rocks in the mountains, the scouts located Geronimo's camp. One of them went in to ask the chief to meet Lieutenant Gatewood for a talk. A meeting place was arranged on a river bank. There the young officer and his few men were faced with forty armed warriors and their leaders, Geronimo and Natchez.

Grim Geronimo stared with burning eyes at the Lieutenant as he delivered General Miles' message: "Surrender, and be sent to Florida with your band to join the other Chiricahuas, there to await the President's decision. Accept those terms or fight to the bitter end."

Belligerent and proud as ever, Geronimo argued endlessly, trying to obtain terms of his own, which were refused. Lieutenant Gatewood suggested that the Indians hold a pow-wow to discuss the situation. After this had been done, the sly old rascal came to Gatewood to ask his advice: "If you were an Apache, what would you do?"

Gatewood replied, "I would trust General Miles and take his word." After this had been solemnly considered the two leaders agreed that their twenty-four warriors, with fourteen women and children, would accompany the troop to meet General Miles at Skeleton Canyon. But they demanded an escort of troops to protect them from the Mexican soldiers.

Lieutenant Gatewood obtained this escort from the camp where he had stopped before, and after many trying episodes he brought his Indians to the meeting with General Miles. Geronimo put on a great show of pride as he argued with the General, but finally accepted the terms. He shook hands with General Miles and said to Gatewood, "Good. You spoke the truth."

So, at long last, the Indian wars were over. The outlaws were escorted to Fort Bowie and from there sent to Florida to join the other Chiricahuas. Peace came to Arizona, and Indians learned to live on reservations. During some of his remaining years, the wily old warrior Geronimo became a sort of sideshow attraction for gaping visitors at county and state fairs in the Middle West. He sold picture post cards of himself and bows and arrows he made. Apparently he enjoyed being exhibited as a genuine Indian chief.

## Chapter XXV

### Schools for the Territory

When the first Legislative Assembly of Arizona Territory met in the log cabin settlement of Prescott in 1864, few of the delegates had education on their minds. They were men who came from ranches, mines, small settlements, and the town of Tucson. These pioneers were too preoccupied with the struggle of making a living under constant threat of Indian attack to think about the needs of children.

Their first Governor, John N. Goodwin, however, did give thought to the future young people of Arizona. He was a man from Maine, a firm believer in education. Addressing the Assembly, Governor Goodwin urged the delegates to set up a public school system and vote funds for its support. He also informed them that by an Act of

Congress any state or territory might establish an Agricultural College and receive help in supporting it, provided they complied with the conditions. Although college education was beyond the planning of the delegates, they considered their governor's request for public schools.

The Committee on Education proposed a donation for schools of $250 each to three county seats — La Paz, Mohave, and Prescott — provided each town raised an equal sum. Tucson, in Pima County, was to receive $500 for a school on the same condition, providing the English language was taught every day — Spanish was the prevailing language of southern Arizona at that time. A donation of $250 was proposed for the mission school at San Xavier del Bac, where Father Mesaya was teaching Mexican and Indian children. It was given "as a fitting compliment to the first school opened in Arizona."

The pioneer legislators had done their best, but no schools were opened because the towns did not raise their share of the money. The proposal for a university was left on the records for future consideration.

Education received a big boost from the third governor, Anson P. K. Safford. Here was another New Englander who believed in education. He was a small man with a big beard, possessed of boundless energy and a most friendly spirit. The people gave him the affectionate nickname of "The Little Governor."

Schools were especially necessary, the Governor believed, because so many of the people were of Spanish or Mexican background. They were required to obey the laws of the United States, yet many of them could not understand English. The Spanish-speaking families must have the opportunity to learn the language, laws, and customs of the country where they lived.

Wholeheartedly, Governor Safford believed in free education for all children of the Territory, regardless of race or religion. He prepared a bill to be presented to the Sixth Legislative Assembly in 1871. Public schools were to be organized by county supervisors and school boards. Each school was to receive money set aside from the treasury in proportion to the number of children attending. The citizens were to be taxed for the support of schools. The Governor knew he would meet opposition from the hard-headed delegates, for they did not think it possible, at that time, to spend money for public schools.

In 1871 the wandering capital was in the possession of Tucson, and Governor Safford lived in the southern town. He had support for his public school ideas from leading citizens: men such as Sam Hughes; L. C. Hughes, editor of the *Arizona Daily Star,* and his wife; and Estéban Ochoa, a partner in the freighting company of Tully & Ochoa. This fine Mexican citizen had lived in the old town since before the Civil War and was greatly respected. Governor Safford asked him to present the school bill to the Legislature.

In spite of its favorable presentation the public school bill met opposition, but it was finally passed. Public schools were to be started. However, the Little Governor did not stop with the act of the lawmakers. Energetically he campaigned among the people for the cause of education. From settlement to settlement he traveled, going from door to door and talking to the families. He met a glad response and there was no doubt he had the support of the people in his campaign.

As soon as the school bill became law, progressive citizens in the three principal towns began to work for their children's education. Classes were started in Phoenix,

Prescott, and Tucson, but they were soon discontinued due to lack of funds and teachers.

The people did not give up. In Phoenix one landowner contributed land for a schoolhouse; other men contributed labor and materials. One man provided firewood for their stove. The school was a one-room adobe building with the usual dirt floor and flat roof. The people were immensely proud of the Little Adobe, as it was named.

This little school for the children of the Salt River Valley settlements opened in 1873 with an experienced teacher from the East, Miss Ella Elizabeth Shaver. She made a long journey to San Francisco by train and from that point an even more difficult trip to Phoenix by stage coach. Undoubtedly she made learning pleasant for the children, which delighted their parents. They were sorry when she married John Y. T. Smith, the hay camp man, since their children were deprived of her teaching.

In Tucson the first public school for boys was opened by John Spring in 1871. The memory of this devoted educator is preserved in the name of a school in modern Tucson. It was no easy task for John Spring to tame down 138 rough boys of all ages, who came to school barefoot or in scuffed sandals, with uncombed hair and unwashed faces. They had never met school discipline before. Rough benches on the dirt floor were the only furniture; there were very few books and not even a blackboard. Many of the boys had to learn English before they could proceed farther with education. Yet John Spring made a success of the school and was appreciated by the parents.

The Spanish-speaking mothers of Tucson were delighted when the Catholic Diocese engaged several teaching nuns of the Sisters of St. Joseph to come to the old town. They were true pioneers, those nuns, for they bravely made the weary, even dangerous journey by wagon from San Diego across the deserts. In rooms located beside the San Agustin Church, they opened the Sisters' Academy and Convent for Females. The Sisters of St. Joseph were valuable pioneers in the growth of Tucson.

Mrs. Josephine Brawley Hughes, wife of L. C. Hughes, was determined to bring free education to the girls who did not attend St. Joseph's Academy. Mrs. Hughes was an unusual woman in such a frontier community. She had had civic experience in eastern cities and was active in women's community work in Tucson. In 1873, she started the first public school for girls in an old brewery building. She paved the way for girls' free education as John Spring did for boys, but could not continue the work for long because of ill health.

Governor Safford then engaged two trained young teachers from California, Miss Marie Wakefield and Miss Harriet Bolton. For them the school board rented a small building of three rooms: one for girls, one for boys, one for the teachers. There were two playgrounds also, one for each sex. This school was soon filled to capacity.

Many of the settlers who changed Prescott from a log cabin village to a pioneer town were educated people, determined to send their children to school. Through Governor Safford they obtained the services of an accomplished teacher, Moses S. Sherman. His school was soon crowded, so the citizens voted bonds for the construction of a proper schoolhouse. It was a two-story building of brick with a number of classrooms. Here Moses Sherman presided as principal with several teachers under him, as education advanced in Prescott. Doubtless this brick school, opened in 1876, was the best equipped in the Territory and the pride of the town.

Governor Safford must have had powers of persuasion when he appealed to educational institutions around the country for teachers. Both men and women of ability were willing to come to uncivilized Arizona. In his opinion women made the best teachers, because they had more patience with children and took their work more seriously than men. Certainly he brought to Arizona devoted young women, accustomed to civilized living, who cheerfully worked with the youngsters under the most primitive conditions.

The first pioneer woman teacher was Miss Mary Elizabeth Post, who came by stage from San Diego to the little river port of Ehrenberg. She was an ingenious teacher for she gathered around her Spanish-speaking grown-ups and children. It was give and take between teacher and pupils as she learned Spanish while teaching them English. Later she taught school in Yuma. She needed courage and resourcefulness, for the only building provided for the school was the former courthouse of three rooms; one of them had been the jail and scrawlings of prisoners were still visible under the whitewash on the walls.

Although Bisbee did not grow up to the point of engaging a school teacher until 1881, Miss Clara Stillman, who came from Connecticut, had equally rough conditions to deal with. Half a dozen children were collected in an unused miner's shack far up the canyon, back of Castle Rock. Miss Stillman made a blackboard by nailing two planks together, and wrote on it with a piece of talc. This meant washing the board with a wet rag between classes. The children sat on rough wood benches.

Every day a Mexican boy with his burro climbed the steep trail to sell the school a jug of water.

The little group of children was soon moved down to the Miners' Hall in Brewery Gulch, that narrow street of dance halls and saloons. Here the boys and girls worked with slates and a few books under their kind teacher. Modern school children have fire drill, but to the children of old-time Bisbee, Indian drill was an excitement, because Apaches were always in the neighborhood. Blasts from the mine whistle — one short, one long — were a signal of danger to the village. Teacher and children, as well as other people, marched into the mine tunnel until the danger was past.

Miss Shaver, who married John Y. T. Smith, was not the only teacher to become a wife in one or another of the towns. In Tucson, Miss Wakefield and Miss Bolton married E. N. Fish and John Wasson respectively. They did not lose their interest in the children, however. They organized the women of Tucson, both American and Mexican, to raise money for a real schoolhouse by benefit suppers, serving Mexican and American dishes. They also arranged balls for which tickets were sold at $2.50 a couple. The school was a long adobe building constructed on Congress Street.

The newspapers were enthusiastic in praise of Governor Safford for his work in developing schools. Thanks to him, the Territory had free public schools in most of the settlements by the time his two terms as governor were ended. He worked with the supervisors and school boards, but also the children knew him as a friend because of his habit of dropping in at the schoolhouses to talk with teachers and children.

The editor of the *Weekly Citizen* wrote in 1874: "Less

than two years ago the free school system was started in
Arizona without schoolhouses, books or teachers. It seemed
a forlorn hope . . . but the same undaunted spirit that
had faced death and torture through a long series of years
said, 'We must have either more schools or more jails, and
we prefer the former,' and results show what people can
do if they will."

Each year more schools were built, more teachers
guided the boys and girls through elementary subjects,
especially English. In 1873 there were only eleven school
rooms with fourteen teachers, but by 1880 there were
about one hundred schools and an equal number of teachers. Going to school was serious business for young Arizonans in pioneer times. They had none of the interesting activities of modern school life, no organized sports
or social doings, no marching bands or cheering squads.
They learned more from their teachers directly than they
did from the limited supply of books.

Leading citizens concerned with education decided
it was time to train teachers from among their own
young people rather than engage all instructors from outside the Territory. The founding of a Territorial Normal School was taken up by the Thirteenth Legislative
Assembly in 1885. The founding of a University was also
under consideration.

This session of the Legislature, meeting in Prescott,
was controversial and hot-tempered. Politicians were competing for territorial institutions for their counties, such
as the Normal School, University, and Insane Asylum. They
were also fighting over the permanent location of the
capital, and were voting unnecessary sums for themselves.
Their actions won for the session the title of the "Thieving
Thirteenth."

The battle over the capital took precedence over the struggle for institutions. Prescott had won it back from Tucson but the southern town was determined to be the permanent location. Pima delegates, after conferring with others, saw no hope of winning the capital and agreed to accept the University. When Tucsonans learned of this, a mass meeting of indignant citizens sent a representative of their own to Prescott, provided with funds to persuade reluctant legislators. To the last day of the session the location of the capital was in doubt, but Prescott finally won.

The Pima delegates accepted the University with doubtful feelings, but Maricopa County came out well. By skillful lobbying, their delegates won the Territorial Normal School, to be located at Tempe. The Insane Asylum was also allotted to Maricopa County.

Charles Trumbull Hayden, leading citizen of Tempe, took an important part in the founding of the Territorial Normal School. A section of land was set aside to be used as a school farm. The people of Tempe promised to give twenty acres of land for a campus and to raise funds for a building. It was finished and ready to receive students in 1886. A long, one-story structure of four rooms was a small beginning for a teachers' college, but it was well furnished and was a source of pride. Hiram S. Farmer, the experienced teacher chosen for principal, opened his large home as a dormitory for girl students from out of town. They rode their horses to school, as the Farmer home was some distance from the campus. It was soon discovered that students must be given high school courses before teacher training began, because there were no schools at that level in Arizona.

A few years later, in 1889, the Northern Arizona Normal School was established in Flagstaff. Both schools, with eager students, began their work of training teachers.

The establishment of the University of Arizona was not so quickly accomplished. The First Territorial Legislature had authorized a University, but it was the famous Thieving Thirteenth that presented the institution to Pima County and Tucson in 1885.

Tucsonans, angered by loss of the capital, did nothing about the gift until the $25,000 allotted by the Legislature for building and equipment was about to be withdrawn. The citizens were required to give forty good acres of land for a site, but no one offered to do so. J. S. Mansfeld, the most efficient member of the Board of Regents, worked hard to obtain land and finally persuaded three prosperous citizens to donate forty acres of desert land they owned northeast of the town. These three were highly respected men, although one was the owner of the best saloon in town and the other two were gamblers. In that period, gambling rooms were a part of community life in most Arizona towns and the proprietors were often good citizens and businessmen.

At last, in 1887, ground was broken for a University building. The structure, which took several years to reach completion, was a long, rambling edifice of two stories, with porches all around it and several towers. On the present-day campus that building, Old Main, is a cherished reminder of the first years of the University.

When classes began in October, 1891, this building represented the hopes of Arizona's young people for a college education. It housed the School of Mines, the School of Agriculture, classrooms and laboratories, and living quarters for students and professors. The School of Agriculture and its experiment station made the University eligible for federal endowment under the act establishing agricultural or land-grant colleges.

When the small University opened there were six professors, all excellent men, and thirty-two students. Preparatory courses were necessary because of the lack of high school training.

Old Main stood on its acres in the midst of cactus, greasewood, and mesquite. It was a school humming with activity through the enthusiasm and confidence of teachers and students. Work began with the Schools of Mining and Agriculture, two fields of study in which the University has been immensely helpful to Arizona throughout its history.

The college was several miles out of town, but before long a line of tracks was laid over which a mule-drawn street-car rattled out to the campus in the desert. Good professors and intelligent citizens helped the University to grow, to become ever more valuable to the State.

## Chapter XXVI

### Water for the Arid Land

The farmers of Salt River Valley worked with courage and persistence to bring water to the good soil of the arid land, to help them make a living from their crops. When conditions of river flow and weather were just right everything flourished. Wheat, barley, alfalfa, and corn sprang up vigorously and ripened to profitable harvests. Orange trees and other fruit trees bloomed and bore their fruit.

Nature was against the farmers much of the time. There were seasons of severe drought and blistering heat, when the flow of water to the canals was too low to bring sufficient water to the fields. The crops withered and died and winds picked up clouds of dust to cover towns and countryside. After cloudburst storms in the

255

summer rainy season, or heavy spring rains in the mountains that melted the snow cover too fast, the river often overflowed its banks in rushing torrents. The simple rock and brush dams were washed out and headgates of canals were broken. Before dams and canals could be repaired hot sun and dry air often damaged the crops.

Floods grew worse every year because pioneer settlers had been careless in protecting the watersheds in the hills. Conservation was a word unknown in the West in the late nineteenth century. The hills had been denuded of trees for the sawmills that processed lumber for building. The ranges were badly overgrazed by too many cattle. Rains and melted snow swept down the unprotected slopes, causing unmanageable floods.

In the early spring days of 1891 came one of the most destructive floods they had known. Days of heavy rain in the mountains sent a rampaging mass of water down the Salt and Verde rivers, quickly overflowing their banks. On February 18, the railroad bridge across the river at Tempe went out, leaving Phoenix cut off from rail transportation. The water cut into a low section of the town, gouging a new channel. A crew of men with sandbags tried to keep the river from changing its course. At some places, below the junction of the Salt and Verde, the Salt was eight miles wide.

The water continued to rise, pushing into the streets of Phoenix, so the chief of the fire department sounded a warning and sent riders south of the town to urge people to leave the districts. The dams and headgates of the canals were washed out on February 19. By morning the roar of rushing waters filled the flooded town. In buildings constructed of adobe bricks water seeped into the foundations, melting the adobe so that walls crumbled and the buildings fell, deteriorating in muddy heaps.

On February 20, the flood was at its height. People climbed the stairs of the courthouse to the flat roof to watch the spectacle; others stood amazed at the edge of the flooded streets. An exploring party tried to reach Tempe, but the bridges over the canals on that road were gone, and a mile of railroad track was washed away, together with telegraph poles.

Trains could not run until a new bridge was built across the river. Although crews worked hard, it was not until May that the bridge was completed. During that period of isolation, mails were carried from Maricopa Junction to Phoenix by stage coach. When the first train steamed into town it was greeted by cheering townsfolk and blasts of whistles.

After recovering from this disaster, there was another great flood in 1900, followed by dry, hot winds that added to the devastation. Many farmers gave up and moved away. The people of the valley got together to study what could be done to manage the water supply; otherwise the valley would return to desert, the towns could not grow. Better methods must be found to avoid waste in sending water through the ditches to the farmers.

W. J. Murphy founded the Arizona Improvement Company to study better methods of distribution and the question of water rights. A reservoir to store water was essential to progress, but how could the county finance such a project?

At that time men who knew the West were working on the problem of reclamation of arid lands. They knew that irrigation was necessary in many regions of the West if the country was to prosper. Major John Wesley Powell was one of these men.

Engineers of the United States Geological Survey visited the arid regions to study the possibility of dams in the rivers to provide storage of water.  In Arizona, Colonel William Breckinridge, Maricopa County Surveyor, thought a dam could be built in a canyon of the Salt River at the junction with Tonto Creek.  When Engineer Arthur Powell of the U. S. Geological Survey visited the site he confirmed the opinion of Colonel Breckinridge.

Prominent citizens of Phoenix took up the idea and won support from the people after months of discussion. It was such a bold plan that it was difficult to convince people that it could be done.  Construction of the dam in Tonto Basin would be carried on sixty miles from the nearest railroad, eighty-five miles from the land where the water would be used.  It would cost from two to six million dollars.  How could the Territory of Arizona raise such a sum?  An appeal to the national government was necessary.

A member of the committee in Phoenix was sent to Washington.  There he found that senators from Nevada, North Dakota, and Texas were working on a reclamation bill.  When Theodore Roosevelt became President the reclamation group found a powerful supporter.  Theodore Roosevelt was an ardent believer in conservation and in the development of the great natural resources of the West, a part of the country he knew well.  He was responsible for setting aside National Forests to preserve the watersheds and protect the timber.

The bill submitted to Congress by the western senators was passed, and on June 17, 1902, President Theodore Roosevelt signed the Reclamation Act.  It was a record-making event for the arid western regions, although people in the East paid little attention to it.

When the news reached Phoenix the people went wild with joy. There were discussion meetings and celebrations in the streets. Although there was much to be done before the dream became reality, the people had hope.

The federal government would assist in financing reclamation projects if investigation proved the plans were economically sound. All the local problems of land, of prior rights to water and various other questions must be settled by the people who were to benefit.

There were mass meetings in every town and village, in school houses and churches, to discuss the problems. A committee was formed under the leadership of Judge Joseph Kibby representing the eleven canal companies and the towns. This judge was an old-timer in the valley, a man honored and trusted by everyone, a man who knew the people's problems and was fair in judgment. With the committee, Judge Kibby worked out a plan that provided for water rights, for the services of the canal companies, and for financing the work by assessment of members in the Salt River Valley Water Users Association. The applications for water by landowners would be met as the supply permitted, in the order of prior rights.

The Salt River Valley Water Users Association was incorporated, owned by the shareholders, with laws to protect the rights of landowners, and a system for the fair distribution of the water. Many later systems for irrigation companies were patterned after this excellent plan of Judge Kibby.

In nearly every village and town, in every farm gathering, the Water Users Association was argued pro and con. It meant sacrifice of some rights by these individualistic pioneers, who for the first time were trying to work out cooperation for the good of all. The landowners were risking their financial security and the future of their families in the belief that the project would succeed. Some were eager, others were skeptical and reluctant, but they finally reached agreement. By July 17, 1903, the landowners of this Association had pledged 200,000 acres to be irrigated from the dam to be constructed in the Tonto Basin. The Salt River Valley Water Users Association became a permanent organization.

The Legislature had authorized a tax of $30,000 for preliminary work to be raised in Maricopa County. The national government had appropriated $10,000 for the same purpose. Return of funds expended by the government was to be made in ten annual installments. Later this term was extended to twenty years.

Six years of gruelling work and tremendous expense passed by while the dam was being constructed. A road was built through the mountains to the site to be used by the great wagons, drawn by teams of twenty mules, that brought supplies to the site. Hydroelectric power was generated at the mouth of the canal that diverted the river water, which was used to make thousands of tons of concrete. Thousands of blocks of native stone were quarried from the mountains for the building of the dam. It was a masonry dam, constructed of native stone, mortar and concrete. In the end the project cost about $10,-000,000, but all that the national government had expended had been paid back by 1955.

That is the story of the magnificent Roosevelt Dam that now spans the Salt River in its canyon at Tonto Creek, with beautiful Roosevelt Lake behind it.

On March 18, 1911, distinguished citizens and guests

from the Reclamation Bureau gathered at the top of the dam, and ex-President Roosevelt came to dedicate the dam named for him.  People made the rough trip to the site on horseback, on bicycles or in buggies, and a few in automobiles.  It was a great day for Arizona, and a satisfaction to them that Theodore Roosevelt was so pleased to have this great work of conservation given his name.

At the close of the ceremonies Roosevelt, by means of an electric switch, opened sluice gates in the northern slope of the dam.  From twin funnels leaped two great torrents of water that filled the bed of the river below.

The Roosevelt Dam was the first of many dams, constructed for water control and electric power, that were built under the Reclamation Bureau of the Department of the Interior.  Lately, the name has been changed to Theodore Roosevelt Dam.  In 1961, Arizonans celebrated the fiftieth anniversary of the completion of the dam with appropriate commemorative ceremonies.  It was the first dam to bring agricultural prosperity to Arizona valleys.

The road to the site was graded and finally paved. It became the Apache Trail, which is one of the most scenic and interesting routes in southern Arizona.  Dams that were built on the river below created Canyon Lake and Apache Lake, entrancing bodies of blue water framed in craggy, multi-colored cliffs.  The whole region is now the people's playground for boating and fishing.

## Chapter XXVII

## Towns and Cities

When the twentieth century began, the hardworking, courageous pioneer families felt that the period of trial and danger was over. Arizona was still a frontier region, but towns were growing all over the Territory with shops and businesses, law officers and courts, churches and schools. There were great cattle spreads, booming mines, and successful irrigated farms in the valleys.

Arizonans were frontier people — independent, vigorous, undaunted by hardship, always ready to try new enterprises. They needed courage, for the land they had chosen was not an easy one for settlement. It was a land of vast distances and of great topographical variety — from precipitous mountains and canyons, forests and high plateaus to semi-arid desert valleys. There were fierce rivers

263

and others so shallow that they were dry part of the year. Alternating drought and flood, desert heat and dust storms, plagued the pioneers. The people had, nevertheless, a land of great skies, translucent atmosphere, and brilliant sunshine. They did not yet realize that they had a commercial asset in climate and natural beauty, since they were too busy developing Arizona's resources in mining, agriculture, and cattle-raising.

Arizonans thought nothing of traveling great distances on horseback or by wagon, but they were proud of the fact that they could also travel within the Territory and to the states outside by train, and that railroad transportation advanced their economy. Two transcontinental railroads crossed the Territory, and branch lines served many mines and communities. There were telegraph lines, electric light and power for the largest towns, and automobiles were appearing on the roads.

Except in the mountains Arizona was horse and cattle country. Herds of white-faced Herefords grazed over thousands of acres, and the raising of fast, sturdy horses and mules was for many ranchers a part of their business. Roundup was the important event of the year when, as a rule, several owners of large spreads joined forces to gather in their stock at a convenient place, to separate the young steers for market, and to brand the calves. Roundup was a strenuous time. Quiet cowboys on their skilled cowponies worked among bawling cattle in clouds of dust. At small ranch roundups the women did their part by providing hearty food for the working men in the middle of the day.

Horses, in frontier Arizona, were men's best friends and constant companions, essential in the work with cattle. A man and his horse were inseparable, for no one walked if he could possibly help it. He mounted a horse to get wherever he was going in the spacious country. These were no mere work horses, but animals wise and well-trained, as skilled as their riders in rounding up cattle. Men trained their best horses for racing, too, for this was a favorite sport. On Sundays and holidays the horsemen gathered to race their mounts through a main street of Phoenix or Prescott, betting wildly on favorites and celebrating the results of the races in the saloons.

In southern Arizona, with its Spanish past and hot, dry climate, life was easy and slow-moving for the people living in flat-roofed adobe houses in settlements, on ranches or on farms. A large part of the population was Mexican; some were descendants of pioneer families, but there was also a constant influx of workers from across the border.

Tucson, whose history as a community dated back to 1776 when it became a walled Spanish presidio, was the leading "city" in the Territory, although Phoenix was fast catching up. Mexican inhabitants had welcomed the coming of Americans, for the new pioneers brought a spirit of enterprise, and troops of the Army brought business. Some newcomers spoke of Tucson as a "foreign" town, and so it was in some ways, because most of the people spoke Spanish, and Mexican customs or fiestas were very popular.

For some time in the territorial period Tucson was an Army town, a central supply depot. Citizens accepted the soldiers since they were a protection against Apache depredations. Troops were camped in the Military Plaza, where Armory Park is today, until 1873. Then the camp of infantry and cavalry was moved to a site on Rillito Creek, a few miles out of town, and was named Fort Lowell. It was an important Army post during the Apache wars.

Fort Lowell was also a social asset to prosperous Tucsonans. Many an evening the ladies and gentlemen drove out in their buggies for dinner and a ball with officers of the Fort. Band concerts, by the Military Band, were given in the former Military Plaza to entertain the townsfolk.

During most of the Territorial period, Tucson was noted among Arizona communities for the friendly mingling of Spanish-American and Anglo-American families. Many Mexican pioneers came from good families in Sonora and Chihuahua. Their daughters often married leading citizens of the community, and these families combined Spanish and American customs in their social entertainments. Men of both nationalities were traders, merchants, and freighters. Tucson, with trade in goods from Sonora and California, was a business center for mines and ranches.

American enterprise led the way in commercial affairs and politics as the town advanced in population and prosperity after the arrival of the railroad in 1880. Well-to-do families had solid, high-ceiled dwellings with garden patios. In modern Tucson, the cherished building of Mexican style with inner garden, called the Old Adobe, is a fine example of the territorial family home. This building has been presented to the Arizona Pioneers' Historical Society and will be preserved as a historic site.

Trade with the port of Guaymas in Sonora, Mexico, was carried on by the old route for pack trains and wagons until the Southern Pacific Railroad built a branch line from Sonora to Benson. It followed the trail through Nogales Pass with its grove of black walnut trees (*nogales* in Spanish). There in 1880, Jacob Isaacson, a peddler, built a rough trading post and shelter for travelers. The small settlement that grew up around it eventually developed into the twin towns of Nogales, straddling the border between Arizona and its neighbor state of Sonora, Mexico.

Tucson advanced in culture and prosperity with the meteoric rise of Tombstone in the 1880's. The population of the mining town reached 15,000, and Cochise County was created, with Tombstone as the county seat.

That was the period, in the 1880's and 1890's, when distinguished theatrical companies and other performers went "on the road" to perform in all the thriving cities of the West. Tombstone and Tucson were their stops in Arizona. In Tombstone plays or concerts were given in Schieffelin Hall, while Tucson had an Opera House. The citizens were treated to good plays and heard some of the best singers of the day. Tombstone also had the famous Birdcage Theater for the lighter and more rowdy song and dance acts.

In Tucson, the University of Arizona was growing, adding new courses, more professors, and more buildings, as fast as funds could be obtained. Educated young people graduated to become useful citizens, while the faculty created a cultural nucleus for the townsfolk.

Both towns had their newspapers, which was true of every settled community. The territorial editors were independent frontiersmen, fiery in their style of writing. They were outspoken in their criticism of the government, the Army, and local affairs. Tucson had two newspapers, *The Arizona Daily Star* and *The Weekly Citizen*. For some time the *Star* was edited by L. C. Hughes, who also served a term as governor. While he was governor his accomplished wife helped to run the paper.

John Clum bought *The Weekly Citizen* after he resigned his post as Indian agent of the San Carlos Reservation. Before long he moved on to booming Tombstone, brought in printing equipment and launched *The Tomb-*

*stone Epitaph,* a newspaper that became famous. Later, John Clum was mayor of the town as well as newspaper editor.

Tombstone and Tucson had their wild elements who frequented saloons and gambling rooms. Lawless men were arrested and tried by local judges; bad men shot up saloons and sometimes held up stage coaches or trains. At the same time, self-respecting citizens were building up civilized communities.

Tombstone's glory was brief, for as the mine shafts were sunk deeper and deeper water began to seep into the lower levels. Pumps were installed which kept it under control for a while, but in 1886 the large pumping system at the Contention and Grand Central mines burned down, and water flooded most of the mines. People began to move away as prosperity dwindled, but Tombstone managed to continue its existence as "The Town Too Tough To Die."

Bisbee, with its great Copper Queen Mine and many others, grew more slowly than Tombstone into a successful mining town. The wooden shacks of miners and more solid houses of managers and officers clung to the sides of the canyon walls. Large groups of miners, the Serbs and Mexicans, brought their customs and festivals with them to add extra color to life in the American town. Bisbee often suffered from seasonal floods that raced down the canyon, drowning out business shops or sweeping away houses in the path of the water. Smoke from the smelter damaged all vegetation until it was moved to the railroad town of Douglas on the Mexican border. Then housewives could grow shrubs and flowers in their handkerchief-sized gardens on the canyon slopes.

Other mining towns in the eastern mountains lived

by the prosperity of deep mines. An important town was Globe, in the great copper and silver district of the Pinal Mountains. It was a business town, and the county seat of Gila County. Besides the mining activities, the town was a market for products of ranches and farms, and lively cowboys came in for entertainment. Hardrock miners from Europe gave the population a mixed character. There were Cornishmen, called "Cousin Jacks," as well as Italians, Slavs, and Mexicans, each settled in its own section of the community. The town had its newspaper, *The Silver Belt,* as outspoken in its editorials as other newspapers.

Until 1899, Globe was so inaccessible in the mountains that mines and population were dependent on the great freight wagons for shipping ore and bringing in supplies. When a small branch railroad was built from Bowie, through the Gila towns, people often called the little puffing train on the line the Gila Monster.

Pioneer farmers had gone into the upper valleys of the Gila and Little Colorado in the early days of American settlement. The Mormons were really the developers of farming lands, especially in the upper Little Colorado Valley. They were poor a great deal of the time, eking out a living now and then by driving freight wagons, but they succeeded. St. Johns, their first settlement, became the most important town, and other settlements followed, such as Snowflake, Show Low, Thatcher, and Springerville.

Between this farming region and that of the upper Gila Valley lay the broad plateau of the San Carlos and Fort Apache reservations, where the once fierce Apaches were learning to become farmers and cattlemen. After the fear of Indian attacks was removed by the surrender of Geronimo, pioneers developed the town of Safford, situated in a broad green valley and overlooked by the high peak of Mount Graham, which is more than 10,000 feet in height. When Graham County was created in 1881, Safford became the county seat. It was a center for ranchers and farmers, whose cattle ranges and fields covered the fertile valley.

While towns were growing in the mountains, the farmers of the Salt River Valley were working hard to increase their prosperity with their irrigated fields and crops. Phoenix, Tempe, Mesa, and Florence were settlements with wide, tree-shaded streets and dwellings of adobe or brick. Tempe had the Territorial Normal School, or Teachers College, bringing professors and students to the community, and Hayden Flour Mills constituted the main industry.

Phoenix was rapidly becoming the important "city" of the valley as the market center for produce from the fields of alfalfa, grains, and vegetables, or fruit from the young orange groves.

A curious reminder of old days came to Phoenix when one day a Mexican came into town leading a camel he had captured in the desert. He parked his animal in the corral of a blacksmith shop until he found a buyer, the proprietor of a traveling circus. Perhaps this camel was the last descendant of the herd brought in by Lieutenant Beale so many years before.

In 1882 the editor of the Phoenix *Gazette* had this to say about his young city: "No railroad trains rush into its midst, no machine shops give employment to large numbers of people, no factories support its populace, no reduction works of mines." He went on to praise the orderly, friendly life of the community. How different a picture was that description from the modern city of Phoenix, which is now a commercial metropolis.

After a branch line connected Phoenix with the Southern Pacific Railroad in 1887 and the politicians won the permanent location of the territorial capital from Prescott in 1889, the ambitious citizens pushed their community ahead rapidly.

The Fifteenth Territorial Legislature, which voted to transfer the capital to Phoenix, also passed an act to obtain a site and to erect a capitol building. The land was donated and commissioners were appointed to plan the erection of the capitol. It was designed in the classical style favored for government buildings, called the Ionic-Grecian, to be surmounted by a dome. Arizona materials were used so far as possible in the construction of the building. The ground floor was of gray granite and the upper stories of tufa, a porous volcanic stone; both kinds of stone were dug from Arizona quarries. After some years of work, the main capitol building was completed in 1901. It housed the government offices, the legislative chambers, and the territorial library. The dome was surmounted by a winged figure representing liberty. Proud citizens dedicated their capitol building with bands, a parade, and appropriate ceremonies. Government officers moved in, and the Twenty-First Legislature met in the handsome building.

Prescott regretted the loss of the capital, but had other assets. Although the gold mines became less productive, the cattle industry grew and cattlemen grazed their great herds on the open plains. The town had its wild days, in the saloons, dance halls and gambling rooms of Whiskey Row, but that famous street and much of the business district was destroyed by a huge fire in 1900. The citizens went to work with determination to rebuild the burned section with more substantial buildings that reflected the common-sense ambitions of the townsfolk. For some years they had one of the most vigorous of pioneer editors, John Marion. In *The Arizona Miner* his controversial editorials were known far and wide.

The people were thoroughly American in their sentiments, so the Fourth of July was celebrated with old-fashioned gusto. There were parades of officials, ranchers and miners, escorted by blaring bands. There were fireworks, patriotic orations and much riotous fun with horse racing and cowboy sports. Prescott was a real cow town, and the inhabitants claim that the great western sport of the rodeo was initiated with the cowboy competitions on the Fourth of July in 1889.

Prescott gave to Arizonans the first poet and historian, Sharlot Hall, and a man who typified western daring and enterprise, Bucky O'Neill.

Sharlot Hall came to live in Prescott with her pioneer parents, arriving by wagon. Women did their part in many communities to bring civilization to the frontier, but Sharlot Hall was unusual in that she devoted her life to preserving Arizona history, customs, and characters. She was a poet as well, producing a book of poems in praise of the romance and beauty of the Southwest. Due to her efforts the old log house which had been the first Governor's Mansion was preserved as an historic site. Here were collected mementos of the early days, and while she lived Sharlot Hall made it a center of historic treasures. Governor Kibby, the next-to-last governor of the Territory, appointed her historian of Arizona, a post she held until statehood.

Bucky O'Neill came to Arizona as a young man, riding a burro, and had a part in many enterprises for the Territory. He worked as court reporter, newspaper editor, judge, sheriff, and finally mayor of Prescott. As sheriff of huge Yavapai County he made a reputation by pursuing outlaws and train robbers and bringing them to justice.

When a romantic war fever swept the country in 1898, with the ostensible purpose of freeing the Cuban people from the rule of Spain, Bucky O'Neill took the lead in Arizona. He organized the Arizonans who responded to the call for volunteers. Westerners were eager to join "Teddy" Roosevelt's Rough Riders, a detachment of the First United States Volunteer Cavalry, for Roosevelt was popular with western men. Bucky O'Neill trained a troop of cavalry to join the Rough Riders, and the people of Prescott sent them off to war with music and waving banners.

Arizona Rough Riders finally reached Cuba and took their part in that strange war. Bucky O'Neill was killed in the charge up San Juan Hill.

After the war the famous sculptor, Solon Borglum, offered to create a monument to the Rough Riders, to be placed in the plaza at Prescott. There it stands, a vigorous mounted figure on a charging horse, a memory to Prescott people of their own Bucky O'Neill, and a further memorial to the dynamic spirit of the West.

While mining diminished around Prescott, to the northeast a wealth of copper was being extracted from the slopes of Mingus Mountain. The United Verde Copper Mines were not very successful until after 1890, but from that time on, and for many years, quantities of valuable copper brought wealth to the owners of the United Verde. Jerome, clinging to the mountain slope in layers of long-legged houses, was one of the liveliest mining towns of the Territory.

High on the plateau, at the foot of the San Francisco Peaks, Flagstaff grew from railroading and lumbering. As the town expanded, citizens built their simple homes on streets climbing the hills towards the meadows and forests of the mountains. People began to notice and appreciate the town's beautiful setting and fine climate. The Teachers College brought people of education and energetic young people. The town gained another asset when Dr. Percival Lowell, a distinguished astronomer, founded the Lowell Observatory in 1894 and endowed it permanently. The Observatory, with its powerful telescope and equipment for study, was built on a volcanic mesa 350 feet above the town. The high altitude and great sweep of sky made it an ideal location for the study of the heavens and for Dr. Lowell's favorite project — the examination of Mars. He had a theory that the planet was inhabited by intelligent beings who had constructed its canals.

The magnificent pine forests of the northern plateau came into use to provide railroad ties and lumber for building. Sawmills, lumber mills and logging camps increased after this period of railroad building, with camps extending into the forests of the Mogollon Rim country.

The rough railroad camps — Kingman, Williams, Winslow, Holbrook — grew into busy towns as shipping points and marketing centers for lumbermen and ranchers.

Arizonans were proud of their achievements. Even in the early days there were some pioneers, led by Charles Poston, with an appreciation of history. They thought it was time to begin preserving historical documents, facts, maps, or other records, as well as pioneer possessions. In

1884 this group met to found the Arizona Pioneers' Historical Society, which has grown in value to Arizonans ever since.

Although their land was a remote frontier, little known in the East, the twentieth century found the people of Arizona ready and anxious for the statehood they felt they deserved.

# PART V.
# ARIZONA THE FORTY-EIGHTH STATE

## Chapter XXVIII

## A Valentine from Uncle Sam

## (1912–1940)

On February 14, 1912, President Taft, with a gold pen, signed the proclamation that admitted Arizona to the Union as the forty-eighth state. In every town and village celebrations were staged with all the enthusiasm of frontier people who had at last accomplished their great desire for statehood. There were parades and bands, orations and showers of fireworks. It was a magnificent valentine from Uncle Sam to his youngest state. Admission Day has been an annual holiday ever since.

Achievement of statehood was the climax of a long struggle carried on by politicians and citizens of Arizona. From the beginning of the twentieth century representatives in the National Congress, and committees from the Territory, had worked for passage of a statehood bill.

277

Constitutional Conventions were held, with influential men from the counties discussing ideas and laws.

Congress, at that time, was considering the pleas of various territories for admission to statehood. Indian Territory and Oklahoma were admitted as one state, Oklahoma. Congressmen intended to do the same for Arizona and New Mexico, but met keen opposition from Arizonans.

The Twenty-third Territorial Legislature, in 1905, went on record with the statement: "It threatens to fasten upon us a government that would be neither of, nor for, the people of Arizona. It would be a government without the consent of the governed. It humiliates our pride, violates our traditions, would subject us to the domination of another commonwealth of different traditions, customs and aspirations. With the most kindly feeling toward the people of New Mexico, we must protest against this proposed union, and would rather remain forever a territory, than to accept statehood under such conditions."

Governor Otero of New Mexico expressed much the same sentiments on joint statehood in the name of his people.

Nevertheless, Congress went ahead with the framing of a joint statehood bill. A senatorial committee traveled out to look over New Mexico and Arizona, making brief visits to Phoenix, Prescott, and Tucson in Arizona. They reported unfavorably; the population was small in both territories, much of it was Spanish, the towns were rough, the country semi-arid. They ignored the mines and agriculture, the cattle ranches, the transcontinental railroads. They recommended that the two territories be admitted as one state. Senator Beveridge had a sweeping plan for this state, which he called Arizona the Great; it was to be second only to Texas in size, with the capital at Santa Fe.

A joint statehood bill was passed by Congress, with the provision that the citizens of each territory vote on it. If one territory rejected the proposal the joint bill would be dropped. Arizona rejected it by a large majority; in New Mexico the vote was closer, but the joint statehood idea was discarded.

Then in 1910, after the people had framed a constitution, Congress passed a separate statehood bill to admit each territory and presented it to the President for approval. This Enabling Act was signed by President Taft.

At that time there was a great deal of controversy in Congress between conservative Republicans and progressive politicians. The progressives were working for reform of state constitutions to give the people more direct control of their government. Several states had adopted constitutions containing such measures as the initiative and referendum, whereby controversial questions could be put to popular vote. At the same time a measure was proposed for the recall of all state officials by the will of the people. Arizona politicians favored those progressive ideas, and won support for their constitution and for statehood from the progressives in Congress.

The Arizona Constitutional Convention met in the capital city of Phoenix on October 6, 1910. George W. P. Hunt of Globe was chosen for president of the Convention. Groups of politicians, railroad and mining officials, farmers, cattlemen, and some labor leaders joined in the discussions. Progressive political thinking won the day, and the initiative, referendum, and recall were written into the Constitution. Measures were passed providing for employers' liability and protection for workers in hazardous jobs; also, provisions were made for good working conditions for women and children. Woman's suffrage and liquor prohibition were proposed, but were not included.

The Constitution had to be approved by President Taft before a statehood bill could be passed. It was expected that the President, a distinguished judge himself, would veto the document. He joined conservative elements in objection to the clause on the recall of the judiciary by popular vote. He did veto the Constitution, and Arizonans then went to work on a compromise.

The New Mexico Constitution was conservative, so it was accepted without much argument, and the statehood bill was passed. President Taft signed the bill admitting New Mexico as the forty-seventh state on January 6, 1912.

The arguments over liberal constitutions brought Arizona's bid for statehood to national attention. A compromise was reached on the Constitution by a measure excluding the judiciary from recall. The Constitution was then accepted, Congress passed the statehood bill, and President Taft signed it on that memorable Valentine's Day in 1912.

Arizonans flocked to the polls to elect their first state officers. George W. P. Hunt was elected Governor. He had risen to important positions in Globe, after arriving as a poor young man. He was progressive and humanitarian in his ideas and a friend of labor. Sidney P. Osborn, later to become Governor, was elected Secretary of State. Senators elected were Henry Ashurst and Marcus A. Smith. Carl Hayden, son of the popular Charles Trumbull Hayden, was elected to the House of Representatives. Carl Hayden then began his long career of service to the State in the National Congress. He became one of the most influential men of his state and has always been deeply respected in Washington.

The officers and Legislature of the new State settled into the fine new capitol building, called the State House by Governor Hunt which title it has retained. Land-scaping and planting had begun in the State House Park, the park which is now such a beautiful setting for the enlarged capitol of the present time. This building, when statehood began in 1912, was on the outskirts of the small city of Phoenix.

One act of the First State Legislature was to rewrite the article of the Constitution on the recall of state officers, to include the judiciary, and to have this article approved by the people.

An Arizona flag was already in existence. It had been designed in 1910 for the use of the Arizona Rifle Team. This organization competed in national matches with teams from other states, and the members wanted a dis-tinctive banner such as the other teams possessed. General Charles W. Harris, their commander, was asked to design a flag. Arizona's colors were blue and gold, but they had no historical significance. On the other hand, red and gold represented the Spanish flag carried by Coronado and other Spanish explorers in Arizona. So General Harris combined gold, red, and blue to design the flag that flies from every public building in Arizona. It has the setting sun, for a western state, with thirteen rays of alternate gold and red; deep blue forms the lower half of the flag; and a copper star, superimposed on the middle of the flag, represents Arizona's copper wealth.

Carl Hayden, soon to be elected to the National Congress, was a member of the Rifle Team. And Mrs. Hayden was the lady who had the honor of stitching that first flag. In 1912 the Legislature adopted the design for the state banner.

Arizona began state government with the Democratic party in control. Their Democratic Governor, George W. P. Hunt, was re-elected in 1914 and continued to serve as governor, with the exception of brief intervals, until 1932.

When Arizona became a state the nation was seriously concerned with foreign problems due to conditions in Europe where events were leading to the outbreak of World War I. Nearer home, our next-door neighbor, Mexico, was involved in the great Revolution out of which the modern nation of Mexico evolved.

The Mexican Revolution began in 1910 with the overthrow of Porfirio Díaz, who had ruled the country with an iron hand for thirty-four years. The whole country was deep in a terrible struggle for more than ten years.

In that period of the Díaz dictatorship, Mexico advanced with the growth of industries — oil wells, mines, railroads, and great haciendas — that were mostly owned and operated by foreign corporations. Mexicans could not advance to good positions in the foreign-owned industries. The mass of the people lived in poverty and illiteracy. The constitutional republican government established by the Mexican hero, Benito Juarez, was not functioning.

The Revolution soon degenerated into bitter fighting between rival leaders. The oppressed people burst out with the violence of a volcanic eruption. They followed peasant leaders to loot and burn haciendas, to seize towns and railroads. They were demanding land and justice. The United States tried to maintain neutrality, but made some gestures of intervention that were greatly resented.

Arizona borders on the state of Sonora, and from that state came some of the most dynamic revolutionists, among them Alvaro Obregón and Elias Calles. Many refugees from the war crossed into Arizona, while some leaders in exile plotted to aid the Revolution from American towns. When the fighting reached Sonora, the people of border towns had a front row seat to watch the battles. Pancho Villa and his wild cavalry fought the Federal troops of Venustiano Carranza, who had captured the presidency and was trying to rule the whole country.

Battles raged between Federalistas and Villistas in Mexican Nogales, separated from the American town only by a barbed wire fence. Camp Stephen D. Little was located in American Nogales, with infantry troops to guard the border. There were several clashes with Mexicans, at times, even in the American town. Soldiers patroled the whole long boundary line, from Texas to California, to prevent Mexican bands from entering United States territory. Mexican towns changed hands so frequently that Arizonans seldom knew which party was in control.

Pancho Villa and his cavalry fought Federalistas in Naco, across the border from Warren. The people of Douglas witnessed battles being fought a few streets away in Agua Prieta. They often sat on rooftops to watch the excitement. But when bullets flew across the border they took refuge in the houses.

Pancho Villa was a swaggering warrior, but he was careful to keep his soldiers on his side of the border most of the time. The Villistas did make a sneak attack by night on the tiny settlement of Columbus, New Mexico, where U.S. troops were stationed. There was wild fighting in the streets and some buildings were burned before the Villistas were chased back across the border to their own territory. Local people were roused to anger. President Wilson sent General Pershing with a cavalry regiment to take up quarters at Fort Huachuca on the border to demonstrate U.S. strength. By arrangement with Carranza's government, which had been recognized by the United States, General Pershing was permitted to send his cavalry into Mexico to pursue Villa. Carranza's officers, however, did nothing to help Pershing's campaign and it was a discouraging one. Pancho Villa continued his attacks on rival Mexican bands.

At the same time that the Mexican Revolution was raging, the colossal struggle of World War I began in Europe. When the United States declared war, in 1917, to join the Allies, Arizonans responded to the call for men.

The First Arizona Regiment was drafted into the Army, and many men enlisted in the Navy, Marine Corps, and National Guard. Air combat, with bombers and fighters, was used for the first time. In this branch of service Arizona pilots had their share. Frank Luke, Jr., a skilled aviator who had shot down twenty-one aircraft, was forced down behind the lines and killed.

Arizona's economy boomed during the war years because of the great demand for beef, cotton, and copper at high prices. Cattlemen profited, as did the mine owners since 40% of the copper mined in the country came from Arizona. The cotton acreage was increased so much to meet the demand that cotton became the most important agricultural product.

World War I ended in 1918, and the Mexican Revolution had settled into a more or less stable government by 1920. The Border Patrol kept close watch on the desolate miles of desert and mountains between border towns. There was friendship between the inhabitants of Arizona and Sonora, and people traded across the border.

After the war, the National Prohibition Act brought smuggling activity to border towns, and the Border Patrol was kept busy trying to prevent bootleggers from bringing Mexican liquor into Arizona. The young state was too far away to be much affected by the extravagances of the 1920's, and did not suffer so much from the devastating market crash of 1929 as did the industrial sections of the country. The great depression of the early thirties, however, affected Arizona along with the whole country.

Government projects helped many unemployed people. The Civilian Conservation Corps gave work to young men. Local writers were helped through hard times by a branch of the WPA Writers' Project, with its scheme for a series of books on the states. The work of the Arizona writers proved useful for the state since they produced the Arizona volume of the excellent series of American Guides.

By 1940 the "Baby State" was rapidly growing into a vigorous adolescent. Irrigation in the Salt River Valley had increased steadily under the management of the Salt River Valley Water Users Association. Acres upon acres of orange, grapefruit and lemon groves, date palms, alfalfa, lettuce and other vegetables patterned the broad valley. Their lush growth contrasted with the uncultivated desert sections and barren mountains. Farmers had a good market for their crops. Phoenix, as the shipping and business nucleus of Maricopa County, became the chief commercial city of the state, in addition to its position as the capital.

The great demand for fine, long-staple Pima cotton, grown in Arizona soil, made cotton-raising a big business. Huge cotton farms spread over former desert areas in Maricopa County and extended into Pinal and Pima counties. Large scale agriculture brought a new element into the population — migratory workers. They followed the crops, traveling with their families in wornout jalopies. Many Mexican workers were brought across the border by the truck-loads to be hired by farmers. The migratory workers lived in primitive shacks on the cotton and vegetable farms during the season of growing and harvesting.

The lively young state attracted people from many sections of the country who came to seek health in the dry, sunny climate, or to start business. Arizona's climate and unique beauty of arboreal desert and impressive mountains were becoming known. Working cattle ranchers found a new source of income by opening their homes to so-called "dudes." These visitors reveled in trail riding and cowboy picnics around camp fires on the desert, as well as watching the work with cattle.

Artists and writers were drawn by the charm of the country and the easy-going manner of living. They settled in and around Tucson, Phoenix, Wickenburg, and the Oak Creek Canyon country. In Tucson the University advanced as an intellectual center when accomplished professional men, attracted by the climate, joined the faculty. Both the University of Arizona in Tucson and Arizona State College in Tempe experienced a period of growth.

## Chapter XXIX

### Dams for Water and Power

People of Arizona have glorious playgrounds that were created by harnessing rivers to serve the needs of farmers and townsfolk. Vacationing families by the thousands flock to Lake Mead and Hoover Dam in the brilliant summer weather of northern Arizona. Lower down the Colorado are the all-year recreation areas for fishing and camping at Lake Mohave, formed by Davis Dam, and Lake Havasu, formed by Parker Dam.

The rushing, turbulent Colorado of old times is tamed now to bring water and electric power to Arizona, Nevada, and California. Where steamboats once chugged up the unpredictable stream, stopping at sun-dried little ports of adobe buildings, the activities of modern life have come to the river. Highways of Arizona, Nevada, and

California cross the stream over roadways built along the crests of great dams. Power lines hum, and their metal towers stride across miles of country, carrying electric power from the great hydroelectric plants to distant cities. Campers enjoy water sports on sparkling lakes. Irrigation projects in the area around Yuma make oases of green growing crops.

The shining blue waters of Lake Mead wind for miles between mountainous cliffs of vari-colored rock which are the tops of drowned canyons where the Colorado once raged in dangerous rapids. The rocky shores are a changing panorama of color because of the rocks and shifting, brilliant light of sun and cloud shadow. At the head of the lake the muddy old river is forced to drop its burden of silt, sand and gravel to the bottom, creating the clean, clear water that reflects the sky in vivid blue.

Lake Mead is fun, but the guided tour through the complexities of huge Hoover Dam and the great power plant is a revelation of the thought, energy, and engineering skill that built this miracle of construction, machinery, and power. It is easy to take for granted these great works of men's minds and ingenuity that now operate so smoothly for the prosperity and recreation of southwesterners.

The people of the Salt and Gila river valleys do not forget so quickly, for they know that their good life depends on the dams and irrigation systems that make their valleys so fertile and productive. Without those works of man the fields would be reduced to scrubby desert for lack of water, and the old days of drought and flood would return.

After Theodore Roosevelt Dam was completed, with its power plant and great reservoir that conserved water for irrigation systems, the reclamation of the desert valleys continued. Lower down the Salt, Horse Mesa Dam created Apache Lake; and Mormon Flat Dam created Canyon Lake. The Verde River was controled by Horseshoe and Bartlett dams. Coolidge Dam was constructed on the Gila in its upper valley to bring water for irrigation to the fields of the Pima Indian Reservation and to farms of non-Indians.

The Reclamation Act had been signed by President Theodore Roosevelt in 1902, thus creating the Bureau of Reclamation under the Department of the Interior. The engineers realized that the arid lands of the Southwest could not become successfully productive unless the incorrigible Colorado with its tributaries was controled. This river system, the second largest in the United States, has been one of the most destructive rivers in the world. Tributaries flow from Wyoming, Utah, Colorado, and New Mexico to make the main stream that secretes itself for hundreds of miles in deep gorges in Utah and Arizona. The powerful river emerges from the Grand Canyon to form the boundaries between Nevada and Arizona and between Arizona and California. The Colorado River Basin includes seven states — Wyoming, Colorado, Utah, Nevada, New Mexico, Arizona, and California.

Carrying along in its tumultuous course the loose earth, gravel and rock from all its tributaries, the river poured tons of silt every year into its lower reaches during the spring floods.

Farmers irrigated crops in the rich soil left by floods in the Imperial Valley of the Salton Basin in California. Water was diverted from the Colorado into a canal to flow south into Mexico, then to turn back into California. This canal was a joint project of an American and a

Mexican company. It was carried on for some years but was not very successful because river floods spoiled their fields many times.

In 1905 the raging Colorado broke through its levee and poured its whole flow into the Imperial Valley, destroying crops. Its waters filled the dry, salt-covered depression, about 280 feet below sea level, known as the Salton Sink. A shallow body of salt water named the Salton Sea was the result. It was two years before the river was restrained and re-directed by levees.

The Bureau of Reclamation was convinced that these ruinous floods, carrying masses of silt from the tributaries, must be controled by a dam. The rights of all the states drained by the Colorado and its tributaries must be consulted in building that dam. For sixteen years the engineers studied canyons of the Colorado in Utah and Arizona to find a site for a huge dam, strong enough to control the river before it emerged from the canyons in its course to the Gulf of California. They chose two possible sites in the deep gorges between Nevada and Arizona, either Boulder Canyon or Black Canyon.

Arthur Powell Davis, Reclamation Director and Chief Engineer, was the man who conceived the control of the Colorado by a dam of greater height and strength than any that had yet been constructed. Many thought his plan was impossible, that he was an impractical dreamer. He was the nephew of John Wesley Powell, the first man to journey through the canyons, and he continued his uncle's interest in taming the rivers for conservation.

The governors of the seven basin states were called to consultation with the Reclamation Director in 1920. They agreed that a treaty should be framed to provide for an equitable division of the Colorado River water, and commissioners were appointed. These men met in Santa Fe in 1922, with Herbert Hoover, then Secretary of the Interior, as chairman. A treaty was drawn up called the Colorado River Compact, or Santa Fe Compact. By this document the available water was to be apportioned annually between the upper basin and lower basin states, with the point of division at Lee's Ferry. The states of each basin were to be allotted annually 7,500,000 acre feet of the available water. This Compact provided a base for future agreements between the states and for federal legislation to authorize multi-purpose projects. Provision was also made for Mexico's share of water, since the Colorado flows through Mexican territory to enter the Gulf of California.

The Santa Fe Compact was ratified by the legislatures of all the basin states except Arizona, whose lawmakers believed the terms of the contract were unfair to Arizona and would not provide water for future developments. Nevertheless, federal legislation for construction of a dam went ahead with approval of six states. The Boulder Canyon Project Act was passed by Congress and signed by the President on December 21, 1928.

A contract for construction of the dam and power plant was signed with Six Companies, Inc., of San Francisco. The sale of power from the future hydroelectric plant was contracted for with California cities before construction began. Much of the cost to the government of constructing the dam and power plant would be repaid from the sale of power.

The engineers first expected to build the dam in Boulder Canyon, but study of the rock walls proved that Black Canyon had the best geologic structure to support such a mighty dam as the plans called for. It was between the somber walls of Black Canyon that Lieutenant Ives' small steamboat, the *Explorer,* penetrated back in 1858. After his boat was wrecked and he escaped by land, the Lieutenant reported to the government that his party was the first, and doubtless the last, to visit Black Canyon. He predicted that the Colorado River "was destined, through most of its majestic way, to be forever unvisited." How wrong he was!

It was in this appalling gorge that the engineers and construction workers began their labors. Everything about Boulder Dam, as it was named although it was in Black Canyon, was colossal and stupendous. The canyon, between Nevada and Arizona, was in stark desert country of dust, heat, and no roads. Roads must be built for trucking, and a rail line built to transport machinery. Men worked in the canyon depths in furnace heat in a scene of roaring activity. Constantly, nature fought them with heat, dust, cloud bursts, floods, or high winds. Workers were suspended over the cliffs to drill the rocks and place dynamite that blasted masses of rock into the gorge. After building coffer dams and diversion tunnels to turn aside the water, the floor to the canyon was blasted down to bedrock.

Four tall intake towers were built above the dam, and spillways were constructed. When pouring of concrete began, which was mixed in a big plant on the rim, cableways carried huge steel buckets of the mixture into the gorge to fill the great frames in which the concrete was to set. Engineers found they must run aluminum tubing filled with cold water through the mass to control the temperature; otherwise heat generated in the hardening process would be harmful. Throughout the months of terrific labor, the engineers and construction workers struggled with problems they had never met before, and finally succeeded in solving them.

On the Nevada side of the canyon a model town, to house workers and officers of the project, was built in the raw desert wastes. Shops, businesses, modern houses and all other necessities were built according to plan for the 5,000 inhabitants. Boulder City was a neat, orderly town. After the dam was finished and the power plant operating, the town became the home of men and their familes employed in the management of the dam and power plant.

By the summer of 1935, all the concrete was in place and the dam neared completion. In twenty-one months 1,200 men with modern equipment had built a structure half the height of the Empire State building in New York City. It was the highest concrete dam in the world, being 660 feet thick at the base and 45 feet thick at the crest.

The diversion tunnels at each side were blocked, the coffer dams were blown up with a roar, and water began to rise back of the dam. The fierce Colorado was trapped. As the water crept up the canyon, old Fort Callville, where steamboats used to land, was drowned. A prehistoric Indian ruin called the Lost City disappeared under the water. The wild creatures of the canyons scrambled for safety up the walls of the gorges when rising water flooded their homes. Mountain sheep, foxes and coyotes, wild burros, hundreds of small rodents and snakes saved themselves, or were rescued by boatmen from small islands that were the tops of former cliff homes. These little creatures were dumped on the shores of the lake to seek new homes. When Lake Mead was filled it became a new wildlife refuge.

The gigantic project was completed. In September, 1935, President Franklin D. Roosevelt dedicated Boulder

Dam with these words: "This is an engineering victory of the first order — another great achievement of American resourcefulness, skill and determination. This is why I congratulate you who have created Boulder Dam and on behalf of the nation I say to you, 'Well done.'"

In 1936 the huge power plant was completed, and the first generators went into operation. Within the following years other generators were added one by one.

For a long time the name Boulder Dam signified a magnificent achievement in which the people of the Southwest took great pride. Then, in 1947, the name was changed to Hoover Dam to honor Herbert Hoover who had been chairman of the Colorado River Compact Commission.

The National Park Service took over the development and management of the great recreational area around Lake Mead, Hoover Dam, and Boulder City, creating the delightful and informative playground that thousands of Americans now enjoy.

The Yuma Project was started by the building of Laguna Dam on the California side, with the help of the Reclamation Bureau. A siphon carried water under the river to irrigate the Yuma area. The farmers of Imperial Valley then had the help of the Reclamation Bureau in the construction of the All-American Canal which they had been planning after the failure of the American-Mexican Canal. This waterway crossed through desolate sandhills, making it necessary to line it with concrete and face its sides with hard gravel to keep out encroaching sand. It carried water to irrigate the fertile soil of Imperial Valley. The Imperial Dam was built on the Colorado north of Yuma to store water. These two projects were ready for operation in 1941.

California had another big project for using Colorado water. The Metropolitan Water District of California wanted a dam and an aqueduct to transport water across miles of desert to Los Angeles and other southern California cities. A contract was made with the Bureau of Reclamation to buy large amounts of power from the Hoover Dam plant to pay for building Parker Dam. The citizens of Los Angeles voted bonds to pay for the construction of the aqueduct and a reservoir at the California end.

Parker Dam and power plant were built near the town of Parker, Arizona, with a reservoir that created beautiful Havasu Lake. The purpose of the dam was not only to serve as division point for the aqueduct, but to store water and provide power for the Colorado Indian Reservation and the Parker-Gila Project.

It was not until 1944 that Arizona joined her sister states of the Colorado Basin by ratifying the Colorado River Compact. It had been a controversial issue, but gradually the people and legislators realized that Arizona must join the Compact in order to share in the benefits of water from the river. Governor Sidney P. Osborn believed strongly in the necessity for signing the Compact and worked skillfully to bring it about. The Governor also worked for a new water contract with the Colorado River Commission and Secretary of the Interior. It would give Arizona 2,800,000 acre feet of water annually from Lake Mead, plus one half the surplus of Colorado water.

In an historic special session of the Legislature, February 14, 1944, Governor Osborn asked for the ratification of this contract and the Colorado River Compact. He also asked for an appropriation to be used in conjunction with the Bureau of Reclamation in planning future developments of water and power. The contracts were approved and $200,000 voted for the reclamation work.

An editorial in the *Phoenix Gazette* of February 14, 1944, stated: "By joining the sisterhood of river states it would seem that only benefit would accrue. We must act now, not in the next few years, because if we wait the waters of the Colorado will go elsewhere, leaving Arizona only acres and acres of parched desert land that could have been productive."

Arizona joined her sister states in their joint efforts to obtain beneficial use of Colorado water. However, controveries with California over rival claims to the use of water would continue for many years.

After World War II, Davis Dam, in Pyramid Canyon between Nevada and Arizona, was constructed to fill the need for more electric power. It was the fourth largest power installation of the Bureau of Reclamation, designed to relieve power shortages in central and southern Arizona and to pump water for Arizona and California.

The dam was constructed 67 miles below Hoover Dam, and its reservoir backs up to the tail race of the power plant in Black Canyon. Long, slender Lake Mohave, winding between the picturesque walls of several canyons, has become a favored recreation area under the National Park Service. This lake and Lake Havasu back of Parker Dam, with their adjacent towns and camping places, have changed the barren desert and canyon shores of the lower Colorado into vacation spots and wildlife refuges. There are also modern communities with permanent populations.

Down the river near Yuma the Wellton-Mohawk and the Gila Project have utilized the waters of the Colorado and Gila, with canals and pumping stations, to turn acres of desert into productive farms. Small settlements have grown up near the fields.

The untamed Colorado, with its history of floods and destruction, has indeed been harnessed, confined, and put to work to serve the arid lands and power-hungry cities of Arizona, Nevada, and California.

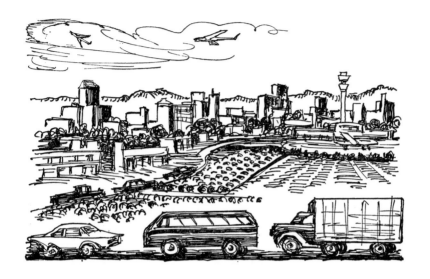

Chapter XXX

A Frontier State Grows Up

(1945 - 1961)

When the Japanese attacked Pearl Harbor on that
fateful day, December 7, 1941, the United States and
many other nations of the world entered a new era of
history, although people did not realize it at the time.
Hitler and Mussolini had begun their steamroller progress across Europe before the United States declared
war after Pearl Harbor, joining Canada, nations of Europe,
and Latin America against the Axis powers.

In that colossal global conflict people of many nations mingled on the battlefields, at Army, Navy, Marine,
and Air Force installations, in distant lands or on islands
in the Pacific Ocean. The whole world was drawn closer
together. Distances were no longer a separation when
aircraft penetrated the most remote regions.

Arizonans joined the nation in the tremendous struggle to preserve freedom. Men and women of the state served in branches of the armed forces in most parts of the globe. Defense industries were established in Arizona, as well as in many other states. The nation was on the move — enlisted men crowding the trains; families traveling to jobs in defense plants; wives and children following their men to training camps whenever possible.

The quietly growing frontier state, Arizona, was thrust into war activities and wartime demands. The state had a strategic location because of proximity to the great aircraft manufactories and other war industries on the Pacific Coast. Ideal flying weather caused a concentration of air training fields to be established in Arizona. Pilots, navigators and crews learned their jobs at many airfields in the vicinity of Phoenix and Tucson. The Davis-Monthan Base, on the outskirts of Tucson, became a bomber base for the training of crews and pilots flying the B-24 and B-29 bombers.

Thousands of soldiers were also trained in the state. There was a gunnery camp at Kingman; companies were trained in desert warfare at Camp Horn near Wickenburg and Camp Huder near Yuma. Many of these men put their training into practice on the battlefields of Italy and North Africa.

Wartime factories were built at Phoenix, such as Goodyear Aircraft, AiResearch Manufacturing, plants for making airplane and tank motors, as well as others. Tucson had the modification plant of Consolidated-Vultee Aircraft Company.

Into the new state, booming from wartime industries and military camps, from the sale of their beef, cotton and copper, came a great migration of people. They came for war jobs, to set up business in town, or to work in mines. Families came to be near the men stationed in military camps.

The State Colleges and University lost hundreds of students to the armed forces, but they carried on steadfastly, helping out with military or air courses and educational programs in home economics and nursing.

Almost overnight Tucson and Phoenix changed into busy cities with more population than they could take care of. Subdivisions sprang up like mushrooms on the outskirts; the schools were overcrowded and short of teachers.

Small Yuma became a lively city due to the military training camps and increased farming on irrigated lands. Every town that was involved in defense work, or was near Army and Air Force camps, was flooded with new people who needed housing and room in the schools for their children.

Winter visitors filled the ranch resorts and hotels because they could not go to Europe for vacations, and Arizona seemed safer than the coastal resorts of California and Florida.

Arizona was changed from a frontier region to a modern state through the influx of people and industries. Many who came for war jobs stayed on, if they could find other work. Some small firms reorganized from defense business and kept going. Air Force personnel remained an important element in the population of southern Arizona. There began a new westward surge of people from the crowded East and Middle West to the wide open spaces of the Southwest.

America was on wheels; and the tremendous increase of automobiles, bus lines, and long distance trucking made necessary the building of good roads. As a result the state acquired an excellent system of highways. Federal highways crossing the state added more traffic to the streams of vehicles on the roads.

The transcontinental railroads, Santa Fe and Southern Pacific, handled rail traffic well, while some branch lines suffered from competition with automobiles and trucks. Travel by air became popular as people took advantage of better plane service to speed up trips across the country.

The handsome Sky Harbor Airport at Phoenix and the Municipal Airport at Tucson saw the coming and going of sleek airliners of transcontinental American and Trans World airlines. A number of regional lines served towns of the state and linked Arizona with neighboring states. There were flying clubs, and some wealthy ranch and resort owners had their landing strips and private planes. The approach of the jet age in air travel caused extra long runways to be built at the Tucson and Phoenix airports. In 1960, service by jet liners began, and arrangements were made for Aeronaves de Mexico to land planes at Tucson, thus giving that airport an international status. Service with Aeronaves began in the summer of 1961. Planes of the Civil Air Patrol (CAP) were carrying on their good work of search and rescue. Squadrons of the Strategic Air Command, stationed at Davis-Monthan Base, added the whoosh and roar of jet bombers and fighters to the flight of planes across Arizona skies.

The constant stream of transcontinental travel on the highways gave a big boost to the motel industry. Approaches to the leading cities were lined with neon-lighted motels, ranging from simple cottages to gaudy establishments with restaurants and swimming pools. Visitors and home-seekers sought out lovely Oak Creek Canyon and Sedona, below the rose-and-cream-colored cliffs. Wickenburg became the center of a guest ranch country, while wealthy winter visitors found entertainment, swimming pools and every luxury in the environs of Phoenix and Tucson.

During the post-war years, colleges and universities all over the country received a stimulus and added enrollment from the hundreds of young men returned from war who were anxious to continue their education by the help of the G. I. Bill of Rights. Arizona colleges had their share as every campus overflowed with G. I.'s and their families. College work became a family affair; children were a part of campus life. War surplus buildings, particularly Quonset huts, were set up on or near each campus to accommodate the young families. These G. I. students were mature young men who knew what they wanted, who were determined to advance in their chosen business or profession by further study. Their interests and work raised the caliber of instruction. Sometimes the wives were also taking courses or were working to help the family income, unless they were tending babies.

As the number of G. I. students diminished, a new flood of college-age young people swamped the institutions, raising the enrollment between 1950 and 1960 to phenomenal heights.

The Teachers Colleges in Flagstaff and Tempe had grown to the point where their leaders petitioned the Legislature, in 1945, to authorize them as multi-purpose state colleges rather than strictly teacher institutions. This bill was passed and the schools became Arizona State College in Tempe and Arizona State College in Flagstaff.

Arizona State College in Tempe expanded rapidly in enrollment because the young people of Maricopa County, which is heavily populated, preferred college education near home. New courses and departments were added; new buildings of excellent design enlarged the campus. In 1954 the Board of Regents granted the college a university-type of organization, and five colleges were established. Dr. Grady Gammage, the dynamic president, guided the development toward university status, and in 1959 the Board of Regents granted his request for a change of name to Arizona State University. This was confirmed by popular vote on an initiative proposition. Arizona State University reached an enrollment of more than 11,000 students. After Dr. Gammage's death in 1960, Dr. G. Homer Durham, his successor in the presidency, became the director of the vigorous, expanding State University.

At the University of Arizona a constant building program attempted to keep up with the need for more dormitories, classrooms and other new buildings to accommodate various colleges and departments. U of A extended beyond the campus in every direction. Enrollment of students increased from 6,044 in 1950 to 12,500 in the season of 1959-60. Foreign students, who have come year by year from many countries for special studies, increased in numbers and profited from their association with American university work.

This modern University, under the presidency of Dr. Richard A. Harvill, has ten colleges and many departments. From the beginning, the institution has served the state with research and experiment in agriculture, irrigation, soil study, animal husbandry; and in the fields of geology, mining, and engineering. The departments of archeology and anthropology have high reputations. Dr. Douglass' tree-ring research developed into the science of dendrochronology. Part of the work is the dating of prehistoric wood by tree-ring analysis or radio carbon dating. The Colleges of Law and Engineering are outstanding. Programs of research and experiment, sponsored by grants from foundations or individuals, have brought distinguished specialists to join the staff.

The expanding State College in Flagstaff has also felt the demand by more young people for college education. New courses and departments have been added, and a building program is under way. Dr. Lacy A. Eastburn guided the growing college as president from 1947 to 1957, when he died. Dr. J. Lawrence Walkup, who was dean of the college at that time, took over as acting president until the Board of Regents appointed him to the post.

A worthwhile school, The American Institute for Foreign Trade, was founded in Glendale after World War II. It is co-educational; its purpose is to train young men and their wives for commercial positions, banking or other jobs in foreign lands, with special emphasis on Latin America. Priority is given to study of the language and culture of each nation, so that those who live and work in foreign countries may fit in better with the national life around them.

Phoenix Junior College, Grand Canyon College, and Eastern Arizona College, in Thatcher, fill part of the need for junior colleges. The state's excellent public school system has been stretched to the limit to accommodate the hundreds of pupils brought to most cities by new population.

Maricopa County, once concerned chiefly with agriculture, cattle, and tourists, has become the industrial center of the state. Manufacturing plants extend into the county from the environs of Phoenix, which has become a bustling commercial metropolis. In 1959 it was rated the most important city in the three desert states of Nevada, New Mexico, and Arizona. Housing developments spread out in every direction to satisfy the demands of increasing numbers of families for homes. Various branches of the electronics industry lead the way in manufacturing, and there are plants, large and small, making aircraft parts and equipment, tools, and dies. Phoenix is also the shipping center for the agricultural products of vast fields of lettuce and other vegetables, citrus and dates.

In the capitol building the governors, state officers, and the Legislature have managed the politics of the young state. Arizona began statehood with the Democratic party in power and continued to be predominantly Democratic for some time. In recent years the Republican party has gained strength and there have been several Republican governors.

Arizona has gained important standing in national political affairs. Senator Carl Hayden, a Democrat, has served in the National Congress since statehood. He served first in the House, then in the Senate, and at present is the dean of the Senate, a quiet man of powerful influence. In 1960, Stewart L. Udall, member of an important pioneer family and a Democrat, became Secretary of the Interior. He is the first Arizonan to hold a Cabinet post. Senator Barry Goldwater is the conservative Republican leader in the state.

Tucson, the other important city of the state, owes

part of its rapid growth to the increase in the number of firms engaged in manufacture and research for various branches of electronics. There is also a large company engaged in aircraft design, electronics, and manufacture of missiles. As resort centers, both Tucson and Phoenix have a fashion industry with a southwestern flare in the design of dresses, frontier pants and other varieties of southwestern garb.

Although manufacturing has reached first place in the state's economy, the basic resources remain the most important assets — cattle, cotton, and copper. The cattle business is modern and efficient; cattle shows and auctions are part of the year's work. Quarter horse shows also attract many devoted horse breeders. Racing of a professional variety is as popular as the oldtime racing of horses in the streets. The stocky, square-built Herefords, excellent beef cattle, are prepared for market in the fattening pens and pastures of Maricopa County and Continental, south of Tucson. Phoenix has stockyards and slaughter houses.

The cotton industry is the largest source of agricultural income, and Arizona ranks fifth among the cotton-growing states of the nation. Irrigation, an ideal climate, and the scientific study carried on in all branches of cotton-raising give this state an average yield of 2½ bales per acre, more than the average in other cotton-growing states. Arizona leads in the production of the high quality, long staple SUPima cotton. Scientific research and experiment, in collaboration with the agricultural specialists of The University of Arizona, has brought the cotton industry to the highest level of production and profit.

In Maricopa, Pinal, and Pima counties cotton-raising is big business. The owners of vast acreages do not live on the farms, but in nearby cities or out of the state. Tenant farmers or managers are hired to direct the processes of growing and harvesting the crops. Arizona's large scale agricultural work has become increasingly mechanized. Cotton-picking machines replace workers to a great extent in harvesting. At the gins, the cotton is processed and baled for market by machinery. Machines also do much of the cotton cultivating and are used in the great fields of vegetables and grains.

For this reason the migrant population in the cotton towns and on the farms has greatly diminished. The central towns of the cotton region — Eloy, Casa Grande, and Coolidge — have grown in stability from a more permanent population.

Next to cotton comes copper, for Arizona is still the Copper State. There may be good years or bad years, but the great demand for copper, used in numberless ways and essential to all kinds of industries, keeps the mines operating successfully.

The great open pit copper mines are the most interesting operations to study. Modern technology, chemical knowledge, and powerful machinery make it possible to extract copper and other minerals, such as gold and silver, from low grade ore that could not be used in former times. When a whole mountainside has been drilled, blasted, and cut by machines into terraces, the huge pit is a sculptured structure that resembles a giant sports arena. The machines working on terraces and the huge shovels gobbling rock to be dumped into ore cars look small in the pit.

The ore cars are hauled to the mill at headquarters. There the rock is crushed to a powder and the copper is concentrated in tanks by a process called flotation.

The concentrate must be sent to a smelter to be reduced to metal. Various processes in the smelter furnace melt the concentrate; the impure elements are separated to become slag, and the copper is poured off.

Metal is formed into copper anode sheets that are sent to a refinery for finishing. By electrolytic processes the pure copper is separated by one method, and the gold or silver is recovered by another process. Most Arizona companies send their copper to eastern refineries, but Phelps Dodge owns a refinery at El Paso where copper from their mines is refined.

Phelps Dodge is the largest of the mining companies that have great influence in the state. Since the old days of the Copper Queen, this company has become chief producer of copper in the Bisbee area. The large open pit mine, Lavender Pit, changed the landscape between Bisbee and Warren when the hills were gouged out. Householders of the region had to settle in the growing towns of Lowell and Warren. Phelps Dodge also operates the old Morenci mine in the eastern mountains. At Ajo, in the western desert, Phelps Dodge took over the New Cornelia Copper Company. It had been a prosperous mine, built up by John C. Greenway who was an influential citizen in the early years of the young state. The New Cornelia became a huge open pit operation with mill and smelter. An attractive, up-to-date company town is near the mine.

Near Superior, the Inspiration, the Miami, and the Magma mines grew out of the old mines in the region and are still producing. The Magma is a deep underground copper mine. The Magma Company also owns and operates the San Manuel Copper Mine north of Tucson. Old claims were bought and developed with the help of the

U. S. Bureau of Mines. By degrees the mine came into operation, with a mill and smelter. On a hill near the mine the company built the brand-new town of San Manuel to house the employees.

The Kennecott Company has a large open pit mine and mill at Ray, with a smelter at the nearby town of Hayden. To the west and southwest of Tucson other companies operate the Silver Bell, Pima, Duval, Banner, and other mines.

In Arizona copper mining employs 11,000 men, as shown by 1959 figures, while copper mining in all other states together employs only 22,000. The money value in the state, according to 1959 figures, shows that the large companies produced metals worth $260,000,000, and the small ones produced $58,000,000.

Gold and silver are recovered in the process of copper refining; lead and zinc mines are profitable, and there are some quantities of other minerals such as asbestos, tungsten, molybdenum, and uranium.

Instead of working with pick and shovel, modern prospectors take to the hills with Geiger counters to crawl over the rocks, scouting for uranium. There is a uranium mine on the Navajo Reservation, with a mill for processing at Tuba City. Prospectors are hopeful they will turn up other deposits of the valuable mineral.

Arizona's forests have been a resource exploited by lumber companies in the northern part of the state. Timber is now to be used in a new way by the Southwest Forest Industries, Inc., operators of mills at Flagstaff and McNary. This company is building a paper mill near Snowflake to produce newsprint and kraft paper. The company hired hydrologists to search for adequate water supply, and it was found from an underground lake. As timber is cut, the cropped areas will be planted with seed-lings and left to grow so the forest reserves will not be depleted. The mill may employ several hundred men and will bring business to the quiet small settlements of McNary, Snowflake, and Show Low.

The great changes brought about by the influx of population and industry have affected most parts of the state. Yet, in the small cities and towns and the spacious countryside, the flavor of living is still that of the easy-going and friendly southwesterner.

Only the two big cities, Phoenix and Tucson, have become so metropolitan, with such a mixture of people from all over the country, that they have lost much of the intimate, southwestern charm. To balance that, the great number of professional people who have chosen the cities for home make them the cultural centers of the state.

Music was the first cultural delight for Arizonans, and as the two cities grew they maintained symphony or-chestras and other musical organizations. Each city has a lively winter season of music, with the symphonies and other groups. The two universities have Artist Series for students, faculty, and the public, bringing to the commu-nities outstanding musicians and ballet companies. Lit-tle theater groups are important, and there are visits from orchestras of national reputation. Painters, sculptors, and craftsmen form active groups in Phoenix, Scottsdale, and Tucson, enhancing the winter season with one-man shows and exhibitions in the galleries.

Tucson maintains close relations with the neighbor state of Sonora in Mexico, through trade, shopping and visitors. Sonora and Arizona join in the Arizona-Sonora Desert Museum, located in the foothills of the Tucson Mountains. This is a living museum that preserves, studies, and displays the wildlife and vegetation of the great Sonoran desert region that belongs to both Arizona and Sonora.

There is stimulating cooperation between The University of Sonora in Hermosillo and The University of Arizona in Tucson. Through exchange programs of dance and theatrical groups, through lectures and music, young college people of two neighbor nations create a friendly spirit of understanding.

Out of a dramatic, turbulent past Arizona has grown into a modern state. In this process there has been an intermingling of people differing in nationality, culture, and customs. They are the Indians; those of Spanish or Mexican origin; many Europeans; Negroes; Chinese; and Japanese; all welded into the modern civilization of the United States by the dominant Anglo-Americans.

Once this section of the Southwest was rather inaccessible and little-known. In the East many people believed that Arizona was inhabited chiefly by Indians, cowboys, and gun-toting bad men. That time is past and Arizona has been thoroughly discovered. While cherishing with pride their stirring history, Arizonans are now contributing their special talents and resources to the advancement of national life.

Chapter XXXI

The Spectacular North Country

The powerful Colorado River has become the center
of attention in northern Arizona, as it was in past years
along its lower course. Snaking in zigzags down through
the carved and colored rock country of southern Utah,
between the walls of Glen Canyon, the Colorado is joined
by the San Juan River before it enters Arizona. These
canyons had a history, but it was known mostly to specialists until the Bureau of Reclamation studied this section
of the upper Colorado River basin as part of their Colorado River Storage Project.

Their plan was to construct dams to control the
water of the upper basin system, create storage reservoirs,
and obtain hydroelectric power. De-silting works were
also necessary to catch some of the tons of earth and

313

gravel the mighty Colorado pours into Lake Mead. Engineers reckoned that in the course of some years silt
would clog Lake Mead, damage Hoover, and other works
on the river.

The winding miles of Glen Canyon, with enchanting
secluded side gorges, had long been the cherished field
for exploration by archeologists, geologists, naturalists,
and adventurous lovers of the wildnerness. For years
rivermen in special boats have taken voyagers from the
San Juan in Utah through Glen Canyon to Lee's Ferry.
The canyons cut through a wide, lonely land, arid and
rocky, inhabited by few people other than wandering
Navajos with their flocks.

Major John Wesley Powell's boat expeditions came
through the twisting gorges of Glen Canyon. He described them for future explorers, besides giving Glen
Canyon its name. Some prospectors and miners searched
for gold and started mines in the gorges, and various
archeologists explored the cliffs and discovered ruins.

Then, in mid-twentieth century, this paradise of
scientists and explorers was invaded by engineers of the
Bureau of Reclamation. They chose a dam site in a
narrow gorge of Glen Canyon about twelve miles below
the Utah border in Arizona, a spot inaccessible except
by an old desert road. There was a good approach, however, by paved highway 89, running north from Flagstaff
to cross the Colorado on Navajo Bridge.

The Colorado River forms part of the northern border
of the Navajo Reservation, and the San Juan River continues along the border of the Reservation as far as Montezuma Creek. A section of the future reservoir would
be on Navajo land, as would the area for the construction
town that was to built. After discussion with the Navajo

Tribal Council, conducted on both sides with respect and consideration, the Navajos were offered by the Bureau of Reclamation an equal area of federal land adjacent to their Reservation in exchange for the land needed for the Glen Canyon Project. They chose the McCracken Mesa area in southern Utah, and Congress passed an act legalizing the exchange in 1958.

When the engineers and road builders began work to reach the site of Glen Canyon dam, Flagstaff profited as the nearest railhead. The work brought business and population to the town and to the whole northern area. A new paved road was built from highway 89 straight through the tall Echo Cliffs and on over the shimmering, empty country of strange shapes and colors to the site. Trucks brought heavy machinery, the gorge was studied, and blasting of the canyon walls and floor began.

It is a matter of history how the Colorado was put to work for multiple purposes by the building of gigantic Hoover Dam. Now people of the 1960's may see a similar colossal project of engineering going on at Glen Canyon.

Huge cranes and trucks, buildings for construction work, power lines, towers that support powerful cable-ways are clustered on the canyon rim. They create a busy scene of man's ingenuity and technology engaged in the conquest of a river.

Standing at lookout points on the rim, visitors can see, far below, tiny figures of men and machines at work on the canyon floor, where huge frames are being filled with concrete to construct the dam. Below this area, where Colorado water is rushing through diversion tunnels into the stream, it is a river of yellow-green, muddy water, twisting and rolling between the perpendicular walls of rough, dark red sandstone.

The graceful arch of the new steel bridge spans the canyon 700 feet above the river. On this bridge traffic is crossing into Utah. The bridge is the highest and second longest steel-arch bridge in the United States.

The Colorado and its tributaries gouged their course deeper and deeper through the sandstone plains in prehistoric ages. The result is that the river is far below surface level and cannot be seen until the canyon rim is reached. From higher ground it is difficult to follow the corkscrew windings of the gorges across the rumpled surfaces of rock. The river and its canyons are dwarfed by the immensity of the country.

On a windswept mesa near the dam, the town of Page was built to house the construction workers and engineers, just as Boulder City was built during the construction of Hoover Dam. The first contingent of men and their families lived in house trailers that are still a part of the community. Within four years Page grew into a small town of energetic families, some of whom have acquired nice small houses with patches of green lawn. The people have all the household conveniences, a community swimming pool (in the desert), a school for their children, markets for food. After a while they may even acquire a few trees to shade the barren desert surroundings from the blazing sun.

Glen Canyon Dam was authorized by Congress in 1956, and work began in 1957. It is hoped that the dam and hydroelectric plant will be finished sometime in 1964. This power plant, with eight generators and a capacity of 900,000 kilowatts, will furnish needed power for intermountain states — Utah, Colorado, New Mexico, and Arizona.

The dam will be 700 feet high from bedrock, second

only to the height of Hoover Dam, and will have a length across the top of 1,550 feet. Millions of tons of concrete will be used to build the colossal structure. From a cement plant at Clarkdale, Arizona, 188 miles away, monstrous trucks travel constantly, bringing cement to the dam. Other materials used in making concrete are quarried near the site. A concrete mixing plant, twenty stories high, has been built on the rim of the canyon against the cliff. The mixed concrete is swung by cable from the plant in huge steel buckets to be poured into the great frames. The mixing process generates so much heat that chipped ice, from a refrigerating plant, is used instead of water. While the concrete is setting, great heat is generated, so aluminum tubing filled with ice water is run through the mass to keep the temperature right.

Glen Canyon Dam is the key structure of four dams being built by the Colorado River Storage Project to store waters of the upper Colorado River system. Thus the flow can be regulated to give a more even distribution of water, annually, to the upper basin states. The other projects are the dam and power house at Flaming Gorge on the Green River near Wyoming, Curecanti Dam on the Gunnison River in Utah, and Navajo Dam on the San Juan River. This last is planned to divert water for Navajo irrigation projects in New Mexico. Bridge Canyon Dam is another project, still in the future, to be built below the Grand Canyon gorges.

When the solid walls of Glen Canyon Dam are completed, the frustrated river will be forced back to fill the gorges behind it, creating a huge reservoir to be named Lake Powell for the first explorer to go through these canyons. The water will drown out the small side gorges. It is expected that the lake will filter through the twists of the canyons for 186 miles on the Colorado River and for 70 miles on the San Juan River.

No longer will boat travelers look up from the river to towering cliffs. They will swish in power launches over a blue lake, rimmed with tawny rock forms. They will have camping, fishing and boating under the direction of the National Park Service. The vast, silent country will be invaded by people and their activities, but they will all be dwarfed by its spaciousness.

A wilderness of beauty and secret gorges will be lost, together with remains of prehistoric Indian life. To anthropologists and those who cherish the rare quality of this primitive region, the drowning of the canyons seems a great loss to America. Many people with energetic, adventurous spirits and the necessary finances have visited the canyons by boat and marveled at them; many more would have done so in the future. But when the lake is filled and recreation facilities built, hundreds of Americans will visit this spectacular region of their country.

To study the canyons and their history before they were flooded and their history lost, the Upper Colorado River Basin Salvage Program was inaugurated by Congress. Contracts were made by the National Parks Service with the University of Utah and the Museum of Northern Arizona for the exploration and study of geology, historic sites, and prehistoric life in Glen Canyon. Teams of archeologists, geologists, and historians of the two institutions cooperated in the project. The University of Utah worked in upper Glen Canyon and areas north of the San Juan, while the Museum of Northern Arizona took over lower Glen Canyon, the San Juan canyons, and areas south of it.

These teams have collected most interesting facts

about past life in this region. Evidently, during prehistoric ages, the steep-walled canyons and barren mesas were populated by bands of primitive Indians who were undaunted by the desolation and difficulties of the country. They cut toe-holds in solid rock of cliff walls to reach the river and find places to ford it. In caves, or on ledges, the people built shelters of various kinds, sometimes cliff houses of stone in caves, sometimes half circle rooms of great boulders set against the protection of a rock wall. A few ruins of stone buildings of the Pueblo type have been noticed by all river travelers. On the mesas above the canyons, ruins of settlements have been found. There are petroglyphs or drawings pecked out on boulders in many places.

Archeologists believe that these primitive inhabitants were of the same racial group as the Anasazi who, in the course of centuries, built pueblo towns and cliff dwellings in New Mexico and Arizona. In historic times Navajos have known this whole region.

Some of these ruins had been investigated in past years by archeologists, but no real study was made of them. When the experts of the Glen Canyon Project finish their work, they will have added a new page to the story of prehistoric life in the Southwest.

Archeology in Arizona is not confined to books, college courses, or exhibits in museums. It is a living thing. Experts are continually exploring ruins of settlements and working on the historical salvage programs. Wherever federal lands are being plowed up by bulldozers for the construction of highways, dams, or pipe lines, archeologists search for prehistoric artifacts.

At Glen Canyon, the historical survey carried on by these teams will also preserve a record of man's activities in the deep-walled canyons after the river explorations made by Major John Wesley Powell, in 1869 and 1870.

In the Utah section of the canyons there is a landmark noted by all travelers on the river — a great cleft in the canyon wall called Hole-in-the-Rock. There is a story connected with this strange cleft in the rock, the story of an incredible journey made by a group of dedicated Mormons.

They were sent by the Mormon Church to found a mission in the region of the San Juan River, now called the Four Corners country — where Colorado, Utah, Arizona, and New Mexico meet. At that time it was almost uninhabited country. Their scouts had decided that the shortest route for such a big company was to cross the Colorado at Hole-in-the-Rock and continue across the barren wilderness.

Late in 1879, the pioneers with wagons, families, and livestock assembled on the canyon rim in wintry weather. Bit by bit, with exhausting labor, the men drilled and blasted the rock walls of the cleft to make it wide enough for wagons to pass. Another group of men transported timbers over miles of desert, slid them down the cliffs and constructed a barge to ferry the wagons across the river.

In January, 1880, they were ready to try the descent through Hole-in-the-Rock. The men braked the first wagon by locking the back wheels with chains. Ropes and chains were attached to wagon gear by which ten or more men could hold back with all their strength at the rear to slow the wagon as it went over the brink. The descent through the slit was "as steep as the roof of a house," one woman wrote later.

With the driver in the seat, reining in the horses, the frightened animals were urged over the edge — and down the wagon went! It scraped the rock walls, the horses slid on their haunches, avalanches of sand hit the wagon, then it skidded over slick rock.

When the first wagon came through without disaster, the work went forward steadily. Every wagon and its team, though battered and splintered, was brought through the steep descent to the river's edge. Some women and children rode in the wagons, others walked down the steep trail. Cattle also were driven down through the slit and urged to swim across the river, while the wagons were ferried across on the barge.

Then these brave people continued their journey over a stark country of huge masses of sandstone, of buttes and mesas. The men had to cut a trail for the wagons through solid rock much of the way. The journey took six months, but the indomitable people came, at last, to their chosen site on the San Juan.

The terrible Hole-in-the-Rock trail was used by several companies going to the San Juan settlement until after 1881, when a better crossing was found. Hole-in-the-Rock will be mostly under water when the reservoir fills. The historic Crossing of the Fathers will also be gone.

After the Mormon pioneers came the prospectors, in the 1890's, following rumors of rich gold and silver in the region. They explored the canyons, climbed the walls, washed gold from gravel bars in the stream bed. The gold was difficult to recover and required panning, sluicing, or dredging to make mining a success. Supplies and machinery were brought in over miles of desert, then transported to claims by any kind of boat available. A man named Stanton tried a scheme for dredging the canyon. His machinery was hauled in from a great distance, and for some time the dredge was operated and recovered gold, but the cost of operation made the scheme unprofitable. Mining activity led to the making of rough roads into the river country from Gallup and Flagstaff.

Modern explorers have found the remains of miners' huts and rusted machinery on ledges or in quiet coves. Stanton's rusted dredge still stands in the river. All these relics of an unsuccessful gold rush will be drowned by the flooding of the canyons, but the history will be preserved in the reports of the historical teams. Thanks to the men of the salvage program, new information is being added to the story of Arizona in this interesting northern country.

In Arizona, the Glen Canyon study is concentrated at the Research Center of the Museum of Northern Arizona. Here, every summer professional people and graduate students in the fields of anthropology, paleontology, geology, or botany are at work on their study projects of the region. Young men set off on field trips to their special areas and return with their findings. Some of them are busy all summer with the Glen Canyon surveys.

The delightful Northern Museum was founded in 1928 by Dr. Harold S. Colton, to further the study by himself and others on the prehistoric Indian life of the northern plateau and the geologic history of the region. Dr. Colton and his wife added to these projects their interest in the contemporary Hopi and Navajo people, who have always been closely associated with the Museum.

Young people of scientific bent, intellectual curiosity, and love of the great outdoors, find opportunities in this northern region to advance in their fields, whether it be the study of Indian life and arts, geology, archeology, or forestry.

The Rocky Mountain Forest and Range Station of the U. S. Forest Service maintains an experiment station in the woodlands for their work with the ponderosa pine, Douglas fir, spruce, aspen, and other trees of the great northern forests. There is a School of Forestry at the State College in Flagstaff where young men are trained in branches of forestry or lumbering.

Hidden away on wooded hilltops near Flagstaff, the Naval Observatory and the well-known Lowell Observatory have busy programs of astronomical research. Lowell Observatory, founded by Dr. Percival Lowell, became famous for the study of the planet Mars in particular, in addition to study of the other planets in the solar system. Dr. Lowell's work was carried on by Dr. E. C. Slipher who had been his assistant for some years. Dr. John H. Hall is now director of the Observatory.

Lowell Observatory owns six telescopes of different types for their special studies. In 1961 a very large and unusual telescope will be moved to Flagstaff by agreement between Ohio State University, Ohio Wesleyan University, and Lowell Observatory. This Perkins 69-inch reflecting telescope, fifth largest in the United States, will be a more effective instrument for research in the high altitude and clear nights of Flagstaff. In Ohio the atmosphere is denser, and there is interference from city lights. Astronomers of the Perkins Observatory, home of the large telescope, will share observations and research through the instrument with the staff of Lowell Observatory. A special observatory to house the big telescope is being constructed on Anderson Mesa, eleven miles southeast of Flagstaff, at an altitude of 7,250 feet.

Scientific and engineering projects are carried on in a region of beauty and variety. The country is popular with people of the state and with hundreds of visitors who come every year. From the world-famous Grand Canyon, the pine forests and volcanic mountains, to the strangely alluring desert land of the Hopi and Navajo people, nature puts on a rare show. In addition, there is the heritage of the past in prehistoric Indian dwellings preserved as National Monuments. They form a background for the busy activities of modern Arizonans in the north country.

Chapter XXXII

Changing Life for Indian Citizens

The original inhabitants of the Southwest, the Indians,
mingle with the daily life in towns, on farms, and ranches
in Arizona and New Mexico, though most of the people
have their homes on reservations, or in the Indian villages
of New Mexico. Quiet in manner, very brief in speech,
Indian men work at jobs in Arizona towns, on the railroads, in industries, and on cotton farms. They are forced
to do this because farming or sheep and cattle-raising on
the reservations cannot support all the people. Except
for their features and heavy black hair these members of
the working population look much like other Americans,
for Indian men have adopted the usual southwestern outfit of blue jeans, shirt and cowboy hat.

Arizonans do not learn much about their Indian fellow

325

citizens from these slight contacts in shops or other jobs, but people who live near any of the reservations are often well-acquainted with them. These white people understand something of Indian character and ways of thought, so different from that of non-Indian; they sympathize with Indian problems and have glimpses of home life on the reservations.

Indian ways are changing rapidly from the pressures of adjustment to the American type of civilization around them. It may be that the old-time habitations and picturesque customs, still held dear by some of the tribes, will eventually disappear.

Work in towns, with money in wages, brings change to Indian ideas. The young people become acquainted with American comforts and gadgets. Money brings them American dresses, shoes, and shirts. The girls adopt the latest fashion in hair arrangement. Young Indians visiting in towns are just as fond of soft drinks, chewing gum, and movies as their non-Indian companions. Money brings the women new stoves, pots and pans. These new possessions filter into Navajo hogans, or Apache wickiups, or the old stone houses of the Hopi. Even radios, sewing machines, and refrigerators have been adopted in some homes. For the men, money from jobs means a pickup truck or an automobile to take the place of the slown, horse-drawn wagon.

To most people, Indians of the Southwest are best known by their beautiful crafts. These native artists were first recognized and encouraged by artists, anthropologists, and some wise traders of the trading posts on reservations. Now the Indian arts are nationally known and appreciated. Every craft and curio shop in Arizona cities has displays of silver and turquoise jewelry, rugs, and baskets. Some of the work has been commercialized, but the dealers who handle only the best work in design and authenticity keep up the standard for the native artists. Some of the craftsmen work at their specialty in the shops selling Indian crafts. Fortunately the sale of their handiwork brings money to the craftsmen to help out on living expenses.

Indian painters, having learned to handle water colors and brushes, have won a reputation for their delightful decorative pictures that represent the costumed dances, the birds, animals, and symbolic designs of their Indian world. They have discovered, however, that they cannot support themselves by painting — a fact well known to many non-Indian artists.

For years past people, with an interest in Indian cultures and ceremonies, have journeyed to the Pueblo villages in New Mexico, or the Hopi mesas in Arizona to see the ceremonial dances of rhythm, chant, and gorgeous costumes. These dances have had great religious significance to the tribes for hundreds of years.

As interest grew throughout the Southwest in these unique ceremonials, businessmen of two towns undertook to organize annual celebrations, to bring visitors to the towns, and to gather Indian tribes for the mutual profit of townsfolk and Indians.

The Gallup Ceremonials, organized by businessmen of Gallup, New Mexico, is an event that brings a gathering of tribes from all over the West for several days in August. Craftsmen exhibit their best work, encouraged by awards of ribbons and many sales. Indian rodeos in the afternoons and ceremonial dances at night by the light of huge bonfires are exciting. During the Ceremonials, the town is jammed with people. The affair has become rather commercialized, but it is a big trade fair and is as well a time of entertainment for Indians and non-Indians.

Flagstaff, Arizona, has always been close to Indian life, since the reservations of the Hopi and Navajos are close by. The Pow Wow, the colorful and thoroughly Indian celebration, grew from an invitation from town leaders some years ago to come and enjoy the Fourth of July with the townsfolk. The Indians were offered free food, games, and dances. From these early celebrations grew the Pow Wow, which is attended every year by hundreds of Navajos, Hopis, Apaches, Pueblos of New Mexico, and even Cheyennes from the plains.

The town is theirs during the three days of the festival. Indian fires burn all night under the pines in the great grove where they camp, as the people visit and sing together. In the daytime, between events, the people display their baskets, rugs, and jewelry at booths near the camp ground, or families shop at the town supermarkets and department stores, buying the same sort of things other Americans want. They enjoy with gusto all the whirligig devices of the Carnival Show, set up close by the rodeo grounds.

Each morning there is a gay parade, bright with color and music; each afternoon Indian cowboys compete in a wild rodeo; and at night the ceremonial dances are given in the rodeo arena. Seen in the flickering blaze of fragrant pine log bonfires, the spectators are drawn into the vivid dancing by the chanting and the rhythmic beat of drums.

In southern Arizona, the desert-dwelling Papagos have an annual harvest festival in their own style, organized by the tribe with the help of Indian Service officers. In the headquarters building in Sells the people display products of their desert farms — beans, pumpkins, wheat, and corn; also displayed, are the beautiful baskets woven by the women, and tasty jam made from the fruit of saguaro cactus. Young and old enjoy carnival sports, Indian food, and Anglo soft drinks sold at booths. Horses and cattle are tried out in a spirited Indian rodeo, with cowboys from various tribes joining the Papagos. The women teams from the different villages compete in the exciting game of taka, which is comparable to the game of hockey. The evening is spent in a lively dance for cowboys and young folks.

Another annual event of great interest is the Navajo Tribal Fair that takes place in September in Window Rock, the Navajo Reservation headquarters in Arizona. This is a tribal enterprise that has grown from year to year. People come from all over the huge Reservation to have a social time, to trade their crafts, and to display cowboy skill in rodeos. The ferris wheel and games of chance attract all comers.

The quiet, happy Indian crowds that stream through the fair grounds, in and out of exhibition halls, create a scene of vivid color with the picturesque costumes of the more conservative people. Each person is decked with a wealth of silver and turquoise jewelry. Many young people show the changing ways of life in their dress; girls with dress and hair arrangement like any other American girls; and Navajo horsemen, cavorting on their rodeo ponies, wear the orthodox rodeo costume of bright satin shirts and big hats.

Navajo families enjoy camping on the hills around Window Rock, visiting around supper fires, sleeping on the ground or in pickup trucks or wagons. They trade with each other, and dicker with white traders who are buying rugs and jewelry for their shops.

The exhibition halls show the great advances made

by these intelligent people from their past life as a pastoral tribe herding sheep or growing small patches of corn. They now have a tribal organization that maintains a saw-mill and lumber industry. Tribal funds are spent to drill wells for watering stock and to build paved roads, re-placing desert trails over the miles of their Reservation. The Tribal Council also built and maintains a motel for visitors at Window Rock and one at Shiprock, New Mexico. The Council has completed the first tribal park at Monu-ment Valley on the Utah border, called Monument Valley Navajo Tribal Park. Window Rock now has a 7,000-foot paved runway for the landing of small planes that transport supplies around the Reservation, or carry officials and other visitors. CAP planes do search and rescue work over the Reservation, using a few runways to land on.

This display of tribal advancement at Window Rock points up the changes in reservation life for the Indians since the Indian Reorganization Act was passed by Con-gress in 1934.

In territorial days, after the Indian wars were over, the tribes were settled on lands set aside by the U.S. Government as their reservations. The Indian people were wards of the government, under the administration of the Indian Service. There were years of changing policies by the Indian Service, mistakes in plans for the Indians, and great misunderstanding between them and the Indian Service officers. Tribes were helped with food when crops were bad; agricultural agents tried to teach the people better methods of farming and stock-raising. Education had been promised, but Indian schools were always too few to take care of the many children scattered over wide reservations. Tribes of strong individuality, such as the Navajo, Hopi, and Apache, held on to their language, their customs, and religious beliefs in spite of efforts by Indian Service officials to change them.

In Arizona there are between 76,000 and 78,000 Indians who live on nine reservations and belong to fourteen different tribes. These great areas of reservation land account for 26.7 percent of the total land area of Arizona. The tribes cannot support themselves entirely by their ancestral occupations, however, even though they learn modern methods of farming and stock-raising. There is not enough good land.

At last, in the 1930's, the government realized that the Indian people must learn self-government and management of their affairs. They must have better education or they would not be able to carry on their lives as citizens, but would have to remain wards of the government.

Within a few years after the Indian Reorganization Act had become law most tribes had created tribal councils for self-government, aided by Indian Service officers. Some of them had tribal laws and constitutions as well. This system has worked successfully in Arizona. Now each tribe elects a Tribal Council from among the people, with a chairman and vice chairman. The Indian Service officers act as advisors and counsellors to the chairmen and members of the Council. The Indian lands are now held in trust for them by the government. Indian enterprises have been encouraged, and many educated young men and women have jobs in the offices at reservation headquarters. The chairmen of Tribal Councils, chosen from Council members, are men of ability who have education and can take the responsibility of leading their people.

Through these organizations the Indians, so removed from the civic life of the states they live in, learn the

American system of law and democratic procedure by discussion and votes in the Council. This self-government has produced valuable Indian leaders.

The Indians are citizens now with the right to vote, and they are learning to manage their own affairs. The national government plans to release direction of farming, stock-raising, and health services to the states, and eventually expects to give up the reservation system. The Indians will then be full-fledged citizens with the responsibilities and advantages of any other citizens.

Tribal Councils on some reservations maintain law and order with native policemen and have tribal courts to try offences committed on the reservation. There are hospitals and health services on Indian lands to take care of the people.

Education has improved with more government elementary grade schools on reservations, but many more are needed. There are a few Indian high schools, but most students of that age must get their schooling off the reservations. Some go to government boarding schools; others attend high schools in towns where they study with non-Indian companions. These boys and girls live in dormitories from which they go to school in busses. Government scholarships, and some from Tribal Councils, help ambitious young people toward college educations. Arizona State University and the University of Arizona have a good many Indian students. In Tucson, these students have the Amerind Club which gives them a social center and a place to exchange ideas and plans.

The majority of the older people on reservations do not speak English, but use their own language entirely. Children learn English in school, and workers in towns soon become at home in the language. Tribal leaders realize that their people must have English and better education or they cannot compete successfully in American life.

World War II gave the Indians a big push into the white man's world. They enlisted or were drafted by hundreds and served in various branches of the armed services in many countries.

Quite a number of girls enlisted in the women's services. The Indian men proved themselves good soldiers and this gave them pride. The Navajo Signal Corps did splendid work in the jungles of the Pacific Islands. Speaking over walkie-talkies in the Navajo tongue, they could convey important messages in a code the Japanese could not decipher. They were commended by their superior officers.

In their wartime travels the Indians received an eye-opening revelation of the white man's complex civilization. They saw cities and skyscrapers, became used to plane travel, to ships on the seas, and to complex machines. Life could never be the same for these young men and women when they returned home. They could not fit in well with the old-time customs or the limited opportunities for making a living. Hundreds of Indian families also left the reservations for war work, and though some returned to the reservations, their ideas had been changed by their experiences.

Through the Tribal Councils, various tribes have responded to self-government and business, according to their abilities and to the qualities of their leaders.

The Apaches of the San Carlos and Fort Apache Reservations, in eastern Arizona, have been outstanding in the intelligence and determination they have used to develop their cattle industry. The government supplied good animals to start the herds, and Indians paid back with cattle when the herds were successful. Agricultural agents gave them help in methods of stock-raising.

These vigorous people took kindly to the management of their cattle industry and their reservation affairs. The San Carlos Tribal Council owns and operates two herds and gives rights on grazing areas to associations of Apache stockmen. One tribal herd is called "the old folks' herd" as the profits from the cattle go to the tribal welfare fund. The other is a herd of registered Herefords, used mostly to supply good bulls to Indian-owned herds. The Tribal Council also manages leases for mining or timber cutting, and for community projects such as fairs or stores.

The Fort Apache tribe also has a communal herd, and provides Indian stock-raisers with grazing ranges. These Apaches have a lumber industry as well, selling timber from their forests to commercial operators.

On both reservations the men operate their cattle business by modern methods. Stock-raising is a good source of income, though not sufficient for all the families.

The Navajo tribe, largest in population, with millions of acres in Arizona, Utah, and New Mexico, is emerging from the old way of life. Reservation lands contain mineral resources that are being developed through leases to companies exploring for uranium, oil, and natural gas. The Tribal Council receives a great deal of money from these leases and from royalties paid on successful operations.

The latest enterprise is a combination coal mining and power plant which is to be placed in the New Mexico section of the reservation. The agreement has been made with the Arizona Public Service Company, the Tribal Council, and Utah Construction Company of Salt Lake

City, and approved by the Secretary of the Interior. Navajos will mine the coal to supply fuel for the steam-generating power plant. Electricity from the plant will be used by the Arizona Public Service Company, but some will be sold to the Navajos at a low figure. The time may come when electric light bulbs will hang in log-built Navajo hogans.

Large funds from the leases and royalties are administered by the Tribal Council. Money is not distributed to families, though those in need are helped, but is used for tribal improvements; new businesses; roads; windmills and water tanks; and improved stock-raising. As Paul Jones, chairman of the Council, says, tribal funds are used "for the benefit of children yet unborn."

The Bureau of Indian Affairs has a Relocation Program for the purpose of moving Navajo and Hopi farming families to the good lands of the Colorado River Reservation, home of the Mohaves and Chemehuevis who have accepted the newcomers.

It was especially necessary for Hopi farmers to find new opportunities, for the Hopi Reservation is small and is in desert land. They have dry farming, a little irrigation, some flocks of sheep. Hopi craftsmen have a reputation for beautiful weaving, pottery, basketry, silver jewelry, and carved kachina dolls. Their artistic work brings income to many men and women. The younger people, more than most Indians, must seek jobs in towns or on farms. Those who have moved to new homes on the Colorado River lands are doing well with farms or small shops.

The Pimas farm their land as they always have, using water from the San Carlos Project on the Gila River. Water is often insufficient, because the Indians must compete with white farmers for the use of it. The people are more thoroughly adjusted to the American pattern of life than most Indians. They live in villages or on farms, some using the same type of houses as their non-Indian neighbors. They mingle with non-Indians, although they keep tribal customs closely to themselves. Some land is leased to white farmers. The Pimas, and the desert-dwelling Papagos as well, have many of their people living away from the reservation, working on large agricultural projects.

The small remnants of other tribes have limited acreage in the Salt and Verde valleys, but they must depend on wage work for most of their support. Another small tribe, the Havasupai, live contentedly in their lovely canyon retreat, Havasu Canyon near Grand Canyon. They have pools and waterfalls and good land to provide crops for the limited number of families. They also make money by organizing horseback trips for visitors into the canyon, with overnight quarters and guides provided. The Hualapais, another small group, have lands in the Grand Canyon area. They expect to profit, by contract, with whichever organization receives permission to build Bridge Canyon Dam in their territory.

The Indian people of Arizona are now caught between two worlds of utterly different customs, feelings, and ambitions. They cannot keep their old, aloof Indian life on reservations, though dear to them and picturesque to white visitors, for it is lacking in health conditions and prospects for making a decent living. They must adjust to the American civilization in which they live, acquire the education and skilled training that will make it possible for them to compete with other Americans. It is especially hard on the young people who have become adjusted in many ways and yet are not completely accepted on an equal basis in trades, professions, or social life.

Great changes are going on in Indian life. The older people try to preserve the ancient customs and beliefs, but the young generation is inclined to break away from tradition and tribal training. For their own happiness they must keep close to the family relationship, close to their Indian ways of thought and feeling that gives them stability. These first Americans cannot become imitation white men, but should contribute their special talents and characteristics to modern American civilization.

Chapter XXXIII

Wildlife, National Forests and Monuments

In the hushed depths of Arizona's great forests, wild animals live undisturbed in their natural habitats; animals such as elk, deer, mountain lions, and bears. In Houserock Valley, at the eastern edge of the Kaibab Forest, a herd of wild buffalo roam and feed under the protection of the State Game Commission. Pronghorned antelope, in their wild flight, skim over the desert valleys they love. In remote, craggy areas the rare mountain sheep still live in safety.

People driving along forest roads may find startled deer beside their cars, or watch them leaping away through the underbrush. Near marshy Mormon Lake, not far from Flagstaff, twilight is the time when the shy elk, the graceful antelope and deer come from their hideouts to drink at the lake's edge. Part of the pleasure of passing through the aisles of tall pines of the Kaibab Forest, in the Grand Canyon National Game Preserve, is to get a glimpse of the herds of beautiful mule deer or to see the Kaibab squirrel. This rare little animal lives only in the Kaibab and is different from other squirrels with its tufted ears and white, plumy tail.

Many small animals, as well as birds, have secure homes in wildlife refuges. Beaver continue to build their dams along little mountain streams; they are watched over and sometimes transplanted by men of the State Game and Fish Commission. They say that beaver do valuable work because their dams help check flood damage and thereby store up water. The Commission also keeps the rivers and lakes stocked with fish.

Javelinas, or wild pigs, have their favorite haunts in rugged desert foothills, as do wild cats, foxes, and coyotes. Controlled hunting throughout the state prevents the animal population from becoming too large, and it also protects them from useless slaughter.

These wild creatures of forest, mountain, and plain would be in danger of extinction without the care and protection of the State Game and Fish Commission and the rangers of the National Forest Service. The specialists of these two organizations collaborate in the work of caring for the inhabitants of the wilderness.

That is only one of the jobs expected of the rangers and supervisors of the National Forest Service. Theirs is the task of preserving the forests by scientific management, added to the equally important work of protecting the watersheds on which farms and towns depend for water supply. The rangers also manage the fire lookouts and bring in crews of fire fighters when devastating blazes sweep through the precious timber to destroy many acres.

In pioneer times, when the great West was being explored and settled, the frontier people used the natural resources of forests, streams, and range lands recklessly, without thought of conserving and developing them for the future. Great areas of forest were stripped of timber by the logging companies, and the need of wood for railroads and for housing brought more destruction of forest reserves. Huge herds of cattle and sheep were allowed to graze on the range lands until the forage was eaten off, and unprotected earth was washed away in spring floods to damage irrigation projects and reservoirs with silt.

It was Theodore Roosevelt, that dynamic American who loved the West and believed in the conservation of its resources, who initiated the federal project to set aside national forest lands. The U.S. Government stepped in to conserve the splendid natural resources for the greatest good of the greatest number of people. The National Forest Service, under the Department of Agriculture, was established in 1906.

All over the country, in every state, there are National Forests on lands of the public domain. Arizona has seven National Forests, preserving the great stands of virgin timber, the woodlands, and great sections of range land. The forest belt extends from the Utah border in a great curve through the center of the state, on into New Mexico, and down to the southern mountain ranges.

In the southern National Forest, the Coronado, travelers might ask — where is the forest? They see rolling hills and gulleys covered with dry grass and desert vegetation over which stride companies of the tall, fantastic giant saguaro cactus. Or they see plains of golden grass and greasewood bushes, palo verde, mesquite, and other desert trees, and white-face cattle browsing here and there in search of nourishment.

The giant saguaro are being protected as part of the Coronado National Forest, and rangelands are being improved by seeding with good grasses. Over-grazing is controled by leasing sections to ranchers on which an allotted number of animals may graze. The Coronado Forest also has real woodlands and tall pines on the slopes of the Pinaleno and Graham mountains in the east, and the Catalinas, Santa Ritas, and Chiricahuas in the south.

Conservation of range lands to improve the grass cover, prevent over-grazing, and erosion from floods, is part of the rangers' work in most of the forests. Sheep may also feed in certain areas by permit, and sheep drives provide a controled trail for driving the flocks between summer and winter pastures.

The National Forests in big timber country — Apache, Coconino, Sitgreaves — are the source of Arizona's lumber industry. Here the chief project of rangers and supervisors is the care and scientific management of the splendid trees. Men of the Forest Service set aside certain acreage for logging, and mark the largest, most mature trees or those least healthy for cutting. Then the timber is sold to logging companies by competitive bid. Forest Service men supervise the cutting to make sure it is done by proper logging practices. The logs are piled on flat cars or trucks and hauled to the sawmills of the lumber companies to be transformed into boards.

Plenty of trees are left in a logged-over area with room to grow, and sections of young trees are left alone until they are full grown. This "sustained yield" practice means that trees may be cut only in relation to their annual growth; so that the forests are replenished and continue to produce timber from year to year. No area is stripped of trees; therefore, the ground covering is not exposed to erosion from floods or runoff from melting snow.

Most of the National Forests include mountain peaks or ranges, not only to protect their forests, but also because the springs and creeks in the high country become little streams that feed the rivers. This watershed must be protected if the rivers are to fill the reservoirs and provide water for the works of man on farms and in towns. The Forest Service also maintains recreation areas where people may enjoy their empire of forests, streams, and mountains.

Some of the National Forests have areas of deep, primitive wilderness in rough, almost inaccessible country, which continues on into equally wild country in New Mexico. Here Wilderness Areas have been set aside to be forever preserved as an example of what the primitive forests were like. There are no roads in Wilderness Areas, no cabins or picnic grounds, just horse or foot trails for those hardy campers who want to explore real wilderness.

Forest rangers are men hardy and expert, ready to deal with primitive territory and wild life, scientific in their profession, and dedicated to their jobs of conservation.

Uncle Sam spends millions on the National Forests all over the nation, but the forest management repays much of the cost by income from timber sales, fees for grazing permits, water power, and land use. Arizona benefits from the National Forests of the State, not only in the services done for the people and resources, but by receiving a third of the income from the state's National Forests for the use of schools and road building.

In the fine weather of spring, summer, and autumn hundreds of Arizona families spend happy vacations on the camp grounds, provided without charge on National

Forest lands. In woodland groves or near a lake or trout stream, they set up camp. Sometimes the family car has a trailer hitched behind in which they sleep, or they may pitch a tent or roll up in sleeping bags. If they camp by a lake for fishing there will be a boat tied on top of the car.

At the camp grounds they find wooden tables and benches, stone fireplaces, a tap of water, toilets, and trash cans. The places are well-kept, and the least campers can do, who have such a treasure of outdoor life offered to them, is not to be litter bugs—no beer cans, boxes, papers, or other rubbish strewn around; no carelessness with matches and fires. "Leave a dead fire and a clean camp" is the rule.

The National Forests in Arizona are: Apache; Coconino; Coronado; Kaibab; Prescott; Sitgreaves; Tonto.

When their work overlaps, the National Forest Service and National Park Service cooperate in many of the preserved areas of scenic beauty and historic value.

The National Park Service, under the Department of the Interior, is dedicated to the conservation of the scenic, scientific, and historic heritage of the United States for the benefit and enjoyment of the people. Arizona has one National Park that includes Grand Canyon National Monument. Altogether the state has sixteen National Monuments, more than any other state. "Monument" is not used in the usual sense of an impressive building, but denotes "natural, historic or prehistoric features of outstanding national interest", as Park Service rangers explain.

The marvelous gorge of the Grand Canyon has attracted explorers from the time of John Wesley Powell, and they have come in large numbers each succeeding year. Various groups braved the rapids in boat trips. Ellsworth and Emory Kolb settled on the rim, explored trails, took the first moving pictures of the Canyon. Miners clambered down the cliffs to stake claims, hoping to extract copper and gold. There was so much interest in the great gorge that the Santa Fe railroad ran stages from their main line to the Canyon to take tourists to the rim. Soon a hotel was built, and before long the Santa Fe had a branch line to the Canyon.

To preserve this region of Nature's marvels from exploitation, the Grand Canyon was set aside in 1902 as a National Monument, and in 1913 an area of more than 1,000 square miles was established as Grand Canyon National Park.

National Monuments in Arizona are scattered all over the state. They have been created for two purposes: to protect the dwellings of prehistoric people, or historic sites, and to preserve areas of unusual beauty and valuable natural growth.

Fortunately, many of the prehistoric Indians built so well that their cliff dwellings and pueblo towns survived the ages, though in ruinous condition. Archeologists have excavated and studied the sites, mended and restored buildings whenever possible. Carefully, they have preserved the records of ancient life they found. There are pottery, baskets, scraps of woven material, and ornaments of shell, stone, and turquoise. Some of these things were removed to museums, but other relics are put on display at the small museum at each site to tell something of the people's story. The same study and display has been carried through at historic sites of later ages. Superintendents of National Monuments need to be well versed in archeology, geology, and natural history to be good at their jobs.

Prehistoric builders, in remote Tsegi Canyon in northern Arizona, constructed the cliff towns of Betatakin, Keet Seel, and many other villages in huge caves. They are preserved now in the Navajo National Monument and can be visited on guided horseback trips. Canyon de Chelly, with its history of Navajo life in the past and present, with its towering cliffs and ancient ruins, is a National Monument of special interest to many visitors.

Pueblo towns of prehistoric times are Wupatki in a red rock valley near Flagstaff, and Tuzigoot, a town on a hill in Verde Valley. Montezuma's Castle is a cliff dwelling and is also situated in Verde Valley. In Walnut Canyon near Flagstaff some ancient people built low shelters under overhanging ledges in the canyon. Tonto National Monument is another village built in a cave in the wild rugged region of Tonto Creek and Theodore Roosevelt Dam.

Standing in the desert near Coolidge is the massive, crumbling tower of Casa Grande, protected from weather by an unbecoming tin roof. Built by the prehistoric Hohokam, it has fascinated people for centuries. It is surrounded with the excavated floor plans of houses and remains of the irrigation canals the ancient people used.

The great ruined church of Tumacácori National Monument, on the road between Tucson and Nogales, preserves in a most interesting way the story of the Spanish missions. Another historic site is Pipe Springs National Monument up near the Utah border. It is a strong stone-walled structure built like a fort, a reminder of the pioneer Mormons who built it to protect themselves from Indians, while they raised cattle.

Two historic sites of value to Arizonans have been declared eligible for the status of national monuments by the National Park Service. One of these is old Fort Bowie, in Apache Pass, famous in the period of Indian wars. The other is the fine old Hubbell Trading Post near Ganado, on the fringe of the Navajo Reservation. The founder of the post, Lorenzo Hubbell, was in former times one of the best and wisest friends of the Navajo people. Since his death, the family has carried on the business. The interesting building houses many historic mementos; such as photographs of Indian leaders and of white visitors, among them Theodore Roosevelt. There is, as well, a valuable collection of old Indian baskets and rugs.

On the Mexican border, near Bisbee, an area of forest and mountains has been set aside as the Coronado National Memorial, to commemorate Coronado's famous expedition into the Southwest. Historians believe that it was through this region that the Spanish explorer entered Arizona. There are exhibits along a foot trail descriptive of the story.

More interesting to many visitors than relics of prehistoric or historic buildings are the National Monuments of unusual value in geology, wildlife, and botanical species. Sunset Crater near Flagstaff, with its dark cinder cones and lava fields, makes understandable the violent volcanic past of the region. The jeweled-stone trees of the Petrified Forest, strewn over miles of the Painted Desert, record a story of prehistoric geologic changes.

Southern Arizona has a prize possession in the great stands of the giant saguaro cactus that grows nowhere else except in Mexico and a small strip of California. One large area of hills and gulleys, over which the angular giants march in droves, is preserved as the Saguaro National Monument, near Tucson. This delightful acreage of unspoiled desert contains many other varieties of cactus, besides desert plants and shrubs where small animals and birds make their homes. The Monument lands extend into the craggy mountains, the Rincons, in the background.

Another rare variety of cactus, that grows thickly on both sides of the Arizona-Sonora border, is preserved in the Organ Pipe Cactus National Monument. The long-armed clumps of organ pipe and countless other cactus plants create an unusual desert garden.

In the southeastern corner of Arizona, the Chiricahua Mountains rise so steeply from desert lowlands to high peaks that they contain five zones of climate, vegetation, animals, and insects. Because of this the Natural History Museum of New York has established here a station for study and experiment.

The mountains are the result of intense volcanic up-heavals, followed by ages of cracking and splitting of rocks by erosion. A large section of craggy, eroded rock pillars and weird shapes is so fantastic that it is set aside as the Chiricahua National Monument, the Wonderland of Rocks.

Each of the Monuments has a headquarters building where visitors may obtain information. There are collections of mineral samples and displays of animal and insect life. Picnic grounds are provided for visitors, with tables and stone fireplaces.

Thanks to these national and state organizations, devoted to the preservation of America's heritage of natural treasures and the works of man, these wonderful places will bring knowledge and enjoyment to the people for all time.

## Chapter XXXIV

### Arizona in the Space Age

Arizona's gorgeous skies and translucent atmosphere have always been special attractions of this southwestern state. Now, in mid-twentieth century, when scientific minds are concentrated on space and astronomers are searching the heavens for more knowledge of the universe the skies and clear air are infinitely valuable.

The spacious skies attract advanced astronomical observations, and climate brings scientists for atmospheric and meteorological research and experiment. Arizona is an ideal region for the study of solar radiation and the various uses of solar energy, as well as for advanced experiments with all phases of electronics, radar and other projects of the space age.

Astronomers in past years have chosen Arizona for one

of the regions for their observatories. The distinguished study carried on at Lowell Observatory at Flagstaff and the research and teaching at Steward Observatory at the University in Tucson have won reputation.

When the National Science Foundation and the Association of Universities for Research in Astronomy (AURA) undertook to find a site for a national optical observatory, the Tucson area was one of the 150 sites considered in the Southwest. This section of the country is the best for astronomical observation. The scientists were looking for good atmospheric conditions, for a place where the night skies would not be blurred by smoke or dust or the reflected light of cities. They also wanted a place where astronomical observation and study was already established.

Far out on the Papago Indian Reservation, southwest of Tucson, they chose their site on the top of a rugged mountain 6,785 feet in altitude, named Kitt Peak. It was miles away from towns, in the midst of sheer desert, and the only dwellings in the region were tiny Indian villages. The mountain top would give observers an unlimited sweep of sky to study, and, in addition, the observatory would be only 45 miles from Tucson with its city advantages and excellent University of Arizona.

The site chosen being on the reservation of the Papago Indians, permission had to be obtained from the Tribal Council to use the land. Kitt Peak and Baboquiviri Peak, farther south, are sacred to the Papagos as the homes of their mythical Indian gods.

After negotiations with the Tribal Council, the Indians agreed to lease 200 acres of land to the National Science Foundation at Kitt Peak and to place restrictions on a large acreage besides, where they would continue to cut wood and graze cattle, but would not interfere with operations of the Observatory. This agreement was made law by Act of Congress and signed by President Eisenhower. When the installations are complete the Papagos will be given space to exhibit and sell their crafts, especially their fine baskets.

The Papagos are practical people, and doubtless expect employment on the heavy tasks of road building and construction of buildings. In their picturesque Indian phraseology they call the astronomers "The People with the Long Eyes."

The National Science Foundation, which finances the building of the Kitt Peak National Observatory, was created to advance research and scientific knowledge through universities and several large research centers. Kitt Peak Observatory is only one of their great projects. After a meeting with astronomers in Flagstaff, a panel of scientists was appointed to investigate sites for a national observatory. When they had made their report, the Association of Universities for Research in Astronomy (AURA) was organized by seven universities and incorporated in 1957, under the laws of the state of Arizona.

It is this organization, AURA, which plans and directs the work of the Kitt Peak National Observatory. AURA maintains its headquarters in Tucson, adjacent to the University campus, with offices for administration and research together with laboratories and optical shops. Here much of the designing of instruments for the Observatory is done, and mirrors for the telescopes are prepared. Kitt Peak National Observatory will cost millions of dollars and will bring to Tucson famous astronomers who will be allotted viewing time with the telescopes.

The Observatory was dedicated March 16, 1960, after

two years of hard work in road building and construction of buildings. Dr. Meinel, then director of Kitt Peak, and Dr. Carpenter of the Steward Observatory were hosts to a distinguished gathering of astronomers. Enos Francisco, chairman of the Papago Tribal Council, was present to represent his people.

Kitt Peak has a large 36-inch telescope and two 16-inch instruments. The 36-inch telescope of the Steward Observatory will be moved to Kitt Peak for teaching and research, because clear-viewing in the night sky over Tucson is hampered by city lights.

Two major telescopes are under construction: a large 80-inch reflecting stellar telescope and a complex solar telescope. The great mirror of the 80-inch instrument is being ground and polished at the optical shops in Tucson.

Solar research — the study of the sun's surface, its sunspots, flares, and the analysis of light rays — will be carried on through the solar telescope, a huge structure, part of it underground. It will be the largest and most powerful instrument of its kind in the world.

While astronomers are studying the universe, other scientists are working for knowledge of atmospheric conditions, the behavior of weather, clouds and precipitation, solar radiation, and meteorology in Arizona and arid lands in general. The Institute of Atmospheric Physics at the University of Arizona, under direction of Dr. Kassander and Dr. McDonald, conducts experiments and studies problems of climate, solar radiation, and meteorology. Part of this program is in cooperation with the University of Chicago's Department of Meteorology. The Institute is supported partly by the University and partly by grants and research contracts.

During several summers, cloud-seeding experiments

were tried to learn whether rainfall might be increased by this method. Cumulus clouds over the Catalina Mountains were sprayed with silver iodide by an airborne generator at certain periods. Records were kept of rainfall on seeded days, and there was an increase, but of course the scientists had to admit that nature might have produced this by summer showers without their help.

The Institute of Atmospheric Physics has a Solar Research Laboratory, a building designed for experiment in trapping solar energy for heating or cooling by moderate-temperature thermal processes. The roof is a collector, or dissipator of energy. It is covered with copper "tube-in-strip" material. For heating, solar energy is absorbed in water circulating through the tubes during the day, then passed on through ceiling panels in the building. In hot weather, the roof at night dissipates the heat absorbed from the building during the day.

The Laboratory is an absorbing experiment to solar energy scientists and to those who hope solar heating may soon be practicable for homes. It is the largest and best equipped Laboratory of its specialized type in the United States.

In Phoenix there is a branch of the Association for Applied Solar Energy which publishes *The Journal of Solar Energy*, as well as a newsletter. Their library of books on solar energy is stored at Arizona State University, and the Association cooperates with the University in research problems.

Research in electronics is greatly stimulated by the increasing number of electronics plants that have been established year by year since World War II, around Phoenix and Tucson. Climate is a factor in bringing electronics firms to southern Arizona, because certain components need low humidity to be effectively produced and assembled. These manufacturers, employing skilled personnel, also like to establish plants in the environs of cities where employees will have advantages and recreational opportunities in a good climate. The technicians and scientists who are associated with the industry appreciate the facilities for study and testing provided by the University in Tucson and Arizona State University in Tempe.

The advanced work in electronics communications, being done at the U. S. Army Electronic Proving Ground at Fort Huachuca, also attracts manufacturers. This project gives them opportunities to test the devices they manufacture.

The old Fort has become a busy center of scientific research and experiment for military purposes, since the U. S. Signal Corps at Monmouth, New Jersey, established the Electronic Proving Ground. At Fort Huachuca, theories and instruments developed by the Signal Corps are tested. Army technicians find large areas of sparsely settled land for their testing, and because no large towns are near, the air is relatively free from the interference of radio or TV waves in their experiments with electronic communication.

Their tests are intended to give field commanders of any future war in this modern age the utmost assistance in maintaining communications on the battlefield by radio and radar. Weather conditions are also studied by meteorology. The technicians develop the survey of terrain in unmanned aircraft, the drones, which are equipped photographically for reports and are electronically guided from ground stations in their flight.

The saucer-like radar receivers, mounted on great operating machines, are tilted to the sky to test radar surveillance and aircraft guidance radars. One of the latest projects is called the Electronics Environmental Test Facility. Control centers, radar sites and radio relay sites will be set up at intervals in a corridor between Fort Huachuch and Yuma. The problem is a military one: how to maintain electronic battlefield communications in an atmosphere that is noisy with electronic sounds from radios, transmitters, radar and generators. Drone planes will be used in these tests of communications.

The mass of data and information that comes into headquarters at the Fort is processed by great electronic computers, the machines of magic brains, in one of the world's largest computer centers.

The men of the Fort and the University of Arizona cooperate in research, and the University has a Data Reduction Center of electronic computers that is at the service of the military and of industrial firms of the state, as well as the departments of the University.

Radar, electronics, atomic energy are all exciting achievements of the space age in which Arizona has a share. Nuclear problems are being studied at Fort Huachuca and at the University of Arizona. Through a grant from the Atomic Energy Commission, a multi-purpose, safe nuclear reactor, the TRIGA, has been installed for research and teaching. It will also be used to aid those who are working in the fields of medicine, biology, chemistry, agriculture, and metallurgy. TRIGA is the first nuclear reactor to become available in Arizona.

Provided that our uneasy world does not become engaged in destructive nuclear war, Arizona may have a bright future in aiding the rapid discoveries of the space age, as technicians and scientists find here the climate and facilities that suit their work. The state may well become an important center of electronic manufacture and research. The University of Arizona will be increasingly useful to students and scientists, because grants from foundations or individuals provide the means for intensive work, headed by men high in their professions. Arizona State University will also aid in this way.

This bright future for enjoyment of living, for economic prosperity and technological advances, depends on Arizona's precious assets of clear air and sun, great skies and plenty of space. Scientists need an atmosphere undamaged by smog, that torment of big cities, and they need space for their technological work. The people need clean air to breathe, and, above all, the inhabitants of towns and cities must have a sufficient supply of water.

In the Southwest of semi-arid land and little rainfall, water is the basic problem as the population grows. The needs of people, combined with the needs of agriculture and industry, make a great drain on sources of water both in rivers and underground. Fortunately scientific specialists are at work on the problem. The utilization of arid lands in general and of Arizona in particular, and methods for preserving water resources are being studied at the University of Arizona by the Arid Lands Research Commission, composed of men from several fields of science.

While tourist agencies boast of Arizona's atmosphere, a murky haze of dust, smoke and fumes from automotive vehicles or other sources frequently hangs over the two large centers of population, Phoenix and Tucson. This is a warning that air pollution may injure one of the state's assets — its clear atmosphere. Civic leaders, with the example of smog-ridden cities before them, are aware of the danger and are studying local causes of air pollution.

Arizona, with its special qualities of space and climate

and its opportunities for research in this scientific age, may well become a vital area for scientists and technologists. Those men whose minds are set on the exploration of space, the great adventure of the present century, will find here facilities for their research and experiment. Thus Arizonans may keep their state a region for constructive scientific experiment and, as well, preserve a rare section of the country for the enjoyment of living.

# THE MARCH OF ARIZONA HISTORY

## BIBLIOGRAPHY

### GENERAL BOOKS ON ARIZONA

*Arizona, Its People and Resources.* Tucson, University of Arizona Press, 1961.

*Arizona, the Grand Canyon State.* A State Guide. Revised by Joseph Miller. N.Y., Hastings House, 1956.

Barnes, William C. *Arizona Place Names.* Revised and enlarged by Byrd H. Granger. Tucson, University of Arizona Press, 1960.

Calvin, Ross. *River of the Sun: Stories of the Storied Gila.* Albuquerque, University of New Mexico Press, 1946.

Corle, Edwin. *The Gila: River of the Southwest.* N.Y., Rinehart, 1951.

Farish, Thomas E. *History of Arizona.* Phoenix, 1914-1918. 8 vols. Vols. 1 and 2 consulted.

Hinton, Richard J. *The Handbook to Arizona.* Tucson, Arizona Silhouettes, 1954. Facsimile of the original of 1878.

Krutch, Joseph W. *Grand Canyon, Today and All Its Yesterdays.* N.Y., William Sloane, 1958.

McClintock, James A. *Arizona, Prehistoric, Aboriginal, Pioneer, Modern.* Chicago, S. J. Clarke Publishing Co., 1916. 3 vols.

Peattie, Roderick, ed. *The Inverted Mountains.* N.Y., Vanguard, 1948.

Peplow, Edward H. *History of Arizona.* N.Y., Lewis Historical Publishing Co., 1958. 3 vols.

Sloan, Richard E., ed. *History of Arizona.* Phoenix, Record Publishing Co., 1930. 4 vols.

Wyllys, Rufus K. *Arizona: the History of a Frontier State.* Phoenix, Hobson & Herr, 1950.

### PART I

#### PREHISTORIC ARIZONA

*Arizona — Its Place in Time.* Phoenix, Arizona Republic, 1960.

Blake, William P. "Some Salient Features of the Geology of Arizona." *American Geologist*, v. 27, pp. 160-67, 1901.

Colton, Harold S. *Days in the Painted Desert and the San Francisco Mountains: a Guide.* Flagstaff, Museum of Northern Arizona, 1932. (Bulletin No. 2).

———— "The Rise and Fall of the Prehistoric Population of Northern Arizona." *Science.* v. 84, pp. 337-343, Oct. 16, 1936.

Cummings, Byron. *Kinishba: a Prehistoric Pueblo of the Great Pueblo Period.* Tucson, Hohokam Museums Association, 1940.

Fenton, Carroll L. *Life Long Ago: the Story of Fossils.* N.Y., Reynal & Hitchcock, 1937.

Getty, Harry T. *Prehistoric Man in the Southwest.* Grand Canyon, Arizona, 1936. (Grand Canyon Natural History Association, Natural History Bulletin No. 7.)

Gilmore, Charles W. "Fossil Footprints from the Grand Canyon." U. S. Smithsonian Institution, *Smithsonian Miscellaneous Collections,* v. 79, no. 9; v. 80, nos. 3, 8.

Gladwin, Harold S. *A History of the Ancient Southwest.* Portland, Me. Bond Wheelright Co., 1957.

————— *Excavations at Snaketown.* Globe, Arizona: Gila Pueblo, 1937-48. 4 vols. ("Medallion Papers," Nos. 25-26, 30, 38).

Halseth, Odd S. *Arizona's 1500 Years of Irrigation History.* Phoenix, Pueblo Grande, n.d.

Haury, Emil W. "The Lehner Mammoth Site." *Kiva,* v. 21, pp. 23-24, Feb.-May, 1956.

————— "The Naco Mammoth." *Kiva.* v. 18, pp. 1-19, Nov.-Dec., 1952.

McKee, Edwin D. *Ancient Landscapes of the Grand Canyon Region.* Grand Canyon, E. D. McKee, 1931.

————— "Sedimentary Basins of Arizona and Adjoining Areas." *Bulletin of the Geological Society of America.* v. 62, pp. 481-505, 1951.

Markham, Harvey C. *Fossils: a Story of the Rocks and Their Record of Prehistoric Life.* 3rd ed. Denver, Colorado Museum of Natural History, 1954. (Popular Series No. 3).

Maxwell, Ross A. "Rocks Tell Stories." *Region III Quarterly,* U. S. National Parks Service, v. 2, pp. 15-19. July, 1940.

Patrick, H. R. *The Ancient Canal Systems and Pueblos of the Salt River Valley, Arizona.* Phoenix, Phoenix Free Museum, 1903.

Parker, Bertha M. *Life Through the Ages.* Chicago, Rowe, Peterson & Co., 1954.

Robinson, Henry H. *The San Francisco Volcanic Field, Arizona.* Washington, 1913. (U. S. Geological Survey, Professional Paper No. 76).

Schellbach, Louis. "Grand Canyon: Nature's Story of Creation." *National Geographic,* v. 107, pp. 589-629, May, 1955.

Smiley, Terah L., ed. *Climate and Man in the Southwest.* Tucson, University of Arizona Press, 1958. (University of Arizona Bulletin, v. 27, no. 4).

Walton, Matt. "Geology of the Painted Desert and Petrified Forest." *Arizona Highways,* v. 24, pp. 1-12, July, 1958.

Wormington, Hannah H. *Ancient Man in North America.* 3rd ed. Denver, Colorado Museum of Natural History, 1949. (Popular Series No. 4).

———— *Prehistoric Indians of the Southwest.* Denver, Colorado Museum of Natural History, 1947. (Popular Series No. 7).

## PART II
### SPANISH AND MEXICAN ARIZONA

Bolton, Herbert E. *Coronado, Knight of Pueblos and Plains.* N.Y., Whittlesey House, 1949.

———— *The Padre on Horseback.* San Francisco, Sonora Press, 1932.

———— *Rim of Christendom.* N.Y., Macmillan, 1936.

Cooke, Philip St. George. *The Conquest of New Mexico and California; an Historical and Personal Narrative.* Oakland, Biobooks, 1952.

Emory, William H. *Lieutenant Emory Reports; a Reprint of Lieutenant W. H. Emory's Notes of a Military Reconnaissance.* Albuquerque, University of New Mexico Press, 1951.

Jackson, Earl. *Tumacácori's Yesterdays.* Santa Fe, Southwestern Monuments Association, 1951. (Popular Series No. 6).

McDermott, Edwin J. "The Saga of Father Kino." *Arizona Highways,* v. 37, pp. 7-27, March, 1961.

Manje, Juan Mateo. *Luz de Tierra Incognita; Unknown Arizona and Sonora, 1693-1721.* Tucson, Arizona Silhouettes, 1954.

Martin, Douglas D. *Yuma Crossing.* Albuquerque, University of New Mexico Press, 1954.

Newhall, Nancy. *Mission San Xavier del Bac.* San Francisco, 5 Associates, 1954. Photos by Ansel Adams.

Paylore, Patricia. *Kino: a Commemoration.* Tucson, Arizona Pioneers' Historical Society, 1961.

Thayer, John. *Desert Padre: Eusebio Francisco Kino.* Milwaukee, Wis., Bruce Publishing, 1954.

White, Helen C. *Dust on the King's Highway.* N.Y., Macmillan, 1947.

## PART III
### ANGLO-AMERICANS TAKE OVER ARIZONA

Beale, Edward F. *Wagon Road from Fort Defiance to the Colorado River.* Washington, 1858. (35th Congress, 1st Session, House Exec. Doc. 124, Serial 959).

Bents, Doris W. *The History of Tubac, 1752-1948.* M.A. Thesis, University of Arizona, 1949.

*The Butterfield Overland Mail across Arizona.* Tucson, Arizona Pioneers' Historical Society, 1958.

Colton, Harold S. "A Brief Survey of the Early Expeditions into Northern Arizona." *Plateau.* v. 2, pp. 1-4, March 1930.

Cosulich, Bernice. Articles from the *Arizona Daily Star.* In scrapbooks, Special Collections Division, University of Arizona Library.

Hall, Sharlot M. *First Citizen of Prescott: Pauline Weaver.* Prescott, Arizona, 1932.

Johnson, Enid. *Cochise: Great Apache Chief.* N.Y., Julian Messner, 1953.

Lockwood, Francis C. *The Apache Indians.* N.Y., Macmillan, 1938.

Martin, Douglas D. *Yuma Crossing.* Albuquerque, University of New Mexico Press, 1954.

Mulligan, Raymond A. "Down the Old Butterfield Trail." *Arizona and the West.* v. 1, pp. 358-67, Winter, 1959.

Poston, Charles D. Address delivered at a banquet, 1891. Manuscript in the Arizona Pioneers' Historical Society Library.

Pumpelly, Raphael. *Across America and Asia.* N.Y., Leypoldt and Holt, 1870.

Sonora Exploring and Mining Company. *Report made to the Stockholders.* Cincinnati, Railroad Record Print, 1857.

Stacey, May Humphreys. *Uncle Sam's Camels: the Journal of May Humphreys Stacey, supplemented by the Report of Edward Fitzgerald Beale (1857-1858).* Cambridge, Harvard University Press, 1929.

Woodward, Arthur. *Feud on the Colorado.* Los Angeles, Westernlore Press, 1955.

## PART IV
### TERRITORIAL ARIZONA

Bachman, Lucy Nash. *Roles Played by the Gila Bend Area in the Development of the Southwest.* M.A. Thesis, Arizona State College, Flagstaff.

Barney, James M. "The Great Flood of 1891 in the Salt River Valley." *The Sheriff,* v. 8, pp. 12-13, April 1949.

Blake, William P. *The Silver King Mine of Arizona.* Typewritten copy in The University of Arizona Library, from manuscript in Yale University Library.

Brown, J. Ross. *A Tour Through Arizona, 1864; or Adventures in the Apache Country.* Tucson, Arizona Silhouettes, 1950.

Clum, Woodworth. *Apache Agent. The Story of John P. Clum.* Boston, Houghton Mifflin, 1936.

Cosulich, Bernice. *Tucson.* Tucson, Arizona Silhouettes, 1953.

Cremony, John C. *Life Among the Apaches.* Tucson, Arizona Silhouettes, 1951.

Dunning, Charles H. and Edward H. Peplow, Jr. *Rocks to Riches.* Phoenix, Southwest Publishing Co., 1959.

Golzé, Alfred R. *Reclamation in the United States.* N.Y., McGraw-Hill Co., 1952.

Hastings, Virginia M. *A History of Arizona During the Civil War, 1861-1865.* M.A. Thesis. Tucson, University of Arizona, 1943.

Hastings, James R. "The Tragedy at Camp Grant in 1871." *Arizona and the West,* v. 1, pp. 146-160. Summer, 1959.

*History of Arizona Territory, Showing its Resources and Advantages* San Francisco, W. W. Elliot, 1884.

Kelly, William H. *Indians of the Southwest.* Tucson, University of Arizona, Bureau of Ethnic Research, 1953.

Lockwood, Francis C. *Pioneer Days in Arizona.* N.Y., Macmillan, 1932.

———— *Tucson, The Old Pueblo.* Phoenix Manufacturing Stationers Inc., 1930.

Lutrell, Estelle. *Newspapers and Periodicals of Arizona, 1859-1911.* Tucson, University of Arizona, 1950. (General Bulletin No. 15).

Martin, Douglas D. *The Earps of Tombstone.* Tombstone, *Tombstone Epitaph,* 1959.

———— *Tombstone's Epitaph.* Albuquerque, University of New Mexico Press, 1951.

McClintock, James H. *Mormon Settlement in Arizona.* Phoenix, 1921.

Myers, John M. "The Tempe Story." *Arizona Days and Ways,* pp. 26-36, March 17, 1957.

Powell, John Wesley. *The Exploration of the Colorado River.* Chicago, University of Chicago Press, 1957.

Raine, William M. and Will C. Barnes. *Cattle.* N.Y., Doubleday, Doran Co., 1930.

Rockfellow, John A. *Log of an Arizona Trail Blazer.* Tucson, Arizona Silhouettes, 1955.

Stegner, Wallace E. *Beyond the Hundredth Meridian: John Wesley Powell and the Second Opening of the West.* Boston, Houghton, Mifflin, 1954.

Summerhayes, Martha. *Vanished Arizona.* Tucson, Arizona Silhouettes, 1960.

Tuck, Frank J. *History of Mining in Arizona.* Phoenix, Arizona. Dept. of Mineral Resources, 1957.

Underhill, Ruth M. *The Navajos.* Norman, University of Oklahoma Press, 1956.

United States Bureau of Mines. *Gold, Silver, Copper, Lead, Zinc Ore, Progress Report.* Washington, *Minerals Yearbook,* U. S. Bureau of Mines, 1942.

Wallace, Theodore Russell. *A Brief History of Coconino County.* M.A. Thesis. Flagstaff, Arizona State College.

Wells, Edmund. *Argonaut Tales.* N.Y., F. H. Hitchcock, 1927.

Willson, Roscoe. "The Territory Was Old When Phoenix Emerged."
Phoenix, *Arizona Days and Ways*, pp. 94-96, March 11, 1956.

PART V

ARIZONA THE FORTY-EIGHTH STATE

Adams, William Y. *Ninety Years of Glen Canyon Archeology*.
Flagstaff, Northern Arizona Society of Science and Art, 1960
(Museum of Northern Arizona Bulletin No. 33).

Angle, Jerry. *Federal, State and Tribal Jurisdiction on Indian Reservations in Arizona*. Tucson, University of Arizona Bureau of
Ethnic Research, 1959.

*Arizona's National Monuments*. Santa Fe, N. M., Southwestern
Monuments Association, 1945 (Popular Series No. 2).

"Arizona's Stand on Boulder Dam." *Arizona Republic* (Phoenix),
May 14, 1931.

Barnes, William C. *The Story of the Range*. Washington, U. S.
Forest Service, 1926.

*Colorado River: Natural Menace Becomes National Resource*. Washington, U. S. Reclamation Bureau, 1946.

*Colorado River Storage Project*. Washington, U. S. Reclamation
Bureau, 1959.

Crampton, Gregory C. *Outline History of the Glen Canyon Region,
1776-1922*. Salt Lake City, University of Utah Press, 1959
(Anthropological Papers, No. 42).

Denton, John H. and William S. King. "The Tucson Central Business District as a Changing Entity." *Arizona Review of Business and Public Administration*, v. 9, pp. 1-13, May, 1960.

"Eloy: a Cotton Town in Transition." *Arizona Review of Business
and Public Administration*, v. 9, 4 parts in issues for July, Aug.-
Sept., Nov.-Dec., 1960.

Gates, William H. *Hoover Dam*. Los Angeles, Wetzel Publishing
Co., 1932.

*Glen Canyon Dam*. Washington, U. S. Reclamation Bureau, 1960.

Hopkins, Ernest J. and Alfred Thomas Jr. *The Arizona State University Story*. Phoenix, Southwest Publishing Co., 1960.

Kelly, William H. *The Changing Role of the Indian in Arizona*.
Tucson, Arizona Agricultural Extension Service, 1958 (Circular No. 263).

*Kitt Peak National Observatory*. Tucson, 1960.

Kleinsorge, Paul L. *The Boulder Canyon Project, Historical and
Economic Aspects*. Stanford, Calif., Stanford University Press,
1941.

*The Lowell Observatory*. Flagstaff, The Observatory, 1960.

Martin, Douglas D. *The Lamp in the Desert*. Tucson, University
of Arizona Press, 1960.

McCleneghan, Thomas J. and Kit Scheifle. "Bisbee, Historic City With a Future." *Arizona Review of Business and Public Administration,* v. 9, pp. 1-14, October, 1960.

Miller, David E. *Hole-in-the-Rock.* Salt Lake City, University of Utah Press, 1959.

*Research in Science and Technology at The University of Arizona.* Tucson, University of Arizona, 1959.

Shadegg, Stephen C. *Arizona: an Adventure in Irrigation.* Phoenix, 1949.

*Story of Boulder Dam.* Washington, U. S. Reclamation Bureau, 1941. (Conservation Bulletin No. 9).

# INDEX

Note: In the following index the abbreviation *ff.* refers to scattered items on following pages. All other references are to exact page.